P & O. S. N. Co.
S.S. Ranpura
en route to Marseilles
October 24, 1933.

My dear Dr. Cohen :-

My warm thanks to you for your wishes for the New Year. Your fine letter made me feel humble and contrite. I am so neglectful of my friends that I don't deserve to be remembered by them as you did, kindly and graciously. When they do come to me, letters from across the ocean, they warm the cockles of my heart. As the years grow apace, I long to get back to my American anchorage. Indeed, last spring I determined to cut loose from Palestine and return to America for my remaining years, to be coddled by my sisters. Hitler disposed otherwise. I should have felt like a renegade, if I had not remained on to do my bit, seeing that my many years in Palestine naturally mean experience of the sort useful in the emergencies created by a large immigration.

I am not, indeed, as you write, "in charge of the settlement in Palestine of exiles from Germany." I have been heading the "drive" for funds, and in connection with this enterprise I am a member of the executive committee of three which allocates the monies collected. The result of the campaign, £P 12,000 seems pretty good for the old Halukah land, doesn't it? It must be remembered that this was the first campaign of its kind in Palestine, that the Arlosoroff memorial (which reached £P. 18,000) was running parallel with it, and that the Keir campaign for £P. 15,000 had only a short time before been completed. Presently our ad hoc Committee will merge its allocation activities into the new Department for German Jewish affairs recently formed and attached to the Executive of the Jewish Agency, under the Chairmanship of Dr. Weizmann in London, and of Dr. Ruppin in Jerusalem. The new Department insures centralized co-ordinated action. I am now on my way to the

Henrietta Szold

LIFE AND LETTERS

By Marvin Lowenthal

1942

NEW YORK · THE VIKING PRESS

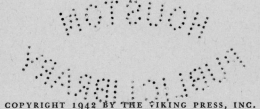

TO

Julian W. Mack

IN TRIBUTE TO HIS FRIENDSHIP FOR

HENRIETTA SZOLD

Acknowledgments

The present book owes its existence to the generosity of the friends of Henrietta Szold who, together with members of her family, placed at my disposal nearly five thousand of her personal letters. Not only the letters which space has permitted me to print but hundreds of others have aided me in tracing this biographical portrait; and I wish to extend to the donors my deep gratitude, only regretting that their number prevents me from thanking each one by name.

I am likewise indebted to published and unpublished accounts of Miss Szold's childhood and family background by her sister, the late Mrs. Thomas Seltzer; and to similar articles and counsel by her sister, Mrs. Bertha Levin, who in addition allowed me the use of scrapbooks, notebooks, manuscripts, and other illuminating documents. Hadassah, the Women's Zionist Organization of America, gave me files of material; and its officers who have been Miss Szold's comrades and disciples have accorded me invaluable advice and information.

The final selection and compilation of the letters could not have been made without the patience, judgment, and yeoman's service of my wife.

MARVIN LOWENTHAL

Contents

CHAPTER ONE

A Baltimore Girl

I

It was a winter during the Civil War. In the back room of a house on Eutaw Street, Baltimore, two or three women were gathered around a small red-hot stove. They were picking lint to be sent to the army for bandages. A little girl, not more than three or four years old, was seated on the floor, gravely helping to shred the lint. "This," says Henrietta Szold, "is my earliest clear recollection." She can remember, too, the tramp of marching soldiers on Pratt Street. She remembers the slave-block which her mother pointed out to her on the corner of Eutaw and Camden. A deserter from the Union armies, she recalls, was driven from the house by her father. The front room, like the back, is consecrated with an imperishable memory. April lilacs are in bloom. The room is filled with people crowding to the windows. Her father raises her on his shoulders and bids her look—and she sees the funeral procession of Abraham Lincoln.

In those days she must have heard her father dubbed "the rabbi of Timbuktoo." *Timbuktoo* was a derisive nickname given to a local society of liberal-minded citizens who proposed to aid the newly freed Negroes to secure an education. The clergy as a whole refused its support; but Rabbi Szold, a born humanitarian who as a youth had fought on the barricades of Vienna in '48, immediately joined the society's board of directors. The little girl will never forget, either, that her father once had a dramatic interview with Lincoln.

1

Using a Bible marked at an apt passage he drew the President from a Cabinet meeting and pleaded for the life of a captured deserter. Lincoln permitted him to go to military headquarters on the Rappahannock and appeal to General Meade; but the plea was in vain. The next day at dawn Rabbi Szold, promising to stay till the end, stood by the side of the deserter and four similar delinquents while the firing-squad spoke the last word.

Seldom has a Jewish father brought to his children a richer heritage. Benjamin Szold was born in 1829 at Nemiskert, a Hungarian village in the Nyitra valley, lying east of Pressburg, a region inhabited largely by Slovaks. From the days of the "enlightened" Joseph II the Szold family were landowners and cultivated their vineyards with their own hands—a rare experience for European Jews. Years later, Henrietta visited her father's birthplace and her mother's as well in a similar village, and she was amazed to discover that "the Jewish society of these insignificant places possesses more wit and intelligence than many metropolitan gatherings of notabilities; anecdotes, bons-mots, trenchant criticisms are bandied in the incisive manner of Frenchmen or Talmud disciples; they are well versed in books and in the reading of German and Hungarian authors; they are commonly ambitious, hospitable, generous, and endowed with an extraordinary taste and love for art and science." Extraordinary vine-dressers indeed.

Benjamin absorbed the fundamentals of Jewish learning in the neighboring towns and won his ordination as a rabbi at the tender age of fourteen. He sought his fortune in Vienna, fought in the democratic revolution of 1848, and was banished from the city for his pains. For several years he tutored in private households among his native Hungarian towns and villages; and in one of them, the home of the

Schaars, Jewish landowners near Tyrnau, he met his future bride. His horizons were widened in Breslau by studies at the university and close relations with the faculty and student body of the newly established "conservative" rabbinical seminary, where Heinrich Graetz, his great history still unwritten, was only one of a constellation of luminaries. In 1859 he accepted a call from a synagogue in Baltimore—"in America," the head of the seminary told him, "you have the world before you." He hastened to the village near Tyrnau, married Sophia Schaar, the girl in whose family he had tutored; and by September they were landed in the New World.

Their baggage was considerable. Rabbi Szold's culture, a distillation of Judaism and the humanities, was as deep as it was broad. The Hebrew Bible he knew by heart; and, according to his youngest daughter Adele, "to the end of his days he could read Horace with ease and recite long passages of Homer from memory." German was his habitual speech, and its literature and arts were a large province in his spiritual homeland. He brought to America ripened political convictions which had already stood the test of gunfire and which enrolled him at once as a "War Democrat," that is, a Jeffersonian who in the paramount issues confronting the nation stood for the abolition of slavery and the preservation of the Union—no timid stand in a Baltimore that sympathized with the Southern cause. "He stood as firm and fearless against the excited masses," writes his contemporary, Marcus M. Jastrow, "as he stood by the unfortunate deserter for whose life he had pleaded in vain." Like himself his wife possessed a strong and warm nature; and in both of them the strength and warmth kept the tang of the vineyards, the soil, and the sun of their childhood.

I I

A little more than a year after the Szolds arrived in America their first child, Henrietta, was born—December 21, 1860. Seven more daughters followed, of whom three died in infancy. In this family of girls Henrietta occupied the place—at table it meant sitting to the right of her father—and received the attention of a first-born son, and as the eldest daughter she helped in mothering the procession of newcomers. From her earliest years, bit by bit as her age permitted, fond parents brought the world to her ken and she in turn took a share in its responsibilities. Bit by bit, her innate character with the aid of these congenial circumstances shaped her life into an avid pursuit of knowledge and duty.

However, little Henrietta was neither an angel child nor a prig. She was known to hug a brood of newborn chicks to their literal death. She could naïvely insult visiting members of the congregation. She dreaded taking Passover gifts, "for the good of her soul," to a filthy home in a near-by alley. She hung ringlets of pine shavings about her head and admired her own loveliness. She was seduced by uniforms and dreamed of becoming a Quaker lady. And like many children she persuaded herself that she was a foundling. "I always thought I was a stepchild, because mother had blue eyes, rosy cheeks, and was altogether fresh and fair, and I was such a sallow dark little thing I could not imagine I was her daughter."

A term in something called a "nursery school" passed without a trace. Then came years of the "German School" where, in the basement of her father's synagogue, Lehrer Jonas Goldschmidt, clad in dressing-gown and slippers, a long-stemmed pipe in one hand and a rattan cane in the other, taught the children the elements of German, English, "secular studies," and Judaism. Henrietta's finger-tips were not unacquainted with the rattan cane and her ears were known to tingle with the rebuke, *"Und du, du Szold, schämst du dich nicht?"* ("And you, you Szold, aren't you ashamed of yourself?")

In the classroom German was reserved for religious instruction and carried with it something of the sacred air given to Yiddish by East European schools. But in the Szold home and for perhaps a fifth of Baltimore's population German was the prevalent household speech. Like other American cities of the period with a large German immigration, Baltimore possessed its Männerchore, Turnverein, Waisenhaus, Greisenheim, Schützen Park, its German churches, schools, clubs, and bookstores as well as two German newspapers and a theatrical stock company.

Gathered in this miniature Germany were samplings of all the Teutonic strains. A quick mind such as Henrietta's mastered not only the classic tongue of Goethe—she read *Hermann und Dorothea* at the age of eight—and the dreary language of encyclopedic histories, a favorite diet of her father; but, merely by talking with the neighbors, she absorbed a collection of provincial dialects, Swabian, Upper Bavarian, Hessian, Plattdeutsch, which to accumulate in the fatherland would have taken years of travel. As a tot of five she innocently talked the leading actor of the German stock company into giving her a ticket to Gutzkow's *Uriel Acosta*. The result proved devastating in an unforeseen way. Her exploit was published in the German press, grown-ups sought out the child, and exclaimed over her as though she were a prodigy; and the embarrassment left a scar, making her shy and ill at ease with strangers until well past middle age. "I wasted half my life as far as human contacts are concerned, because I was bashful," she once said, and added: "It was agony."

Whatever the cause, her shyness if anything intensified her receptivity—the gift for lodging other people's ideas in her own little head and for placing herself in other people's shoes. In this respect her primary school was the Szold home. Not that her father played the schoolmaster, but he rejoiced in this intelligent young creature, talked to her as he would to a contemporary, and together they viewed and judged the world. Adopt a central idea, he urged, never depart from it, but relate everything to that idea—advice that she later said "was a determining influence in my life." Her mother imposed no chores as discipline, but out of abundant vitality and a keen practical sense she swept her children enthusiastically into the arts of sewing, canning, pickling, marketing, cleaning, piano-playing, gardening, every household art of the period except indeed the one on which, as a good Hungarian, the pride of her heart was set—cookery. "I think my whole intellectual make-up is my mother's," Henrietta came to believe, "because I am practical; my mind runs to details and I have a very strong sense of duty."

Behind this bustle of brains and hands, the ultimate teacher and monitor was Judaism. As a matter of cultural and congregational history Rabbi Szold bore the label of a "conservative." He could not accept the radical abandonment of ceremonies and dogmas along with the radical innovations advocated by Isaac M. Wise, David Einhorn, and the American "Reform" group; but, on the other hand, he was willing to discard unessential traditions and rites which he felt no longer applied to the modern world. Like the men with whom he studied back in Breslau, he walked the middle of the road, surer that by doing so neither he nor his faith would get lost.

But it was not the formal label that counted in the Szold home. Battles that now make a scholarly page in the annals of American Jewry echoed with living force around the dining-room table. Should public prayers be read in Hebrew, German, or English—in what proportions and which prayers? Rabbi Szold had drawn up a middle-of-the-road liturgy accepted by his own and more than a score of other congregations; and he and the little Szolds had their answer. How scrupulously should the Sabbath be observed in an economy that made Saturday almost perforce a day of work? The father was both a stanch observer himself and an uncompromising advocate of similar observance for others. Was the Talmud an authority on a par with the Bible? Was God a person or a philosophic idea? What was the Messiah—a man, a symbolic aspiration, or Israel itself? Was the redemption of the Holy Land an obsolete myth or a remote but nevertheless certain reality? What was the mission, the ultimate destiny of the Jews, and what were they —a sect or a people? And how shall a people be defined? What did Progress, the unquestioned watchword of the age, say to all this? The answers were seldom certain; many of them time alone could give. It was the questions, not the answers, that taught; it was the debate, not the decision, that trained the muscles of the mind and heart.

Speaking through the father's lips, Judaism likewise took Henrietta for a pupil on more universal terms. By example rather than by precept, by Talmudic tales, Old World anecdotes, and Biblical quotations directed at every passing event, Henrietta learned that Judaism was a way of life. Foreign politics, American domestic issues, Baltimore's civic affairs, and household crises, one and all were interwoven with Jewish texts and traditions until it was apparent that the fabric of life was of one piece. "If there was a murder trial in the city," she recalled, "my father would point out how it would have been conducted according to Jewish law." For him "Judaism was not only a faith or a creed but a way of life, and he stressed the development of the law"—that is, the canon and mold of daily behavior. He believed that "you cannot have Judaism in full flower unless you have a normal human life in which you illustrate your Jewish principles through the exercise of the law."

Law and tradition are formidable words, but translated into normal human actions they can be lovable things, enjoyed for themselves and imperishable as memories. It was not a law, a principle, or a symbol, but a happy way of his Jewish life that led to Rabbi Szold's disappearance on the one day of 1874 when his presence was most wanted. It was moving day. Bag, baggage, and vanload, the Szolds were leaving Eutaw for Lombard Street. "My father could not be found," Henrietta tells us, "and my mother was beside herself. 'Where is your father, where is your father?' she kept crying. We followed the vans up to Lombard Street, everybody carrying something. And there we found my father in the garden back of the house, planting a vine and a fig tree."

III

The house on Lombard Street, to be the family center till 1896, lived on like a shrine in the Szold memories. Fifty years after her father did his planting, the scent of fig trees on the road to Nablus brought back to Henrietta the Lombard garden gate and a white-haired Negro holding a horse in the alley beyond. The garden with its grapevines, berry bushes, fruit trees, and all sorts of blossoms which flourished in spite of pet chickens, dogs, cats, and the children, and where Henrietta brought her books, Hebrew, German, and French, to study in summer; the cellar, where a living spring cooled the great jars of dill pickles, where shelves groaned under inexhaustible rows of preserves, jellies, and pickles, and where under the shelves stood a barrel of sauerkraut and another of pickled meat; the second-floor sitting-room with its long-suffering square piano, at which Henrietta and her sister Bertha "played duets by the hour, with great satisfaction to ourselves"—Strauss waltzes and Beethoven sonatas rendered with patience and laughter if not with inspiration; the library, book-lined from floor to ceiling, where Henrietta, acting as her father's secretary, learned to marshal facts and ideas and express them not only with accuracy but, as her father insisted, with abundance; the dining-room, where the resources of the cellar, kitchen, and library combined to satisfy the appetite for plain living, Hungarian style (that is, with the best or second-best cookery in the world), and for high thinking, Jewish style—nothing of that house, steeped and overflowing with affection, could die. Sixty-two years old, writing home from Jerusalem, Henrietta Szold tells her sisters: "It is Lombard Street that makes for sympathy and understanding; the rest may do its worst or best—it can't eliminate that."

In 1873 occurred a significant event in Henrietta's girlhood. Following a spell at a public grammar school and before she had reached her thirteenth birthday, she entered the Western Female High School. There, for four years, she studied the usual subjects and others which present tastes might find unusual: astronomy, mensuration, elocution, and "mental philosophy." Her record pleased her father. Semi-annually he attested on her report card that he judged her average marks, which hovered around 95, to be "satisfactory," "favorable," "very good," "excellent"; and in the final flight, when the average soared to 99.8, he found or wrote no word for it.

Her record, it is said, was never excelled—"a reflection," dryly observes her sister Bertha, "on the learning standards of the time." Henrietta, too, considered the instruction superficial, in some subjects a "farce," and that little encouragement was given to youthful curiosity. Yet to students of education her yellowed and faded notebooks, while not refuting the charges, would reveal another side of the story. Their penmanship, spelling, and command of language illustrate standards neglected today. A rusty newspaper clipping informs us that when she was fourteen she burst into print with "A Dialogue between Two Schoolgirls the Day after Washington's Birthday." Its imagery may be absurd, its sentiments insufferable for their pretentious rhetoric and moralizing, but the language is clear and fluent. City officials visited the school for an "afternoon exhibition"; Henrietta read a paper on "Great Men," "showing evidence of unusual talents in one so young." Not yet seventeen, she published in the Baltimore *Elocutionist* an article on "The Troubles in Turkey" in which the Eastern question, no doubt debated in the family dining-room, was handled with an assurance that would have done credit to Mr. Godkin's *Nation*. Somewhere, in her father's study if not at high school, she had learned to think and write.

Botany, a subject not in the curriculum, became a passionate hobby of the Szold girls. Field expeditions far into the Maryland countryside, with Mother Szold of the party, took the place of sports. "No hockey or even basketball or

tennis in my days," recalls Henrietta in later years; "at the
utmost croquet . . . and I knew enough to run away from
a game of croquet." Trees were made into friends and called
by name. "I have a foible for trees," she writes from Jerusalem at the age of seventy-five; and the longing for the
"unique" forests of Maryland in their autumn colors wrings
from her the cry: "I feel I must fly to see them and revive
the memories which even the Zionist adventure in Palestine cannot push into the limbo of forgotten things." When
homesickness overcame her, it was first for the family and
next for those unique forests.

Her girlhood interest did not stop at the analysis and
identification of plants. Experiments were made in trans-
planting wild flowers to the backyard garden. Eventually a
paper was written for the Maryland Academy of Science
on "Essential Organs of Plants." A friend of her youth res-
cues from the limbo of forgotten things their walks together
in the springtime. "Henrietta would greet every bursting
bud, every thrusting leaf and blade, every reddening twig
with a word of recognition: 'The bloodroot is early this
season; this patch will be white with anemones in another
week; look! the dogwood is just beginning to push up.' Nature's book was as open to her as a child's primer."

Boys, younger and older than herself, began to enter her
life. She collected stamps with the lad Harry Friedenwald,
later to be the president of a Federation of American Zionists as yet undreamed of. She listened at her father's table
to the astute youth, Fabian Franklin. The opening of Johns
Hopkins University in 1876 brought to the same table
through the succeeding years a redoubtable son of Marcus Jastrow, the Flexner and Heilprin brothers, and omnis-
cient Cyrus Adler.

Meanwhile, graduation from the Western Female High

School brought Henrietta's girlhood to a close in a blaze of glory. The commencement exercises were held in Ford's Grand Opera House, June 28, 1877. On the stage sat the class of forty-eight young ladies attired in white dresses with "sprays of flowers" in their hair. Among the dignitaries on the stage was the Reverend Dr. Szold. As first in her class, his daughter delivered the honorary address on "Our Public Schools," which was "applauded to the echo." The mayor distributed the diplomas, and the Peabody Institute bestowed gold medals on Miss Szold and four other brilliant students—brilliant indeed in a class of which almost half received scholarship marks averaging 90 and higher. Henrietta's address was printed in the English press, and a condensed version appeared in translation in the German press, where the applause was described as *stürmisch*.

Henrietta was the only Jewess in the class. Most of the Baltimore Jewish families had not yet taken to sending their daughters to high school. Baltimore itself, Southern provincial Baltimore, had not taken, either, to the notion of sending Female High School graduates to college. "We didn't dare mention Vassar," said Henrietta, addressing a graduation class twenty years later, "except in terms of awe with which one speaks of a remote object one has never seen and dare not hope to approach." So she hung the gold medal on a chain around her neck, ready for the commencement of life.

CHAPTER TWO

Widening Horizons

I

Henrietta no sooner left school as a pupil than she returned again as a teacher. For a brief period she substituted for the English instructor and the principal of the Female High School. Then, for nearly fifteen years, she taught at the Misses Adams's school, a private institution "run by Southern gentlewomen whose fortunes had decayed in the Civil War and attended by the daughters of their friends." Her subjects were German, French, algebra, and whatever else was in demand. From time to time she taught in other private schools, too, and tutored individuals in German and Hebrew.

Her temperamental dislike for amateur work as well as her later experiences with modern education in Palestine led her, when she looked back on these young days, to think poorly of her own work. "I feel," she said, "I was a humbug. I was not trained to be a teacher. But I got much interest out of it." It was this interest which must have inspired a different opinion of her skill among its beneficiaries. A lifelong friend says of her teaching at the Misses Adams's: "Some of the pupils at that private school, middle-aged women now, still recall with pleasure the classes she taught. She brought a fine enthusiasm, a fresh point of view, a delight in her subject, and an eagerness to share it with her pupils that made of her teaching a rare art."

After a decade of experience she unburdened her heart on the business of teaching. In a paper read to the state

13

teachers' association (1887) she set forth principles and a prophecy: "Do we constantly bear in mind that conveying information is only a subordinate part of the teacher's work? Do we always labor with the sole end in view of *training* the minds entrusted to our care? . . . The true utilitarian will confine his attention to those elements that educate the *man,* be he in the guise of a carpenter, a banker, a shoemaker, a hod-carrier, or a college professor. . . . It is the living, the organic, the concrete, that in which life throbs and pulsates like his own quickening blood, that attracts a child. In every study he must be shown growth— which is life. . . . Take a flower one day, an insect the next, dwell upon such familiar things as rain and dew, make it a rule never to overstep the horizon of the child's actual or possible experience. . . . There is one study that should be found in the curriculum for the last year of every boy and girl—the study of how to read the newspaper. I am witness to the broadening intelligence, culture, and sympathies of a class of girls (ranged in age from fifteen to seventeen) constituting a news class and reading a weekly journal. . . . Everywhere we discern prognostics of the fact that life in the twentieth century will not be easy to live, that it will require high courage to face the truth, steadfastness and unflinching purpose. The work we have to do is to prepare them for a struggle from which they will not be spared." Such a teacher at twenty-seven must have been an artist.

Newly founded Johns Hopkins University, the educational wonder of its days, was no doubt partly responsible for her advanced ideas. She attended its public lecture courses (as well as those of the Peabody Institute). Students frequented her home and agitated the strange and novel features practiced in its classrooms. A lengthy article on the university which she published in 1883 testified to her keen interest in these innovations. She likewise formed relations with prominent local educators, such as Miss M. Carey Thomas, the founder of Bryn Mawr and later its president; Mary Garrett, who gave Johns Hopkins a half-million dollars to open its doors to women; and Lizette Woodworth Reese, still to be remembered for her poetry. The Botany Club and later a Woman's Literary Club, in both of which she was a leading spirit, made her welcome in Baltimore's most cultivated circles. She was growing in every fiber.

A great portion of her teaching career lay in the Jewish field. At her father's synagogue, Oheb Shalom, she taught in the religious school early Sabbath mornings and again on Sundays. On Sabbath afternoons she conducted a two-hour Bible class for adults. For the upper set of Baltimore Jewesses she led a "select class" in Jewish history.

She quickly learned and published the fact (in an article dated 1880) that "the religious instruction of our youth cannot be trusted to the questionable abilities of a laity where, moreover, the female sex predominates." Piety is not enough to qualify them to teach. Bible lessons, although fundamental, are not enough to furnish the knowledge required. "A Jewish youth must be instructed in the glories of our history and thus learn to know the exigencies of his time and be ready to do battle with them." Above all, youth must acquire a mastery of the Hebrew language, "which is the key to the understanding of all this." At twenty Henrietta Szold was seeking and selecting weapons for a battle she sensed was to come. Young Hebrew-steeped intellectuals in Russia were arming for the same battle, which was to be loosed the next year. Not two years before, a handful of Jerusalem Jews had laid the cornerstone of the first Jewish agricultural colony in Palestine—Petach Tikvah, the "Door of Hope." Henrietta knew nothing of these remote circumstances that were being linked by destiny, not even that among them were the vine and the fig tree on Lombard Street and her father's dictum that Judaism is a way of life.

I I

From the year she stepped out of high school she likewise began instructing others and herself by serving as the Baltimore correspondent of the New York *Jewish Messenger.* Her weekly letters or articles, signed "Sulamith," mirror the age.

Their growing pains at an end, the American Jewish communities had taken mature shape. The immigrants from Germany of the previous generation, who comprised the vast majority of the Jewish population, had established themselves economically. During the lull in immigration between 1860 and 1880 they had consolidated their communal life. Synagogues and Reform temples rose on every side, supplanting the rented, casual quarters and testifying to the stability and comfortable circumstances of the community. Philanthropy, proverbial and obligatory to Judaism, took concrete form. In the opening paragraph of her first letter to the *Messenger,* March 1878, Sulamith describes dozens of communities when she writes of Baltimore: "Our inherited charity and benevolence are well represented by our Orphan Asylum, our Benevolent Society, our Hospital, and other institutions." The organization of philanthropy in a wider sense was represented, too, by the creation of Young Men's Hebrew Associations—one had just been formed in Baltimore—and the growth of the fraternal order of the B'nai B'rith with lodges first in American and then in numerous foreign cities.

Men, however, do not live by bricks and stone or even by the machinery of organization. American Jews had an equipment, but they were sorely divided or at a loss over what to do with it. Cultural content and clear purposes were wanting. "The extensive fields of Hebrew lore, philosophy, poetry, and the noble language in which it is expressed," complains Sulamith, "all have been allowed to remain barren."

In Baltimore, at least, the synagogues were not empty. "While the services are woefully neglected on Friday eve, when there is usually a ball at one of our principal clubhouses, liberally patronized by the Jewish community, on Saturday mornings, however, our ministers deliver their sermons to large numbers." The sources of the trouble lay elsewhere, deep in American life. "Apparently there are but two central ideas to which all is subservient—business and pleasure, the fluctuation of prices or a round of dissipation." Mark Twain had called it the Gilded Age. As one result, "the very mention of Jewish literature and history is sufficient to blanch their faces and strike their hearts with terror." Sulamith observed that when a lecturer closed his talk at the local Young Men's Hebrew Association, "there was a general uproarious movement as if the audience had been liberated from prison."

The drift from Judaism as a way of life was lamented and derided in detail. "I heard a lady, on telling the name of her child, which was that of the heroine of a very popular novel, remark that she hated Bible or so-called Jewish names, they seemed to her so homely, discordant, and inexpressive. . . . Why need we adopt the Christmas tree, ridiculously baptized a Chanuka bush? . . . As long as the head of the family plays solo [this was an aeon before bridge and rummy] evening after evening, the mother gossips with the neighbors, and the young folks rush from pleasure to pleasure, so long will there be no sensible improvement."

Though some of the counter-attractions were on a higher level than solo or business, Sulamith was not to be taken in by their pretensions. While defending the personal integrity and idealism of Felix Adler, who had recently founded the Ethical Culture Society, she dismissed "the bulk of the members" as "apostates not because new ideas have dawned upon their minds, but because they are swept away by a glittering phrase or a foolish desire to appear fashionable." The followers of Robert G. Ingersoll and other evangelists of free thought received similar short shrift. "The fact that a large number of our young co-religionists crowded to hear the blasphemies of Colonel Ingersoll gives force to my remark that some of us are ashamed to avow our noble faith." She is canny enough to detect that, like Voltaire but with less reason, the Colonel is a cautious warrior. "Coward as he is, he makes his objections refer only to the Old Testament, for he well knows that Christians would not tolerate a shadow thrown upon their own holy book; he would be despised and ostracized were he to speak of it in such scoffing terms."

A hitherto ignored if not unknown aspect of the free-thought movement during the seventies is revealed. In several articles Sulamith describes and assails the anti-Semitism of a number of its leaders. A Mr. Reitzel, "the speaker of the congregation of free-thinkers in Washington," attacked the Day of Atonement on the ground that "it shows the animosity which the Jew bears toward his fellow-creatures of other creeds." The Baltimore society of free-thinkers, moreover, made it their special aim "to fight all sectarian encroachments, especially that against [sic] the Hebrews." In virulent letters to the press, leaders of both groups supported the exclusion of Jews from fashionable hotels. Sulamith had learned from Moses Mendelssohn, and promptly quoted him, that "even atheism has its fanaticism."

Sulamith was quick to give her reactions to Germany's outburst of anti-Semitism in 1880, with its attendant riots. The optimism of her judgment on the German Anti-Semitic League and court chaplain Stöcker makes wry reading today. "That the Germans, a nation of philosophers, can be roused by such a demagogue as Hofprediger Stöcker to the unworthy demonstrations which the cable reports daily proves by no means that the true sentiments of the Germans have been expressed." She finds it encouraging "that professors and students at the universities, the elite in the ranks of intelligence, have entered indignant protests against these shameful proceedings," and she adds: "If we have such friends, we can bear the almost certain connivance of the German government and the half-sneering defense of the Jews by the press."

Both her love for German culture, so warmly cultivated in the Szold home, and her belief in the progress of mankind, shared without tinge or scruple of doubt by her whole century, made any other judgment impossible. When next year Russia followed and bettered Germany's example, it was different. Russians were recognized barbarians. Still, her convictions were troubled and her mind harked back to Börne. "Some men reproach me with being a Jew," she quotes sadly, "others forgive me for it, others again even class it among my merits; but *all* remember it."

In Sulamith's sprightly articles a religious battle still

lives, though otherwise all but forgotten now. No one today can quite recapture the bitterness of the Reform advo-
cates and their opponents over details of Jewish ritual and
observance: whether hats should be worn in the synagogue,
the dietary laws maintained, the Sabbath meticulously observed, and the like. The death of Rabbi David Einhorn
(November 1879), a leader in the Reform wing and at one
time an outspoken antagonist of Rabbi Szold, moved Henrietta to sincere but somewhat left-handed eulogy. After
praising his character, intelligence, and scholarship, all
qualities "most needed at present," she found it remarkable that in the flood of laudatory articles about him "nothing is emphasized so much as his work as a reformer of religious observances." The barb came when she concluded:
"It is by no means a distinction for him to be lauded for
that in which he is surpassed by hundreds of men infinitely
his inferiors in every respect." A little later she acquitted
herself brilliantly in a none too gentle controversy with the
peppery Dr. Isaac M. Wise, dean and leading exponent of
the Reform movement. In 1883 the *Messenger,* hoping no
doubt for more fireworks, asked her to report from Cincinnati the commencement exercises of the first class to graduate from Hebrew Union College, which Dr. Wise had
founded and over which he presided. She came with preju-
dices, "disposed to criticize severely and perhaps unjustly."
The criticisms were not lacking, but she left conquered and
showering blessings—"May the institution and the newly
ordained rabbis prosper!"

A recurrent note in the letters of Sulamith expresses one
of her ingrained attitudes. It finds expression again and
again throughout her young womanhood. She often spoke
of it as a hatred of materialism, but it was more pointed
and concrete than that. A single example must serve. In

1879 a convention of synagogue congregations was held at Baltimore. Among the subjects discussed was a colonization scheme to settle Jews on the soil. Reporting on the scheme, Sulamith remarked that "the land of that Jewish colony will most likely be situated in Utopia so long as there are no funds to locate it in less visionary regions." Thereupon she launched into a denunciation of the rich for their lack of imagination, generosity, honor, and, above all, social responsibility.

"Why it is I don't know, but it is a fact that when an insult is offered to a Jewish banker, our nation rises like one man and cries and clamors until the imagined wrong is avenged. I suppose this means that the honor of a rich man is the honor of the nation—the former being tainted, the latter reflects the tarnished point. Well, if that is true, where are our bankers now? The honor of our nation is involved; let them show it is a point of honor with them to regard it as their own reputation. What are they doing to pay for being constituted representative men, a distinction which they have accepted as a matter of course, as their due, indeed as their right? Now is the time to show that they identify themselves with Judaism, that they deserve to have the whole of Jewry as their bodyguard. . . . I should like to know who is to be blamed: the American Jewish public for being too cringing and too ready with praise and laudations, or the American Jewish nabobs who are so ostentatious and boastful."

These are sentiments that Theodor Herzl, who was born in the same year as Henrietta Szold, took almost another two decades to manifest. The heart that dictated them—that demanded *noblesse oblige,* justification, conscience, and responsibility from the wealthy and powerful—was the heart that led many youths in far lands to radical democ-

racy and socialism and was soon to bring many others to
Zionism. Hearts like that sooner or later lead the feet into
new upward-bound roads, to heights where if there be no
road either a path or the heart itself is broken.

III

Meanwhile, in 1881, Henrietta's survey of the Jewish
scene extended to Europe. In the company of her father
she had brief glimpses of Germany, Austria, Hungary, and
the French capital—brief but varied. Prague, with its ancient ghetto, synagogues, and cemetery, cast its wonted spell,
despite "the loquacity and obsequiousness of the guiding
sexton." The tales and legends she had absorbed in childhood from her father's lips, the printed pages of history
which had held her captive in the Lombard Street study and
garden, now were clothed in the grim but romantic reality
of stone. The Hungarian villages where her parents were
born deepened her sense of a personal link with the past.
The villagers and the neighboring townsfolk as well as their
history became identified with herself in heightened vivid-
ness. "My chief impression of that first trip to Europe," she
felt in later years, "was my sense of belongingness to my
father's and mother's people."

Pressburg, where her father had studied and taught as a
stripling, gave her a spiritual shock. Her father pointed out
the arched gateway leading to the ghetto. The gate itself
had vanished. "But he recollected the time when it used to
close upon the last belated Jew, panting under a load of
merchandise, with the spiteful click and ponderous noise
that all prison doors know how to produce. Soon after his
coming to Pressburg, the jailers consented to leave the gate
ajar, and time and again a Jew dared slip out and establish

himself just beyond it. Each one who escaped pushed it open slightly further, until sunshine and air were admitted without stint."

Hitherto, when she had read of Jewish sufferings in past ages, "pity and sympathy," she wrote, "filled out my whole heart" and "there was no room left for anger." But now when "I stood in the place where gloom had brooded, where misery had flourished, where men and women had existed hermetically sealed up, so far as new, fresh, vigorous life was concerned, and whence they had been driven only to be plunged into a deeper abyss of misfortune and pain—such reflections could not but arouse the resentful feelings of a Shylock." Her enjoyment of the charm and talents of the Pressburg Jews—introduced to her by her father—was spoiled. Though nothing in their looks or actions called for it, "bitter feelings" welled up within her. An empty ghetto gateway, her father's memory of a wooden door—substantially these were nothing; but in spirit Henrietta passed beneath the arch and clasped hands not only with a dead and better forgotten martyrdom but with millions who were to suffer in the years to come.

It was a relief to spar with the modern intellectuals of Germany. When the subject of religion was broached, she came to feel that the European, for all his devotion to ritual, was a hypocrite; and she sensed that he in turn looked on her, despite her profession of faith, as a quasi-apostate. It was a relief to have the sexton of the leading synagogue in Paris invite her, in the midst of the services, to attend a "four-thousand-franc wedding," and when she declined, to have him announce, as an irresistible bait, that the bride was no less than "the daughter of a member of the Consistory." It was a relief to learn with care and detail the system of communal organization, the administration of philanthropies, and the training and duties of the rabbinate on the Continent.

By and large she learned to recognize the strength and weakness of European Jewry. "In appearance and with much better cause for being so, they are as materialistic, irreligious, and indifferent to the call of Judaism as we are." Both German and American Jews had absorbed, in their faults as well as virtues, the coloring of their native lands. In Germany the Jews stayed away from synagogues on Sabbath in the same droves as the Christians stayed away from church; but, as became a citizen in "a nation of philosophers," the German Jew assiduously cultivated Jewish learning. On the contrary, in America Jew and Christian alike were stanch at sitting in pews but shy on poring over books. Therefore, despite its cynicism and materialism, "Continental Europe will remain the nursery of Jewish thought and research" and "the hearth of Jewish feeling."

The reasons, she felt, go deeper than social imitation. The Jewish past in Europe throws a living net around the present. Try as he may and does, the European Jew cannot escape through its meshes. "The struggles of his parents and their friends come back vividly to his memory; he recollects their toil and grief; in his ear the cry of 'Hep! Hep!' resounds; in his bosom the remembrance of the wrong, though not of the wrong-doer, rankles. There is not a foot of ground in his vicinity which has not been consecrated by the blood of his own race, his brethren and kindred. And for the sake of what did that blood flow? For nothing less than the very religion he is treating so shabbily—and which he now wishes to obliterate from his life and from the consciousness of his children. It is impossible for him to do this. In their sight he must remain a Jew and even a strict Jew. For every observance, the most minute and trivial, has been sanctified and made inviolate by blood." As proof she calls to mind that in Russia, "where persecution is still rife, the Jews are most religious."

She did not go to Russia, but within a short while Russia came to Baltimore. And Russians were to bring the electric charge around which the atoms of her youthful experiences, thoughts, and feelings would cohere into a living whole.

CHAPTER THREE

Destined to Be Read in Berlin

BEGINNING with this chapter, Henrietta Szold's life will, as far as the material permits, be illustrated through her letters. Few of them, however, pertain to life in her twenties probably because, since she remained at home, few were written. But in 1887 one of her close friends, Harry Friedenwald (born 1864), began a three years' stay in Berlin and Vienna. The Szold family with its five daughters and the Friedenwalds with their five sons were intimate neighbors. After collecting stamps with Henrietta in her high school days, giving her a lift in Latin during his college years, and debating the universe on Sunday evenings at the Szold home, Harry set off for Germany to complete his medical studies, laying the groundwork for his later eminence as a professor and surgeon in ophthalmology and otology. Almost as dear to him as his profession was his interest in Jewish culture.

For the present he is an American student abroad, and Henrietta's letters to him carry on the discussions and bring something of the flavor of the Sunday evenings at her home.

Baltimore, September 21, 1887

This summer was for me as void of work as yours was replete. I do not remember ever to have spent two months in such absolute idleness.

In the early part of July, Sadie, Bertha,[1] and myself, en-

---

[1] Sadie Szold (1867–1893). Bertha Szold, later Mrs. Louis H. Levin (b. 1873), and the sole surviving sister.

ticed by the cheap fare and board offered to the Teachers
Association of Maryland, went for a week to Old Point
Comfort. I cannot say that it was a week of uninterrupted
pleasure. While I enjoyed the ocean, the bathing, which,
however, cannot be compared to Cape May, I was on the
other hand disgusted with the people I met.

The hotel was crowded with that despicable class of people—the Virginia aristocracy with their unjustifiable purse-
pride and shoddyism, or, if possible, even more ignorant
pride of blood. On the other hand, we were thrown with
the teachers from the counties. Since I have seen them I
have heartily wished never to become known to others as
a teacher.

But whatever I missed there I was richly compensated
for in the latter part of the summer when, meeting Rachel
and Joe [2] at Germantown, we three went to New York to
attend the sessions of the American Association for the
Advancement of Science. Rachel and myself, certainly, attended those of the botanical section. While the meetings
were truly interesting, the chief charm of that week lay
in the people we met. What a fine set of men, physically
and intellectually, those scientists are!

After all this good time, you can imagine with what
reluctance I shall tomorrow wend my way schoolward.

Your letter betrays that you do not hold a very high opinion of the morality of the German people. My experience
is indeed very much limited with regard to their conduct
at home. But what I see of them here, as well as other
Europeans, forces me to agree with your estimate. I hear
from them a great deal about the corruption prevalent
among Americans. Now, if it did not smack of Know-

---

[2] Rachel Szold (1865–1926). Joseph Jastrow, who married Rachel
in the summer of 1888.

Nothingism I should venture to assert that three-fourths of the immorality laid at the door of America is traceable directly to foreigners; and when one considers our mixed masses, so loosely welded together, one must concede that the hard work forced on everyone has created a moral atmosphere which reacts beneficially also upon the generally low class of emigrants that the Old World annually disburdens herself of.

There is no doubt that German social life has many commendable features, especially by way of contrast with American ideas on the subject. But the German of the lower classes, still more the Austrian, is so eager to avail himself of pleasures and amusements that he often shirks duties of the most sacred kind. These pleasures, instead of refining him as their character might lead us to suspect, bestialize and materialize him.

Unfortunately, my experience has taught me that our co-religionists in Europe suffer most from that rampant materialism that I speak of. They are indeed intellectually superior to the average German, for which reason they have conjured up against themselves the specter of anti-Semitism; but on the other hand, they have ethically deteriorated from the standard of two or three generations ago—a standard which has up to very recent times prevailed among us in America.

Baltimore, January 2, 1888

Matters over here are much quieter than they are with you in Germany. Our last news reads that Bismarck is intriguing to force the Crown Prince to resign the regency in favor of his reactionary son. Whether this be true or not, it shows that the peace of Europe hangs upon a thread—

depends upon the caprice of some crowned or uncrowned despot in Russia or Germany.

Your allusion to young Prince William's anti-Semitic predilections did not arouse the same feelings of indignation I might have felt at other times. American Jews, American rabbis, are giving the world at present such a sad spectacle of their own utter worthlessness that I am beginning to understand the scorn which the anti-Semite harbors for our co-religionists.

Our [local Jewish] paper, that has made the pretense of being conservative, has actually addressed the leading rabbis of the country for their opinions upon substituting Sunday services for the old Sabbath—thus magnifying into a problem what has heretofore been the consideration of only a handful of extreme radicals, who, however, it must be remembered, are wealthy and hence must be flattered. Cyrus Adler took an admirable stand in the matter.

His scholarly scientific calm is really enviable. I have been in a stew and at a boiling point ever since it occurred. Add to all this that my father received a private letter from Sweden, stating that there is a strong party in favor of Sunday services—testifying to the fact that the Jews of the Old and New Worlds are running a mad race to see who can mold the other in the worship of what is sensuous and material. Can we be surprised if even good people join the ranks of our opponents?

I am sorry to have to close my letter with so discordant a note; indeed, it was not my intention to write of it, but I do not possess Cyrus Adler's calmness and tranquillity—allied with earnestness. I am like my father, who has really been made sick by all these occurrences.

Baltimore, March 30, 1888

I must confess that some evenings are altogether incomplete without you; and, at such times, it is hard to realize that it will very soon be a year since you left Baltimore. All the more earnestly do we hope that your return will restore every bond and refresh every expression of friendly intercourse.

To know that you are hard at work, as we do, conveys nothing to our mind. It is a satisfaction to know only what particular work you are doing—where, how, and with whom, at any stated time. I suppose that is the reason travelers soon conquer the sadness of separation; they can enjoy the picturing of what is being done in the old scenes, which are unchanged by their withdrawal.

To write a letter in Baltimore destined to be read in Berlin is not a slight undertaking—especially if the Berlin be the Berlin of this day and moment. What great things have taken place under your eyes!

I confess to but a small grain of sympathy with the Germans in their *Germanentum* and *National-Bestrebungen* —too often *National-Hochmuth*. The successful victor over Austria and France is too aggressive, too vulgar in his successes, especially when we must concede that the nation in other respects is great beyond expression, and that, if power must be vested in one nation more than another, it is by far preferable it should be in Germany than in another Continental people—Russia, for instance. But in spite of all this antipathy—coupled with a good deal more solid hatred of the Hohenzollern family—I must say that I remember no events of a public nature, except Garfield's martyrdom, to have stirred me as deeply, as pathetically, as this melancholy transfer of the German crown, and the noble, single-minded devotion of each individual German to the cause of a hero-monarch.

The scene, described in our papers, that was enacted before the royal palace, of a vast throng, silent as death itself, gathered under the dying monarch's window, was to me an illustration of the Germans' real greatness.[3] Not force, but reserve of force; not the heroism of deeds but of thought. Is not the calm suffering on the part of the present Emperor,[4] yet unswerving loyalty to the trust his birth entails upon him, the best illustration of it? No one will hesitate to proclaim him a far greater man now than he was eighteen years ago before Paris: not greater as a general, a diplomat, a sovereign, but as a man; and that is saying that he has accomplished the greatest feat and conquest of all.

From day to day I learn to respect and venerate pure simple morality—humanity in the original acceptation of the word—beyond all other things. Not that I am so pessimistic as to consider it a rare virtue. There are many that have acquired it among those I come in contact with, but none, I am sure, without having struggled for it. And it is the accomplished conflict that compels my admiration. Life is hard, we are told, and full of duties and temptations. But the assimilation of this truth is a matter of experience only.

You will infer that I have had such experience. That is a true inference, and the most noteworthy thing about it is that such terrible experiences do not choose unusual events as their messengers. The trivialities of life merely assume another hue which strikes the eye—heretofore color-blind. That is the philosophy evolved during the long quiet winter just ended.

[3] Refers to death of William I.
[4] Frederick III, who died of cancer three months later.

Baltimore, April 21, 1889

As for your stay in Berlin, I think you have chosen wisely
to prefer it to Vienna. News from the latter city has of late
months been of so disappointing, nay, so revolting a nature, that I am well satisfied not to have to identify any
friend with its unpleasant memories.

However, it strikes me that the choice is puzzling between Hapsburg impotence, disunion, and vacillation on
the one hand, and Hohenzollern-Bismarckian arrogance,
despotism, and superciliousness. In the first case, there is the
consoling thought that want of success paralyzes the malign
influence that may have been exerted. In the latter, there
is no palliating circumstance—it is despotism, successful,
vulgarly, provokingly successful. Though the municipality of Berlin may be a model, though the policing of the
state may be perfect, and though the country may be pro-
gressing materially and educationally—I hate even the despotism that does good. It is worse than the despotism that
works evil, which is thereby recognized, detested, and resisted. The other passes for good unalloyed and gathers
strength in secrecy.

How I hate your young military Kaiser,[5] with his wordy
admiration for his grandfather, his unabashed silence concerning his noble father's life—both but a foil for his own
prowess and courage. How boastfully he even enumerates
his grandfather's merits, only to make the climax the
stronger when he can add at the end: "But, see, my grandfather was of the old school; here, look at me, I am of the
new generation, I condescend to be your equal." Have you
become sufficiently Germanized to be hurt by what I have
been saying about Berlin's idol? I trust you are still loyal

---

[5] William II.

to America no matter how well pleased you may be with social life in the Old World.

Just now your patriotism would be stirred to its depths by the preparations going on for the centennial celebration of Washington's inauguration. The reminiscences so crowd the papers that it is quite an education for us Americans in that much neglected branch—the history of our own country.

I am not very much interested in home politics—my man, Cleveland, was ousted. But I am not going to touch on that vexing question, knowing you to be your father's son and remembering that the former and myself had some excited discussions during the campaign.

As for myself, I have been so busy all winter with routine work that I feel dull and unprogressive. In addition to Miss Adams's, I teach at a school in the country, about fifteen miles from the city; and that was an ill-advised step. It has worn me out without compensating me by an enlargement of my sphere of work.

Baltimore, December 31, 1889

It was indeed good news to hear of your early return. This is the last day of 1889. Tomorrow we shall be able to say: "*This* year he comes back."

Your letters have testified to the full to your enjoyment of all your European experiences; still, I am looking forward with delight to the time when you can enter into details and relate your impressions. I am presuming that these three years have not changed you, that you will be as willing as before to describe the effect which sights and incidents make upon you, in short, that the old Sunday evenings will be restored.

What right I have to expect any such delightful restoration I do not know. It seems to me that everything has changed. Naturally, Rachel's going away has made a different family of us. I still miss her as deeply as at first. In fact more so. I am becoming conscious of the irrevocableness of the change. It is a fearful thing—this setting aside a certain period of one's life and saying in one's mind: "That is done with, that is a sealed book; nothing to be added, none of its pleasures to be tasted again," and much more such misanthropic rubbish.

In Baltimore we go on in the humdrum conservative way. When you get back here and have been made to admire the post office and Mr. Fiteman's "improvements," you will look upon your three years' stay abroad as a dream sent by a fairy god-mother—so stable is everything.

I am particularly anxious to hear your personal observations with regard to the Jewish question—both sides of it, the religious status of the Jews and their social position. If one can form an inference from conflicting statements, it appears that anti-Semitism is rampant and that the Jews themselves are little more than race-Jews. It is enough to make one weep tears of blood. As I grow older I can believe what I used to repeat with a cynical air: namely, that Berthold Auerbach died of a broken heart.[6]

Why are we so hated, and why indeed are we so hateful? For, in spite of our experience, which is as long as history itself, that the Jew has had to suffer from unjust discrimination, nevertheless we treat less fortunate co-religionists exactly in the same way. The pride of the rich Jew, the parvenu, is intolerable. His bearing toward the Russians, for instance, is inexcusable. And as for anti-Semitism—what

---

[6] When in 1880 the fire of German nationalism turned against the Jews, Berthold Auerbach, the novelist of German folk life, confessed broken-heartedly: "I have lived and worked in vain."

can be worse than the action of that young jackanapes, the
German Emperor? I am alluding to the restoration of 400
marks' fine to the editor of an anti-Semitic journal. Well,
we shall hear from you.

CHAPTER FOUR

The Coming of the Russians

Across the Eastern sky has glowed
    The flicker of a blood-red dawn,
Once more the clarion cock has crowed,
    Once more the sword of Christ is drawn.
A million burning roof-trees light
The world-wide path of Israel's flight.
                                —EMMA LAZARUS

I

IN March 1881 Tsar Alexander II was assassinated by revolutionary bomb-throwers. Under his successor and with the blessing of the Church and the hearty support of the nobility, Russia entered a long reign of repression and reactionary terrorism. The governmental policy for the Jews was defined in a cynical program: a third were to be converted, a third to emigrate, and a third to perish. The program was inaugurated by a country-wide wave of centrally directed pogroms, in which hundreds died. Then a series of enactments—beginning with the notorious May Laws of 1882—supplemented violence and bloody death by economic starvation. As the government, the Church, and the ruling classes had foreseen, a vast exodus followed. Western Europe and America became the goal of the largest Jewish migration since the fifteenth-century expulsion from Spain.

Within a short while Baltimore made its acquaintance with the refugees. After public protests against Russian tyranny and inhumanity had been made and the clarion poems of Emma Lazarus applauded, the business of what to do with the penniless newcomers was considered, agitated, and then on the whole forgotten. A few agricultural colonies—Sulamith reported on them in her articles—were settled in Maryland and Virginia and neglected.

A provincial community so set and staid in its ways as Baltimore Jewry could not direct the destinies of the immigrants or cope with their problems. A Russian "ghetto" sprang up haphazardly, an abode of hunger, filth, and scantily paid toil, in an eastern district of the city which the German Jews were deserting. The latter were properly outraged over Tsarist intolerance, a little frightened, and profuse in vocal sympathy. But with few exceptions they remained unaware of the practical daily needs of this swarm of ragged outlandish co religionists, ignorant or contemptuous of its spiritual resources and longings or else helpless in devising aid and comfort.

Among the few exceptions was Rabbi Szold. His home became a confessional, a wailing wall, a free boarding-house, and an unofficial one-man employment bureau. Coming himself from the fringe of Eastern Europe and permeated with Jewish tradition and lore, he could not only meet the Russians as man to man but talk to them soul to soul. The intellectuals among them found in him a colleague.

A common love of the Hebrew tongue drew both the rabbi and Henrietta into close relations with a group of young Russians who discussed by the hour modern Hebrew literature and thought. They pondered and debated the new impulses actuating Russian Jewry and crystallizing through the pressure of dire need. They watched words take the form of deeds. Pinsker's startling pamphlet, *Auto-Emancipation,* which appeared in 1881, was a word, its title a program. But a dozen colonies established in Palestine were deeds—a living appendix added to the pamphlet in less than a decade. Societies of Lovers of Zion (*Chovevei Zion*) and Returners to Zion (*Shovei Zion*), which spread through Russia and won adherents in Western Europe and America, were furnishing the plans, money, and men for more deeds.

After casual fellowship and loose sessions of talk, the Baltimore group of Hebraists organized themselves in 1888 as the I.B.L. Hebrew Literary Society—the name a memorial to Isaac Bar Levison, pioneer of the modern revival of Hebrew in Russia. Henrietta continued a give and take with the society, exchanging facts for facts and inspiration for inspiration. They told her about Russia and she told them about America. She read before the society an account of the checkered history of religious tolerance in Maryland. She brought them the life and flaming words of Emma Lazarus. We can hear her begin: "I want to introduce you to a young American Jewish poetess who died a little more than a year ago, and for whom you will feel love and attachment when I tell of her love for you." Then she resumed in the poet's own language the appeal to action, to a revival of the Jewish nation in Palestine, and to a return to physical labor and practical education and with it normal life in other lands. And we can hear her conclude: "I chose to tell you of Emma Lazarus because she is a fit model for you, my young Russian friends, to follow. The flame which burst forth in her bosom—warm yourselves by its warmth and kindle in your hearts a similar light."

Not being an orator or overfond of words, she then proposed to her young Russian friends a deed. In accordance with her bent, it was a deed immediately at hand. Hundreds of Baltimore immigrants were bitterly handicapped in making a livelihood by their ignorance of English and sometimes by their almost complete illiteracy. The same handicap hopelessly barred them from attaining their most cherished goal: American citizenship and a full participation in American life, its liberty and happiness. Public night schools did not exist. She suggested that the Literary Society foster "practical education" then and there by founding and maintaining a night school for their own people. They accepted her project joyfully; and, likewise in the nature of the woman, she left its entire direction and control in their hands. All she consented to do was the hard work.

The second floor of a store was rented on Gay Street in November 1889. The young men of the Literary Society swept, scrubbed, and painted. Yiddish circulars were distributed through the "ghetto." Tuition fees—this was to be no charity school—were fixed at thirty cents a month. The Society taxed its members for the purchase of books, slates, pencils, blackboards, and fuel. Kerosene lamps were lit. Thirty pupils registered. And as superintendent, teaching-staff, and janitor, Henrietta Szold opened the night school—among the pioneers of its kind in America.

"Two classes were put into operation at once," she tells in an article written subsequently, "one consisting of those able to read, the other of such as knew no more than the alphabet. . . . Two volunteer teachers were found [Grace Bendann, 'a little aristocrat,' and Deborah Cohn, 'a young woman of Russian birth']. At the end of a few weeks it became apparent that the volunteer system was vicious, no matter how loyal and efficient the teacher may be. Regardless of the poor state of the finances, the Society employed the required number of teachers [at $15 a month]. One hundred and fifty adults were taught during the semester.

"The curriculum consisted of English, English, and again English. All else was treated as collateral and subsidiary.

The more advanced pupils—that is to say, all such as could spell out words—were given Eggleston's *History of the United States*. The first lesson consisted of reading a paragraph of not more than eight lines. Every word was explained by pantomime, amplification, simplification, analogy, or etymology. German was resorted to only in extreme cases. One of the teachers, in fact, knew no language but English, yet her success was undisputed. After the meaning of the paragraph had been made clear, the historical allusions were discussed, the geographical references explained by means of a map, and as much incidental information as possible introduced. Questions were asked—questions were encouraged and forced; and answers given and required in English. Then a grammar lesson of the most elementary kind was illustrated by examples still drawn from the same paragraph, and finally a spelling and writing exercise elaborated from the same material.

"The history book thus became a universal text-book whence lessons in history, geography, grammar, spelling, writing, and conversation were drawn day after day. For the adults, most of whom were intelligent, well informed, and abreast of current events, the method seemed more effective than using a different text-book in each department of instruction.

"The eagerness of the pupils was often painful to witness, and nothing more pathetic can be imagined than the efforts made by men well advanced in years to crook their work-stiffened fingers around a pen. Although all were hard-worked during the day, their interest never flagged."

The school grew rapidly in the ensuing years, and with it grew anxieties and responsibilities. Funds were always on the point of exhaustion. The Literary Society sweated, taxed itself, and paid. Miss Szold supplemented her hours of teaching with hours of money-raising. An occasional sympathizer made a donation, the Baron de Hirsch Fund was induced to contribute $30 a month, and various "bands" from well-to-do women's societies supported one or another department of the school.

Difficult problems were created by the character of the students. They ranged from boys and girls to aged men and women. They were in every stage of education, and in none at all. Most of the adults were strict Sabbath observers, and they worked overtime during the week to make up for the hours lost from their jobs on Saturdays and, in mid-winter, on Friday afternoons—to the detriment, irregularity, and confusion of their schooling.

The youngsters, especially those born in America or with several years of American life behind them, were, as Miss Szold writes, "in a pitiable condition. They know only drudgery and grinding work. Their home life is not enticing. They have become Americans in naught but levity, shocking grammar, and the despicable smartness of the street and factory. Often I see these young boys and girls openly ridicule the uncouth pronunciation of their classmates, the humble men of thirty and forty who have not been deterred by the false feeling of shame from becoming learners. My heart bleeds for them—they are so well satisfied that they are far superior to their elders who have been tried and purged in the school of sorrow. The national stomach will be able to digest all the Russian Jews whom the cruelty of a despot sees fit to drive to our shores. But the danger lies with their children. The history of our own ancestors reveals the same phenomenon. The second generation of German Jews, more affluent, less hard-worked than the immigrant generation, was notoriously less open to educative influences. Whatever [our] course, let us remember that 'The child's sob in the silence curses deeper than the strong man's wrath.'"

Before the school was taken over by the city in 1898, it had instructed more than 5000 pupils. Christians—Slovak and Czech immigrants—attended it as well as Jews. It maintained seven English classes, besides courses in arithmetic, bookkeeping, and sewing. The general lectures held under the auspices of the Literary Society in the school quarters attracted hundreds of auditors. Its lending and reference library fed hundreds more of hungry minds. But such triumphant details give merely an external picture.

In the letters of Henrietta to her sister Rachel, married and living in Madison, Wisconsin, and in a concluding note to her sister Sadie, we can see the Russian school from the inside looking out.

Baltimore, October 17, 1891

Have I told you that my winter work is in full blast now? The Botany Club, the Woman's [Literary] Club, the Sabbath school, the daily school—and Monday evening the Russian school is open. About the latter I am very much disturbed. I do not see where the money is to come from to keep it going beyond about one month. What we shall do after that, I cannot guess. In other respects the school is bound to be a success.

My work during the week promises to be very heavy this year. I find that, congenial as the arithmetical classes are, they entail considerable work in the way of examining and marking slates. I find it difficult to reach home before 3:30 p.m. Perhaps when I become more accustomed to it, I shall be able to work more quickly. But you know dispatch has never been my strong point.

I must again return to the Russian school. I was much

gratified this week at receiving a note, the purport of which was that Mrs. Dr. Frank guaranteed the whole sum of money required to cover this year's expenses in the dress-making department. You know I was given $150 last year. But of that I managed to save about $45. This year I shall not need more than $55 in addition to what I already have. But, after all, the English classes are the important thing.

One other very gratifying thing occurred this week. On Thursday afternoon—when the Jewish History class used to be in the habit of meeting—I was surprised to find one pupil after another dropping in, until all were assembled; and there could be no doubt that they had done so by appointment. They had come to present the gift (of which I told you) in a formal manner and to express their appreciation of my services—all of which pleasant nothings and formalities I accepted as ungracefully, I suppose, as I usually submit to such proceedings. But my cynicism received a wholesome rude shock by what followed. I had never believed that at bottom any good had been done by my having the Jewish History class. But I am now convinced that lasting good has grown from it. For their main object in coming was to get from me various plans of work for the coming winter, among which they might choose the most attractive, since they mean to continue to study Jewish subjects by themselves. I had never supposed their protestations to amount to anything more than idle words.

Baltimore, October 25, 1891

If you were here at this moment you would not get much conversation out of me. I have so miserable a cold that my voice can scarcely be heard. Shall I therefore shorten my letter? I am afraid it will be a short one because this week has been very unexciting.

The only thing I can talk about is the opening of the [Russian] night school. Against the judgment of my Russian friends I opened during the holidays. The presumption was that few would come. On Thursday evening, however, we had 205 registered. This week, when the holidays are over, there will be a tremendous rush, and we shall have to turn many away for want of room. We cannot possibly take in more than 235. Certainly if we had more money, we might rent rooms in the neighborhood.

If the proper people would take an interest in the school, it might be made an institution of incalculable benefit to the new Jewish community. But you know the narrow-mindedness and the puny-heartedness of our friends. I am convinced that my prominent connection with the school has something to do with its orphaned condition. It takes social influence to make a success of things—not only among our friends but in all circles, even the best.

I must indeed confess that my late experiences have taught me that the "Jewish heart"—the boast concerning which used to anger me—is not a myth. Others, to be sure, do good, and do it on a grander scale. But the *feeling* does not permeate all classes as it does with us Jews. Our difficulty lies in the fact that feeling after all usually keeps pace with knowledge. Uneducated people as a rule cannot conceive of the higher charity involved in giving the opportunity of an education to the needy. They remember that they themselves acquired the good things of this life without night schools, etc., and let others go and do likewise. They refuse to take into account altered conditions, economic and social. The argument which is gradually bringing them around turns on the prospect of suffering in common with their Russian brethren, a prospect looming up distantly but distinctly upon the social sky of this free country. This, too, is doing much to eradicate the ridiculous hatred and scorn of the Russian Jew as such. Strange, is it not, that we Jews must suffer in order to be noble? Is it evidence in our favor or against us?

So far as I personally am concerned, I am my father's daughter. Prosperity has something vulgar and repugnant about it. I feel very much more drawn to these Russian Jews than to the others—a prejudice as vile, doubtless, as the contrary one. Nor do I mean only the suffering Russian Jews. I mean those, too, who are earning a competency. There is something ideal about them. Or has the suffering through which they have passed idealized them in my eyes? At all events, I have no greater wish than to be able to give my whole strength, time, and ability to them.

Baltimore, October 31, 1891

I am sure I shall wear you out with the only subject I am able to write about. But console yourself—you would not fare any better if you were here on the spot. I eat, drink, and sleep Russians. *Ergo,* there is nothing to do but to write Russians also. In fact, the Russian business so absorbs my thoughts that I have gone back to my early girlish longing to be a man. I am sure that if I were one I could mature plans of great benefit to them. I send you a later copy of *Darkest Russia* which you may keep. Perhaps you can do some missionary work among your friends.

Now my especial fad—the school! As was predicted, a tremendous rush of pupils came in on Monday after the holidays: 340 have been enrolled. As we can with difficulty shelter 300, a great many were turned away. But the rush has been so great that we have determined to rent two rooms elsewhere and open two new classes. This is of course a serious matter, for the simple reason that we have no money or

none worth talking about. We shall want two new teachers, several dozen schoolbooks, slates, chalk, pencils, besides
the rent.

In the face of all this, our community remains cold and
indifferent. If we decide to open two new classes, we have
more than sufficient material in the way of pupils. We shall
have seven English classes, a bookkeeping, an arithmetic, a
Hebrew, and a dressmaking class running. That is tremendous, is it not?

Baltimore, November 8, 1891

Now my Russian record: the two extra classes of which
I wrote it was decided (late Sunday night) to open in two
large rooms, two squares away from our building on High
Street. In my heart of hearts I was opposed to the move,
because there was no money and because I felt that it would
be going beyond my strength to superintend them.

But whenever I go to a board meeting, I carefully refrain
from influencing my Russian friends directly on any subject under discussion. This is their school and they must
run it. There was a tie in the committee and the chairman
decided in favor of opening. I immediately set to work to
think out the problem, and I believe I have found a way
by which the last-mentioned difficulty will be minimized
to an insignificant item. I have sent over my two most experienced teachers, whose classes I had already organized
completely; and they need very little supervision.

I should like to tell you about those two days, Monday
and Tuesday, in order to give you an idea of how I spend
most of my life.

I rose at 5:30 on Monday morning. At 6:30 I was at my
desk, writing to my teachers to meet me earlier than usually,
and writing a lengthy letter to two new teachers whom I

wish to engage, an answer to the Y.M.H.A. refusing to lecture before them, and a note to a young lady who had promised to teach but had told me the day before that going out
at night was ruinous to her reputation (I told her that her
services were no longer needed); besides ringing up Fannie
and Tillie Kahn to ask them whether they would substitute
that evening. This before breakfast.

Then to [the Misses Adams's] school where I am nowadays busy, recess and all, until three o'clock. Thence I
rushed to Cushing's to order the extra books, slates, pencils, etc., for the two new classes, and uptown again for the
meeting of the Botany Club, which lasts until six. Rushed
home for supper, and at seven I was at the Russian school.
That evening I had 300 people to manipulate with, but I
am thankful to say that by a quarter of nine everybody was
at work. I reached home at 11:30.

The next morning before breakfast I had to send out a
number of postals for the Botany Club, which has started
an elementary class in botany. School—then an hour's meeting with the executive board of the Woman's Literary Club
—then a rush for a house up on McCullough Street to a
meeting of the Daughters in Israel. I had been invited there
by the band, which has entrusted me with the management
of the dressmaking class, with the hope that I might arouse
the community in general to take an interest in the night
school. It was hoped that the various bands might give us
the profits of a joint entertainment. But to that scheme I
was opposed. It is time for recreative charity to be given
up. And my night school is not ready to beg at any rate. My
Russians are glad to work for it and pull it through. However, I spoke at length about the work of the school, of the
existence of which most of the ladies had up to that time
been ignorant, and of the society under whose manage-

ment it was operated; and in ten minutes I had $111 sub-
scribed as annual subscriptions, the subscribers asking that
their names be enrolled as members of the Russian society.
Besides that, one of the bands which was not yet provided
with work took from my hands the maintenance and repair
of the house occupied by the school. I met this band later
and showed them our needs: ventilators, curtains, bonnet-
hooks, and cleanliness. I was also able to suggest work to two
other bands that would bring them into direct contact with
the best class of Russians and force them to work not so
much *for* as *with* them. In this way I hope a better understanding may be brought about between the two large and
largely hostile camps.

Now to return to my domicile. After this exciting meeting I barely had time to get supper before rushing off to
the school where I was to superintend the various classes.
When I reached there, I found that one of the teachers had
sent me a note saying she would not be there that evening,
as she was invited to a wedding. I was infuriated, but had
to teach under the trying circumstances of being called
away once every ten minutes to attend to some detail of
routine. I again reached home at 11:30 p.m., not having
had dinner either day.

These are not exactly sample days. They are the fullest
of the week. But if I wished to do justice to all of the demands made upon me I would not eat dinner except on
Friday, Saturday, and Sunday. I enjoy this after a fashion.
The only thing I regret is that it is impossible for me to
do any reading, not even of the lightest kind.

I have been interrupted twice in the writing of this—
once to be told that Mr. Freudenreich had passed away, and
once to go to the Sabbath school, where my work is as dis-

tasteful as ever. It is so much easier to teach Russians than
Americans.

Next week I shall write a letter to you in which the word
Russian shall not occur.

Baltimore, November 8, 1891

The two new classes which we have organized are fairly
at work, and we have since then had to turn away about 40
pupils for whom we have no room. Of course, in four
weeks' time I shall be howling at the poor attendance. But
I suppose I must make up my mind that this state of affairs,
not being curable, must be endured. Aside from the Russian school, affairs Russian look very black. There is much
misery. It meets the eye wherever one glances. It seems to
me that I do not nowadays get rid of the heartache caused
by these poor unfortunates. What will be the end of it all?

II

In the summer of 1893 Miss Szold resigned from her su-
perintendence of the night school. The Literary Society
assured her that "the success of the school of which you are
the founder is due solely to your strenuous and never-
ceasing efforts." But she reaped from her experience more
than a testimonial of thanks. The discursive Hebraists of
the Society, the martial writings of Emma Lazarus, the old
and young she taught at the school, the entire Russian epi-
sode from the first pogrom to the last graybeard she watched
struggling with his pen, had made her a Zionist.

More accurately, it gave her vision of the world a new
and lasting focus. In a sense nothing was changed, but everything that had been of import in her life fell into a new per-

spective. The vine and fig tree at home became more than
a childhood association or a Biblical reminiscence; they
blossomed into symbols of the Jewish future—of perhaps
her own. The example of her father's daily pattern of living, though he never formally subscribed to the new doc-
trine, was an argument without words. "I was prepared for
Zionism," she recalled in her old age, "because my father's
attitude was that Judaism is a way of life." As Sulamith writing her weekly columns of comment, she had learned to
look at the American Jewish scene with shrewd eyes; abroad
she had tasted something of the cream of the Judaism of
Western Europe; she had felt in both continents the power
of social assimilation—"materialism" was her favorite word
for it. Then Russian Jewry, its intellectuals, its sturdy toil-
ers, its second-generation scum, its burdens and strengths
and hopes, came to Baltimore and for years possessed her
head and heart. The cry she flung at a group of Lady Boun-
tifuls expressed her recognition that *"We* are in want, not
they!" Her sister Adele remembers her "sob of pride" as
"she spoke of the gray-bearded men sitting at the same
bench, studying from the same books as their little ones."
The grandeur and the romance as well as the tears and
blood of the Jewish people conquered her.

Even her acquaintance with the half-dozen German dialects of Baltimore played its part. She learned at first hand
to value the multiple varieties in the botany of human culture. Every flower of civilization, she came to feel, must be
preserved and nurtured for the good and glory of the whole
garden. In 1889—when a view of this nature was indeed
a novelty—she published an appeal for cultural pluralism.
"A Plea for Custom" she called it.

"I confess my agreement with those great men," she
wrote, "who tell us that the salvation of humanity lies in the

leveling of all barriers, in the forcing upon common ground
of all men. But I never fail to remind myself that the common ground they think of is not that claimed by mediocrity,
that the differences to be obliterated are not to be the marks
of individuality and of varied life. Differences, it is true,
do not make civilization; but differentiation does." For the
Jews as for any other people, "there is an exhaustless variety
of customs that have become exclusively [their own] with
time. To them they are the natural unconscious forms in
which Jewish life and character seek expression."

It was but a step to conclude from this that, like every
other species, the Jewish flower, in order to flourish, needed
a soil in which to root and grow. It was a mere detail that
the young Russian friends induced her to take the step.
"When the chores were done," she relates, "and the pupils
were safely closeted with their teachers, there was time for
talk and plotting—talk about the singular absence of national feeling in the American Jewish communities, plotting as to how Baltimore at least might be nationalized."
One little old man, the only old man in the group, never
faded from her memory. When the discussions waxed hot,
he would let his lean frame slip down in his big chair until
it sank almost from sight, and "as he sat there with his arms
crossed he looked Israel the martyr—his spirit was Israel
the seer's." In the fall of 1893—the year she resigned—the
group prepared to organize a Zionist society. "It was their
plot," she said, "to draw Dr. Harry Friedenwald and me
into it, and they laid their plans to that end. We became
members."

This *Hebras Zion,* or Zionist Association, of Baltimore
was probably the first Zionist society created in the United
States. Indeed, three years were to pass before Herzl published *The Jewish State,* a call that summoned political

Zionism into organized being. A few weeks before the first world congress of Zionists assembled in Basel, Miss Szold —already a veteran—described its purposes and constituents to Dr. Cyrus Adler, who apparently had plans of his own to lay before it. Her letter follows:

Baltimore, July 19, 1897

Dr. Theodor Herzl's address is Vienna IX, Berggasse 6, and the date of the Congress is August 29, and it is to be held in Basel.

It seems that the English *Chovevei Zion* are not going to participate in the Congress; and the prominent Berlin representatives, Willy Bambus and Hildesheimer (son), have just withdrawn their support. Their reason will, I think, be interesting to you. They were members of the committee of arrangements, and found that they could not make their opinion prevail that the Congress was to limit itself to colonization in Palestine and refuse to take into consideration other Zionistic schemes. The true Zionists—those of twenty years' standing—have in mind the solution of a world problem, and refuse to be bound by any such narrow interpretation of the Zionist program. Your plan, therefore, will meet with open minds.

I have no doubt that this Congress is going to give us Occidentals our first true insight into Russian conditions and, above all, Russian forces and spiritual resources. As for the Russian representatives, I find upon inquiry that they are compelled to be very secretive about their preparations for the Congress from prudential motives; the consequence is that the names of the delegates have not been published. The leading Russian Zionist—and therefore the leading Zionist—is, as I told you, Reb Samuel Mohilewer, rabbi in Bialystok. He has been prominent in the move-

ment since 1875, and in 1889 probably saved the movement
from utter ruin by deciding against the observance of the
sabbatical year.

III

"When Zionism converted me to itself," said Miss Szold
in one of her early propaganda talks, "I frankly confess I
did not go through the whole list of objections, possible and
actual, that anti-Zionists raised against it, and refute them
to myself. I became converted to Zionism the very moment
I realized that it supplied my bruised, torn, and bloody nation, my distracted nation, with an ideal—an ideal that is
balm to the self-inflicted wounds and to the wounds inflicted by others—an ideal that can be embraced by all, no
matter what their attitude may be to other Jewish questions."

As part of the "underground agitation" to plant this
ideal among Baltimore Jews, her first public advocacy of
Zionism was in an address delivered to the local chapter
of the Council of Jewish Women in January 1896. She imbedded her purpose in a discussion of what she called "A
Century of Jewish Thought." In it she pointed out that
Moses Mendelssohn, by introducing the Jews to the beauties of a pure Hebrew tongue, first awakened them to self-
consciousness and a sense of self-respect. But "if not restrained and disciplined by self-knowledge, this self-respect
degenerates into self-approval and eventually sinks into that
most contemptible of qualities, national conceit or chauvin-
ism." It was Leopold Zunz and his fellow-researchers into
Jewish history who supplied the salutary self-knowledge.
Then, out of a sane and balanced self-respect and self-
knowledge grew the inevitable ideal of self-emancipation:

the determination neither to cringe, nor to blame, nor to complain, but to meet a people's needs through a people's own efforts. This ideal of self-emancipation was Zionism— "a movement that epitomizes the finest Jewish impulses of the day."

Henrietta Szold's Zionist writings as a whole are evidence that she never was exclusively a nationalist or a religionist in her Jewish philosophy. Even before she knew his point of view, she was close to Ahad Ha'am in proclaiming herself a Zionist primarily for cultural reasons in their broadest sense. She rebuked Zionists who did not admit of religious responsibilities: "racial Zionism is a revolting anomaly," and the one vulnerable point of political Zionism is "undue prominence of the racial spirit." No, her ideal was catholic; it called for a Zionism "which is at once spiritual, philanthropic, and political, and in good time—diplomatic."

Meanwhile the audience for her first avowal before the Council of Jewish Women, as well as the majority of Baltimore Jews, "could not even react." As she recollected it, "they hardly knew what I meant." When her address was published, one Jewish weekly found it "almost too profound for an American woman" and called its author "the most learned Jewess in the United States."

CHAPTER FIVE

Dead Ends

THE conversion to Zionism had been gradual and correspondingly profound. But its translation into deeds was even more gradual. Seventeen years were to elapse before Henrietta Szold set herself to hard work in behalf of Zion. This long pause between believing and doing in a person to whom idleness was abhorrent did not spring from inertia, flagging interest, or personal obligations. In it lay a key to her character.

Only an immediate, practical, and concrete task drew forth the full exertion of her powers. Yet even then she could not surrender her life utterly to a practical and congenial occupation if she did not, according to her own tastes and lights, find it expressive of an all-absorbing ideal. Her hand remained aloof unless it had a task to do within fingers' reach; but for the hand never to lose its grip the task had to capture every fiber of her heart. Half of her long life was passed before these two demands of her nature were met—half a life spent in arduous devoted labor that, for lack of one or another of these indispensable elements, led to dead ends.

When she gave up her work in the night school (1893), she likewise resigned from the teaching profession and bade farewell to the Misses Adams, the religious classes, and her private pupils. However practical and immediate, teaching proved to be a dead end, not because the profession lacked an absorbing ideal but because the ideal failed to absorb her.

The Russian night school, as her letters plainly tell, pro-

vided more than enough detailed grind to satisfy her crav-
ing for toil. In founding it—it was the same year that gave
birth to Hull House—she had created an embryonic settlement house before the term or the institution was generally heard of; and if social service for its own rewards,
in itself a powerful ideal, had conquered her imagination
she might have persevered and taken her place with Jane
Addams and Lillian Wald. She never reached the port, even
though she set sail at a time when the voyage was an alluring
and uncharted adventure, for the sufficient reason that her
islands of the blessed and her romance lay in another sea.

Her heart, to its last romantic throb, brooded across the
waters of the *Yam Ha-gadol,* the "great sea" of the Mediterranean. But Zionism, at least in America, had small place
for a practical worker. What little there was of activity
called for the services of an orator and propagandist. Miss
Szold was not and never became an orator; the mere deliv-
ery of a prepared lecture exhausted her courage and nerves.
Nor could she be a propagandist in thin air—debating, agi-
tating, and organizing in behalf of an ideal that had as yet
almost no foothold in reality. She kept in close touch with
Zionist and Palestinian developments, she consulted with
the American leaders, she published an occasional article on
the philosophy and appeal of the movement; but to all ap-
pearances Zionism was likewise a dead end.

Meanwhile she had yielded to the tide of another deep
interest. As "her father's daughter"—a favorite phrase—
she had turned to Jewish learning and letters. In 1888 the
Jewish Publication Society of America was founded, with
headquarters in Philadelphia, to foster and publish books
on Jewish subjects. At the outset she served as a volunteer
on the editorial board or, as it was called, the "publication
committee." The initial publication was Lady Magnus's

Outlines of Jewish History. Together with Dr. Cyrus Adler she wrote for it a concluding chapter on the Jew in America. One editorial task led to another. Soon she was editing the five-volume English version of Graetz's monumental *History of the Jews*. In 1893 she became the paid secretary of the editorial board and, giving up her Baltimore activities, moved temporarily to Philadelphia.

She held the secretarial post for twenty-three years. During this time, under her immediate supervision, the Society published three to four books annually, of which nearly one million copies in all were distributed to the membership and the public at large. Besides performing the secretarial duties, she translated a dozen of its works, compiled a huge one-volume index to Graetz, took the lion's share in compiling and editing the *American Jewish Year Book* from its first issue in 1899, and was its sole editor for four years. In the judgment of at least one admirer (Louis Lipsky), "she was all there was of the Society exclusive of its directors and canvassers." As he puts it, "she gathered into her motherly care the accepted manuscripts, the work of translation, the proofreading, the compiling of indexes and appendices, and the preparation of advance notices."

It was grueling. Again and again her letters dwelt on "the steady daily work" when not on "the crazy orgy of work." The *Year Book*—a several-hundred-page compilation of events, statistics, and directories, together with fact-crammed articles and reports—was a *bête noire*. "Year Book*—by this time those two words ought to suffice to make my friends understand a state of mind, body, and temper not in the least conducive to letter-writing." Even when life seemed good she wrote, "I'd love it more if it weren't so packed with *Year Book*—and its wearisome work."

To be sure, her services were recognized. It must have

gratified her to read, in the volume dedicated to the achievements of the Society on its twenty-fifth anniversary, "that such a work could be brought before the American public was made possible by the Society's good fortune in finding the person of Miss Henrietta Szold. To speak of the literary output of the last twenty-five years is impossible without remembering her services as translator, reader, and annotator, as bringing to bear upon the preparation of the manuscripts her many-sided culture and her great Jewish enthusiasm."

"I had a feeling," she said many years after, "that the Society did not use its possibilities because it was too academic." This was another way of saying that scholarship, even in the tangible workaday form of publication, failed to absorb and kindle her soul. She was too modest to live for recognition, and too self-critical to extract much nourishment from gratification. Her years of "wearisome work" for the Publication Society led to one more dead end.

For a considerable time during the same period she tried her hand at pure scholarship—research and studies untarnished by the mechanics of book-making and free from the presumed needs of a public.

Her father died in 1902. The ties between parents and children were so tightly knit in the Szold home that, after the natural period of grief, she ceased to mourn his absence; for in spirit and counsel he continued to live with her. Two decades later she can write from Jerusalem: "Today was the twentieth anniversary of Papa's death. I cannot say that I thought of him more today . . . for I think of him every day. Not a day passes but his wisdom and *Menschenkenntnis* come back to my mind. Not a day but that I ask myself what his gently strong attitudes would have been towards the acute complicated problems that confront one in these chaotic days. Nothing, nothing is like what he visioned things."

One of his fond visions for his eldest daughter was a life of the intellect. "My father had raised me for Jewish scholarship," she related, "but I don't think I had scholarly instincts at all." Referring to her life in Palestine, she added: "I have often felt in all these years of Palestinian and Zionist work that my father would not have been satisfied with me. He would have said: 'You have chosen to go away from the worthwhile thing for which you should have prepared yourself—that is, scholarship.'"

Obedient to a call of this strength, she left Baltimore for good in 1903 and settled with her mother in New York. There she devoted her spare time to studies in Hebrew and the Talmud at the Jewish Theological Seminary—spare time, it must be understood, for a woman whose notion of a day's schedule was anything from sixteen to twenty hours. Besides following the desire to become a scholar in her father's image, she pursued her courses at the Seminary as a preparation for editing and publishing a large number of his manuscripts (a task she never finished) and likewise to enhance her services to the Publication Society. She helped prepare the material and did the translation of Professor Louis Ginzberg's four volumes of *The Legends of the Jews;* she also aided in the research and organization of his lectures.

Around her, in her mother's home near the Seminary, was attracted a group of young intellectuals—rabbinical students, instructors, and professors—who took warmth from the heart and living interests of this lady Talmudist. "While I objectively believe I have no abilities," she once judged of herself, "I may have a warmth of personality that I don't know about. My father had that warmth. . . .

I think people come to me and I warm them up." However that may be, scholarship did not succeed to the point of warming her to surrender. As she put it, her work on the *Year Book* and other editorial chores prevented her from continuing her studies. In reality, the inner drive slackened and again she was faced with a blank wall. At least in this respect she could rightly say of her father: "Nothing is like what he visioned things."

As in her youthful Sulamith days she continued to turn into print her experiences with men, books, and the currents of Jewish life. "I think I might have become a writer," she confessed. Besides her translations and adaptations for the Publication Society, she contributed scores of articles to the Jewish press—and fifteen to the *Jewish Encyclopaedia.* She delivered numerous lectures to varied audiences, among which two before the World's Parliament of Religions at the Chicago World's Fair in 1893. As a publicist for Judaism and Zionism, their manifold aspects and issues, she earned the title of a learned and widely read writer. But she never became an author in the sense of making literature a career. She probably never tried. Writing was merely a sidewalk along the streets leading to the succession of dead ends.

Then, in the summer of 1909 her life was changed. By accident she took a journey—she thought of it as a vacation—to a world where all the paths of her life joined into one road, a steep, rocky, and tortuous road, but this time a road without end. The accident, if it can be called that in view of her years of toil, was a severe impairment, almost a breakdown, of her health.

Together with her mother she embarked on a European tour. A gift from the directors of the Jewish Publication Society enabled her to extend it to Palestine. A few letters

survive to tell something of her experience. Unless otherwise noted, they are addressed to a newly found friend,
Alice L. Seligsberg.

[TO DR. CYRUS ADLER]   *New York, July 15, 1909*

I wish for words to convey to you my surprise and gratification on reading your letter this morning and fingering
the enclosure. As it is, I can only say—I was overwhelmed
and I am gratified. I must leave it to you to charge these
hackneyed words with the meaning they should carry to
be a complete expression of my feelings.

Loyal, intelligent, conscientious, and effective you call
my service to the [Jewish Publication] Society—your recognition of that will accompany me and sweeten a vacation
forced upon me by regrettable circumstances, and perhaps
be as potent as the vacation itself in restoring me to a normal degree of self-confidence and joy in living and working.

The pleasure of my trip will be enhanced so substantially
by the contribution made to it by you and the other members of the two committees that I cannot allow it to get itself mixed up with the commoner elements in the letter of
credit I shall carry with me. It must be marked as a distinct
entity, a thing apart, and so I labeled it promptly my Palestine Fund. It rarely occurred to me that a European tour
was a possibility in my life, but never did it enter my mind
remotely that the privilege of beholding the Holy Land
could fall to my share. It makes me happy to think that this
rarest piece of good luck, with all it implies of Jewish emotion and education, shall dwell in my memory not as something purchased by my own efforts, but as something due to
the appreciation of my efforts expressed by those under
whose eyes they were made.

Will you say this and more of gratitude than I can express to all for whom you acted as spokesman?

New York, July 23, 1909

I cannot understand why you should be apprehensive about anything I might say. I am not severe, am I? Only positive, occasionally. I assure you that even if it were my habit to be severe, I cannot imagine my being so with you of all persons in the world. You are so earnest and single-minded, so stimulating to me, so whole a personality, that I recognize unity in all you do and say, and harmoniousness as well.

When I write again, it will probably be only a line to assure you that you are in my mind. So after all this is my farewell; and as it is, may I be a wee bit solemn and tell you explicitly what I think you can read between the lines of this letter—that you have become very dear to me and that I hope you love me, too?

Lincoln [England], August 16, 1909

We flew to the south, to York, and I am writing at Lincoln. In both, the cathedrals—vast, superb, massive monuments of the self-forgetful devotion of generations of the faithful—are contrasted in my mind with the past tragedy and present misery of the Jew. Both York and Lincoln have Jewish memorials of the Middle Ages, and in both the Jewish community was clustered at the base of the oppressor's church. I was filled with jealousy when I went to the room used as a synagogue by the seventeen Jewish families of York —a loft in a stable-like building—and one look upward filled my eye with the noble proportions and graceful details of the minster tower. I went to a service in both cathedrals, there and here. They are so sure of themselves in their spacious, vaulted churches; and we, so much older than they, are still seeking and wandering. But the buildings themselves! The York Minster left me speechless. Hawthorne says—according to the *Guide Book*—that it looks as though it had dropped from heaven and aspired to return thither. I can't improve on that.

Saint-Aubin-sur-Mer [France], September 3, 1909

At last a breathing-spell! Saint-Aubin-sur-Mer is the tiniest of tiny Normandy villages, as beautiful as it is tiny, innocent of galleries and museums, but itself a Hobbema, or a Ruysdael, or a Paul Potter. My Rouen cousin has a cottage here for the summer, and he called for us yesterday at Dieppe in his automobile, and brought us here, after a marvelously smooth passage across the Channel, in spite of a shipful of militant Esperantists.

I don't know but that will be the *summa summarum* of my European experiences—that loyalty to an idea, constancy in the realization of an ideal, devotion, that these are what count in human history. They are the essence of tradition. Take the Madonna cult and its expression in painting. An idea! Take the cathedrals—an attempt on the part of thousands to realize an ideal, and realize it so that every detail of its expression may testify to its reality.

One ought to go straight to Italy and become acquainted with the Madonnas and the children, and the saints, on the soil on which they grew. Then one is prepared to go northward and enjoy understandingly the works that the others stimulated into life and those which the Northerners ruthlessly carried off. But I am satisfied with what has been granted to me. If a note of dissatisfaction creeps in, it is that this opportunity did not come earlier in my life. Many things might have been different.

No, the holy families are not objectionable to my Jewish sense and sensibilities. On the other hand, I am not afraid of them. I wonder whether you really need be? I wonder whether they would now affect you as you seem to think? It is true, we are different. You mention *one* picture, you have carried it in your mind's eye for years, it influences you. I, alas, fail to remember all things—particular pictures, particular scenes. I carry away only impressions, and I remember them. I recollect what effect the Botticellis have upon me, what Rembrandt means, how Velasquez grips me, what objection I have to Rubens and Veronese, how I felt when I entered Peterborough Cathedral, or the old Norman church at Iffley (wonderful this last one is—I believe I shall remember it as a picture by itself); and so I am favored but not influenced, at least not influenced away from my original bent. Is that age too?

Jerusalem, November 16, 1909

How much I shall have to tell you when I return, of the misery, of the beauty, the interest, the problems of the Holy City. If I were twenty years younger, I would feel that my field is here. As it is, there are heroic men and women here doing valiant work. If only they could be more intelligently supported by the European and American Jew. The colonies and the cities of Palestine, they have taught me so much that for the first time in my life I feel the impulse to speak out in public. Will you hold me to it when I return? Should I do it after a month's visit? You see that I am quite the ordinary traveler.

Milan, December 12, 1909

It was a happy fortune that brought us from the East to this Christian-pagan land. The Palestinian experience was tense. Here there are for us only things—no people. There, at Jerusalem and in the colonies, there was pulsating life, and life coupled with misery, poverty, filth, disease, and there was intellectual life, coupled with idealism, enthusiasm, hope. There was debate and demonstration, and argument and persuasion. And when I saw Jaffa recede from sight, I felt that all my powers had been called forth and kept alert during the whole of the four weeks I spent in Palestine.

Here in Italy I have no responsibility, I may enjoy, I need not weigh and criticize and doubt and wonder—or, if I do, I wonder only at the rich beauty poured out upon this favored land.

When I return I shall tell you much about Palestine and Zionism and the Jews. Briefly now only this: the prophecy of many of my friends that Palestine would unmake my Zionism has not been verified. I am the same Zionist I was. In fact, I am more than ever convinced that our only salvation lies that way. The only thing I admit is that I now think Zionism an ideal more difficult of realization than ever I did before, both on account of the Jews themselves and on account of Oriental and world conditions.

And do you know when that apprehension weighed upon me most heavily? When I listened to High Mass at St. Mark's Church in Venice, on the Feast of the Madonna Immaculate. There was the wonderful basilica, with its domes, its mosaics, jewels, and porphyry. There was the soothing music, the almost angel choir. There were the surpliced acolytes, the richly robed dignitaries, the cardinal-archbishop seated on his regal chair in vestments that beggar description, attended with pomp and ceremony. There was the crowd of decorous, devout worshipers, intent upon the (to me) unintelligible service. And I saw these symbols of a vast unseen power, and I thought of my poor little eleven-millioned people knocking at the door of humanity and begging only for the right to live. That was when I almost lost courage. If I have regained it, it was by means which you will call unfair—the more I see of Italy and her treasures, the more I see paganism in Christianity, and I feel that Judaism can conquer it. But of this, too, more when I can speak with the mouth rather than the pen.

Soon I shall—I am quite ready to—come back to dear old ugly New York. It is home!

[TO ELVIRA N. SOLIS]   *Milan, December 12, 1909*

The Oriental trip was really an overwhelming experience. I have found it difficult, even in my full letters to my people at home, to sum up the Palestinian impressions I received. I shrink from using any formula. None can be sufficiently inclusive, none can convey an idea of all the elements and factors that went to make it up; and I do not want to give a false notion of what I feel.

Before I left, many, and also my relatives in Europe, warned me I should probably be disappointed and return anything but a Zionist. Their prediction has been falsified. Not all that I saw deserved to be bathed in the azure and gold of the radiant Eastern atmosphere. I saw much that was saddening, especially in the cities, and if I had taken the route of the usual Jewish traveler—hastening up from Egypt, which English rule has indeed transformed into a well-disciplined land, to the seaport of Jaffa and then to Jerusalem and back again—I should probably weep and abhor.

Fortunately I saw much more. To begin with, I had a not despicable Oriental experience in Constantinople, Smyrna,

Alexandria, Beirut, and Damascus before I reached the Holy Land. That gave me a background. Then I traveled through Palestine from the northern mountains to Jerusalem, and traveled on a wagon, which gave me the opportunity of smelling the very soil and of rubbing shoulders with the people. That was a proceeding calculated to open my eyes and keep me sane. The result is I am still a Zionist, that I think Zionism a more difficult aim to realize than I ever did before, and finally that I am more than ever convinced that if not Zionism, then nothing—then extinction for the Jew.

Among the many things she told on her return were anecdotes which had to do more with her mother—or so no doubt it seemed—than with herself. At Tiberias her mother remarked that the children had only sticks for legs. "She never forgot it," Henrietta said, "and when she would start to talk about the beauty of Italy, tears would come and she harked back to Tiberias." In Jerusalem the two visitors were told that if American women wanted to do something for Palestine they should establish a Jewish lying-in hospital.

At Jaffa they visited the Jewish Girls' School. "As we walked to the school," Henrietta would relate, "we saw a most horrible sight: children with a wreath of flies around their eyes. My mother was horrified. We entered the school and inside there was not a child whose eyes were afflicted. My mother asked the principal, Dr. Turoff: 'How is it that all these children are perfectly healthy while outside there are children in such awful condition?' He replied: 'That is simple; we have a physician who visits us twice a week and a nurse who comes daily, and we take care of the eyes.' As we emerged my mother said to me: 'That is what your group ought to do. What is the use of reading papers and arranging festivals? You should do practical work in Palestine.'"

CHAPTER SIX

The Healing of My People

I

THE return from Palestine signaled no abrupt change in life. Miss Szold pursued her accustomed tasks and merely added to them. The small band of women on the fringe of Zionist activity which her mother had referred to as "your group" was left in obscurity. But in February 1910 she became secretary of the Jewish Agricultural Experiment Station, an undertaking established in Palestine by Aaron Aaronsohn, discoverer of wild wheat, and now incorporated in America. This was "practical work." Julius Rosenwald was president of the station, and among its supporters were Julian W. Mack, Nathan Straus, and other men of means and influence whose paths she was to cross many times on the road to Zion.

In the summer of the same year she was elected secretary to the Federation of American Zionists, itself none too practical and for the most part busy nibbling at the rind of American Jewish opinion. As her first duty she undertook to unravel the administrative and financial jumble in its affairs. "It was a terrible mix-up," Louis Lipsky recalls, "and she was commissioned to search the records, set them in order, and then attempt to interpret them. For months, with relentless tenacity that produced consternation among her friends, she devoted herself to the task of getting the records straight and identifying every item. Nothing daunted her, even if she had to go over the same set of figures scores of times and linger days in a suffocating atmosphere on East

69

Broadway and then travel uptown late at night." For seven months, five days a week, from five in the afternoon to all hours of the night, she battled with dust, grime, and confusion. Meanwhile she continued her regular occupations and, as though to tempt fate, increased the burden by trying to redeem an old promise to the American Jewish Historical Society. Her letters tell the story.

[TO ALICE L. SELIGSBERG] *New York, July 11, 1910*

The very last sentence in your note is the clinching matter—my election as secretary to the Federation of American Zionists. It is not a matter for congratulation—far from it. I was asked to undertake the task because things are in an almost hopeless condition. Those who asked me knew and acknowledged that they were asking a serious personal sacrifice, and I went into the thing with my eyes open—only they have been opened still wider since the fact is accomplished.

It looks as though there would be no leisure for me for a twelvemonth. I am sorry that I won't have at least the summer to work off arrears, one big job in particular, which I may have mentioned to you—the indexing of the Publications of the Jewish Historical Society, which I promised to do some years ago. There are 1600 pages to be done, and I have done about 200. I should say that, reckoned in hours, I have six hundred hours' work to do on it, if the work were consecutive. But as I must snatch the time in driblets, it will amount to much more, because I have to be retracing my steps almost every time I return to the job. It sounds suicidal, doesn't it? Indeed, it is so bad that I think it will teach me never to undertake anything like it again, no matter how worthy the cause. I am not young enough for such dry-as-dust work, I must husband the working time still left for me.

This week it is expected that I shall take hold of the [Zionist] Federation office. But even if that were not going to happen, I should not be able to come to Tuckahoe, because the proof of the *Year Book* is being delivered by the printer day by day, and it is my business to read it consecutively, forward it to the editor, and receive it back from him, and re-forward it to the printer, only to hold myself ready for a repetition of the process with the second proof. And I must have a stenographer by me all the time. What I am hoping for now is that the proofs will be passed so propitiously that I can enjoy my visit with my sister Bertha and her children. We go to her on July 30, choosing that time because it enables us to visit my father's grave on the anniversary of his death. If I can get the *Year Book* off by then, I can take the week as a holiday. If not, I shall have to read proof when I'd rather read to those blessed children, whom I am longing to be with.

As for my mother, I am afraid that not even a special letter would suffice to overcome her indisposition to go away from home (unless it be to Palestine).

[TO ELVIRA N. SOLIS]   *New York, July 11, 1910*
Curiously enough, at the moment when your postcard was handed to me I was contemplating suicide with the sword of David Hays, said (by the Publications of the Jewish Historical Society) to be in your peaceful possession. For I had been driven all but wild by the Hays complications—the Jacobs, and the Davids, and the Charitys, and the rest of them. I never had any head for genealogies, I suppose because I never had much of a family to deal with;

and now it is my fate to have to index other people's families. You and the sword came as the climax, and that after the intense heat of the last few days, and Jonas Phillips's 21 (I won't write that out, so that you can get the full enormity of his crime toward one who is not his descendant)— yes, 21 children, very few of whom had the grace to die in infancy, though some others at least refrained from marrying. That Phillips tribe, as displayed to an admiring but fortunately not emulous world by the Deputy Collector of the Port (I wonder whether *he* himself ought to be indexed under that designation—I didn't, it just occurs to me), I put into categories and headings last night, only to find today that the Hays tribe awaited me in Publications 2:63–72.

In other words, I am at last redeeming an old promise to the Historical Society—to index the first ten volumes of the Publications. I wonder now how I ever came to make so rash a promise. As you see, I have reached only the second of the ten, the end is by no means in sight. But it is "do or die" now.

[TO ELVIRA N. SOLIS]   *New York, July 15, 1910*

Yesterday afternoon I went to the Federation office to install myself as secretary there. Eheu! West End? Impossible, at least not possible this month. You know, do you not? that I was made secretary of the Zionists—they call it honorary secretary. The Zionist dictionary, however, defines honor as work. My first trip of investigation and exploration has simply appalled me. To be sure, if I can justify the confidence others seems to feel in me, the Zionist office will be set to rights and garnished in a jiffy. But I have not the same confidence in myself—as you know—and then, too, I haven't much confidence in other people's confidence.

It springs from that comfortable way we all have about the work other people do—I have always found it the easiest of all work to do.

[TO ALICE L. SELIGSBERG]   *New York, July 15, 1910*

To him who hath shall be given, and from him who hath not shall be taken away. I thought Monday afternoon had been rescued from the general wreckage of my time, and that it was quite safe from depredation. But just now it became imperative to sacrifice it, too. A meeting of the new Executive Committee of the Federation has been summoned hurriedly to meet an emergency, and Monday afternoon suited everyone but me, so I had to yield. The Federation business is in an appalling condition. I doubt Hercules' ability to clear that stable—excuse the unsavory comparison. I was there yesterday afternoon to permit myself to be installed, and I came back uptown with my head swimming. If I could go down to the office for a solid week, I think I could grasp some of the threads firmly. But, unfortunately, this is my busiest proofreading time for the Publication Society—the *Year Book* must be passed very quickly. I had counted on Mr. Jason's staying in over the summer, and giving me a chance to take up the work gradually, but he has already stepped out for good and all.

But please do send me anything you want me to look at —I cannot afford to be cut loose from real living entirely.

[TO DR. SOLOMON SCHECHTER]
                    New York, November 10, 1910

In my former letters to you, I carefully refrained from letting you know about my secretaryship to the Federation of American Zionists, and what it means. I am truly ashamed of having allowed myself to be entrapped again.

Not that those who urged me to become secretary knew that it was a snare. They said and they thought and believed, I am sure, that it would require only two afternoons of the week from me. Instead of which, I have been laboring night and day—and, alas! laboring in vain. The affairs of the Federation were in a hopeless muddle when I took hold of them; I can say that the muddle has been cleared, but the hopelessness remains. So, you see, there is endless work, and no gratification. I cannot flatter myself that I am doing Zionist work; cleaning up other people's Augean stables is too far removed from Jewish ideal hopes to be a solace. And the personal result for me is that I am not living—I have committed suicide—I am merely counting the days until the next convention shall release me.

Last Sunday I was in Philadelphia at a Publication Committee meeting. There, too, everything went as usual—the same abstract discussions about practical details, the same smoke-filled atmosphere.

Fate met the challenge by laying her low. "I went to a hospital in Baltimore and I had an operation performed. I can't remember the amount of dust I had swallowed." The summer of 1911 was spent in slow recuperation.

[TO ELVIRA N. SOLIS]   *Baltimore, June 1, 1911*
When I was well on the road to recovery, and the trivialities as well as the solemn things of life began once more to take hold of my attention, I had to confess to my surgeon, who is a large man, that such an experience as I had passed through was an enrichment of one's spiritual being, but I hastened to add that I was rich enough—I wanted no more.
My progress is steady from day to day, and yet I must admit, with no little reluctance, that the surgeon well un-

derstands my physical needs in ordering so long a period of recuperation. Doubtless my mother told you that I am to do nothing until the fall. And *nothing* is literal, for my bewitched eye deprives me even of the convalescent's traditional pleasure—endless reading. I have always said that only imprisonment for a minor offense will give me a fair chance at that!

[TO ELVIRA N. SOLIS] *Mount Desert, Maine, June 23, 1911*

I have been moved northward, and my two days' experience here makes me very hopeful of regaining my full strength by the end of the summer. Whether my eyes, too, will yield to the fine air and quiet remains to be seen. They have not revealed the secret of their malady to any one of the many oculists I have consulted. So I am hoping they only shared in the general breakdown of my system and will equally share in its general upbuilding.

It was time for me to come away from Walbrook. The last two weeks of my stay there saw no improvement whatsoever. Here I have practically doubled my walking capacity and for many hours of the day I am not conscious of the various discomforts on my right side, which often depressed me and made me despair of the recovery everybody promised. You are good enough to want to know minutely about my condition, therefore I am telling you these details. In character the pains I have are the same as before the operation and they extend from head to foot, but it seems they are not important. Sometimes they bothered me so much that I charged the surgeon with having performed a mock operation. All that is practically over now, and I feel comforted. A little more steadiness of nerve and a little more sleep—they are what I need.

II

Some while before Miss Szold visited Palestine she joined a study group of young women, the remnants of a Zionistic society called the Hadassah Circle. "We met weekly and read papers, and the Zionist Federation looked upon us as organizers of strawberry festivals." This was the group her mother had in mind when, revolted by the fly-infested children of Jaffa, she urged a program of practical work. Upon the return to New York she proposed that the circle drop its paper-reading and make itself responsible for a specific piece of health work among the women and children of Palestine. "A responsibility that requires funds for its execution," she insisted, would insure life and vigor to the group. Her views were supported by Mrs. Richard Gottheil and Miss Eva Léon, both of whom had likewise visited Palestine in the summer of 1909. Moreover, the idea of a nation-wide organization of women Zionists was in the air. Gertrude Goldsmith (later Mrs. Bernard A. Rosenblatt) returned from the world Zionist congress of 1911 under the pledge to work for the establishment of such an organization.

Preliminary agitation, discussion, and meetings resulted in the gathering of a handful of women in the vestry rooms of Temple Emanu-El in New York on Purim (February 24) of 1912. They constituted themselves the Hadassah Chapter of a national organization to be known as the Daughters of Zion. The Feast of Purim, on which the meeting was held, made the name Hadassah almost inevitable, for the word, which means "myrtle," was the Hebrew name of Queen Esther; and eventually it supplanted the "Daughters of Zion." Thirty-eight women subscribed as members.

Miss Szold spoke on the need of a "definite project," and shortly after that she was elected president. Professor Israel Friedlaender supplied the society with a motto from Jeremiah (8:22): "The healing of the daughter of my people." The motto described the program—the propagation of Zionism in America and the furtherance of health work among women and children in Palestine. After much debate, with many counter-proposals from Palestine itself, the first definite project to be adopted, especially because of its advocacy by Dr. Harry Friedenwald, who had been on the ground, was the establishment of American visiting-nurses in Jerusalem. Out of this, it was hoped, would grow a nurses' training-school and a maternity hospital.

Purim of 1912 was not only the birthday of Hadassah but of Miss Szold's life-work. Thereafter, for many years, the organization of Hadassah chapters and the financing and execution of its program became her paramount interest.

"By the end of 1912," as she remembered it in after years, "we had in our treasury about $283. Then Mr. and Mrs. Nathan Straus appeared on the scene and asked me to visit them. They told me they had heard our purpose was to introduce visiting-nurses in Jerusalem; they wanted to know why we didn't do it. I said we had only $283 in the treasury. They said, that doesn't matter—start! I said there was no money; and Mr. Straus repeated, that has nothing to do with it. Mrs. Straus kept nodding her head behind his back as if to say: 'The Lord will provide.' "

The Strauses undertook to pay the passage of two nurses. Eva Léon found in Chicago funds to guarantee $2000 annual expenses for five years. In January 1913 the two nurses, Rose Kaplan and Rachel D. Landy, were on their way to Jerusalem in the company of the Strauses, who rented a little settlement house for them.

And Miss Szold took to the road, seeking daughters of Zion who would aid in the healing of their people.

[TO ELVIRA N. SOLIS]   *New York, July 4, 1913*

It is very close to *Shabbes* [Sabbath], but I should hate myself if I allowed another week to end without sending you at least a line.

You were to have had a letter from Cincinnati. That intention was formed before I knew what Cincinnati could be in summer. The nether regions have no terrors for me any more. Otherwise the experience was enjoyable while it lasted, and it has been stimulating in the retrospect. The Zionist convention was good—respectable enough to satisfy an assimilationist Jew. It was, of course, severely boycotted by that sort of Jew, unless the vice-mayor of the city was their representative. There was very little pyrotechnics, and I was greatly impressed by the earnestness and idealism of the small-town Jew, for whom this is the only opportunity to display feeling. Of course, we have our men who are in the movement for what they can make out of it for themselves. But no one is duped by them, and so they do no mischief.

My own mission I found to have been premature. I had an idea there would be many more women delegates present than are in the habit of coming, it appears. The lesson I learned is that nothing can be done easily. It all takes hard, concentrated work, and we shall have to put in a year of outside agitation to produce concerted action at the next convention. But it was good to become acquainted with the forces existing elsewhere.

I was at the hotel that had been chosen as headquarters, and that gave me the opportunity of talks and discussions between sessions—the best feature of a convention. I spoke at a little theater on the Hills, to the other sort of Jews. Of course the heat melted the audience; but if I may judge by the letters I have received since my return, what I had to say made some impression. Indeed, it seems probable that I may go to Cincinnati in the fall on my way back from Chicago.

In Cleveland my visit produced a Zionist women's organization, Shoshannah Chapter. It promises well. There, too, I spoke to a hot temple audience. But by that time I was unable to keep myself on my feet, and I really do not know what impression I made. I got home sick, and scarcely had my mother nursed me back to comfort, when our little apartment was made topsy-turvy by painters and paper-hangers. Imagine confusion plus heat!

[TO JESSIE SAMPTER]   *New York, July 15, 1913*

I do know all about your meeting with Miss Seligsberg, and I think the result excellent. She showed me the folder when she was in town a week ago. If we can keep up this folder propaganda as the winter's work of Hadassah, we shall be doing admirably—for ourselves at home and for the chapters elsewhere, too. My trip to the convention convinced me that much, much is needed everywhere; and the people outside look to New York for guidance. There are now chapters in Philadelphia, Baltimore, Cleveland, Cincinnati, and Boston, the last two still incomplete in organization. Chicago is ready.

At the convention not much could be done in the way of centralization. It was folly to think we were ready for it after so short a period of effort. The Daughters of Zion scheme was received very sympathetically, and the men delegates promised moral support in their home towns. Of women delegates there were too few. That is what we must work for—to secure a large delegation of women at the next convention.

The convention was satisfying to me. It seems not to have been extraordinary in any way. That in itself held the assurance that we are secure in ourselves. We no longer need pyrotechnics to keep up our enthusiasm. Cincinnati was not a favorable environment. The heat was intense, and the people at large as cold as the frigid zone produces them.

I am glad you are going to write. You will serve Zionism best in that way. I believe it is what we need most—good writers, from whose work Zionism will radiate as a fine aroma. We have had the brochures, the apologia, the party pamphlet, the disquisition, the essay—now we should have literature based on Zionism as a pervading conviction and life philosophy.

Yes, I do know your clover—Turkish clover, I believe it is called. It was introduced into the United States years ago, but within my time and memory; a field of it is a beautiful sight.

I hope the summer arrangements will prove comfortable and conducive to all the studying you want to do—but don't want to do *too* much.

[TO ALICE L. SELIGSBERG]

Madison, Wisconsin, October 10, 1913

I am writing to you within the hour of leaving for the synagogue. That, I hope, will dispose you to deal leniently with me. I know that I shall seek atonement tomorrow, among many other sins, for that of having left two such fine letters unanswered so long, and of having failed to express to you the good wishes I cherish in my heart for you for the New Year and for many years, and for our friendship throughout all the years. When I get back to New York, I shall try to tell you, though even then in as few words as possible, how I have been overrun with letters requiring immediate replies, letters on account of the Jewish Publication Society, and on account of Hadassah, and on account of my present trip and speaking engagements, not to mention my epistolary obligations to many charming hostesses. You will forgive me, will you not? And you will believe that my neglect of you has not been caused by indifference, either to you or to what you write about.

In general, as to the latter, I have one great regret, that I shall not be present at the meeting on the eighteenth. It seems to me admirably planned, and I am happy to think that Hadassah has acquired you and that you are happy to have been acquired.

I rejoice with you that the Harlem Federation relations worked out so well. Of course, your girls are to be called "the little Hadassah girls," and I hope they may be the pioneers of what I think is Hadassah's real American work—the young. I have been talking to Dr. [Horace M.] Kallen—illuminating talks—and in talking it has more than ever become clear to me that the women must make themselves responsible for Zionism among the young. But we ourselves are not yet ready to educate—we must first educate ourselves.

Your Hebrew program is fine. You will gain much from Dr. [Israel] Friedlaender. Dr. [Mordecai M.] Kaplan I do not know as a teacher. Only do not do too much. You ask me what is too much. I cannot tell. But be careful. So far as the writing is concerned, I should not hold off from studying. The writing will be improved if you wait for another year. But think of yourself, your health. If you can study and do the Hadassah work, too, let the writing go.

When I return I shall have much to tell you about Judaism here and elsewhere in the West. We need Zionism as much as those Jews do who need a physical home.

III

The outbreak of the first World War rocked when it did not shatter the optimism of an age. Its impact on Miss Szold and on all that was dear to her in the Jewish world is revealed in the ensuing letters.

[TO JESSIE SAMPTER]

Mount Desert, Maine, August 24, 1914

My real vacation reduced itself to less than a week—there was so much proofreading to be done on the *Year Book*. And in three days from now I go back to New York—to continue to read proof of that same luckless *Year Book*. I knew it to be a mistake to come away from home while the book was under way; but I acted against my better judgment because the whole family, every last member of it, was assembled here, and it was the first time in years that the opportunity of being together was granted to us. In spite of my preoccupation it has been worth while.

The spot is the embodiment of all that is charming in nature, the climate is ideal, and it has been delightful to be with my sister's children, and with my sister, their mother, who is taking her first vacation during her married life. It was something, too, to come here and find my mother greatly improved. The disappointment is that none of the writing or reading or thinking I had planned and hoped to do this summer has got done.

Physically being away from New York has benefited me, but otherwise I am as tired as I was—I mean, I have gathered no inspiration to do more than I have been doing all

along, attending to routine duties. Perhaps even a long un-
disturbed vacation would not have achieved a better result
in these dreadful days that rob me of all confidence in the
perfectibility of humankind.

The war makes joy impossible. Whenever I have tried
to turn my thoughts away from it, all I have succeeded in
doing was to think of some department of life which it is
sure to affect to its detriment. You know what havoc it has
already played with Zionism. The whole administration in
Berlin is disorganized. Some of the members of the Actions
Committee are serving in the Russian army, one in the
German army, one in the Austrian. Next Sunday a conference is to take place in New York for the purpose of de-
liberating what we can do over here to keep the work going.
What can we do? Can we look brave when we see how Bel-
gium's neutrality was made mock of? And I am not a little
anxious about our own practical work. How are we going
to secure the means to keep it up? The whole cataclysm is
too horrible to be conceived of.

I am going home a couple of weeks earlier than I had
expected on account of the conference next Sunday. They
telegraphed to me to come. I do not know of what use I
can be—as the German has it, *mein Verstand bleibt mir still
stehen*. But I obey orders—I go to the front.

I am ashamed to say that I have not read your article
—but then I have done nothing. Yes, I have read the Herzl
biography, and—I wept over it, it was so beautiful, one of
the most beautiful pieces of literature I have ever known.
And now Herzl's work is nigh to destruction! My feeling
is that a half-generation will have to elapse before we attain to the point occupied by Zionism before this barbarous
outbreak of greed and passion came to throw us back into
medievalism. We shall probably not lose everything we have

achieved, but we shall in equal probability unlearn the marching step toward Zion.

Instead of all this pessimistic jeremiad, I should have been telling you of all the comeliness that meets my eye whenever I look up from my writing—purple mountains, blue sea, smiling apple-planted lawn, and the roofs of the village houses nestling in foliage.

I hope that, when we meet, the bloody specter will have been banished; and if the world will have learnt its lesson and the people rise in their might and demand the end of all autocracy in their affairs, then even the war will be called a blessing.

[TO ELVIRA N. SOLIS]
Mount Desert, Maine, August 25, 1914

News has come from abroad that the war has completely disorganized the Zionist administration. Some of the members of the Actions Committee are at the front in Russia, one in Germany, one in Austria; and Dr. Schmarya Levin was on the *Kronprinzessin Cecilia,* and therefore is here. Under his headship, an effort is to be made to reconstitute an administrative body here [1]—with the records in Berlin, with the sympathizers in Russia! There you have an illustration—not that you or anyone needed it—of how destructive this outbreak of passion and greed is of all the works of peace.

[TO MRS. JULIUS ROSENWALD] *New York, January 17, 1915*

Your night letter has come to hand, and you will receive a copy of all recent telegrams that have reached the Pro-

---

[1] The effort resulted in the creation of the Provisional Executive Committee for General Zionist Affairs, with headquarters in the United States.

visional Executive Committee for General Zionist Affairs
concerning the situation both in Palestine and among the
refugees in Jaffa. Most of our information at present concerning Palestine comes from a group of Palestinians who
have taken up their abode in Alexandria, in order that
they may serve as intermediaries between Palestine and
ourselves. If it were not for them, we should lack information about many points, and we should not be able to get
money to our people in Jaffa.

I asked them to do so in order to make up for the meager-
ness of the letters received from our own nurses. I am enclosing the most recent *Bulletin* issued by Hadassah, in
which you will see that we received only postcards.

You will notice that though Mr. [Aaron] Aaronsohn ad-
vises the nurses to return to the United States, they have
made no move to do it as far as we know.

Let me congratulate you and Palestine upon having secured, as you tell me in your telegram, a "splendid response
from local organization." I wish there were a way of Hadassah's being kept informed of all you do. I have requested
Mrs. Lesser to employ a stenographer at our expense and to
dictate to her a full account of what has happened for our
benefit. It would be so valuable to us from the point of view
of propaganda.

However, the paramount consideration is that you are
advancing the cause of Palestine. From my point of view,
as I need not tell *you,* that is the cause of the Jew and, most
important of all, of Judaism. In many respects the war catastrophe has left me bewildered and uncertain. In one respect I see more clearly than ever—that is in respect to
Zionism. The anomalous situation of the Jew everywhere—
the distress, misery, and in part degradation (witness Poland!) of seven millions, more than half, of our race; the

bravery of the Jews who are serving in all the armies; the size of the contingent we are contributing to every front— means to me that the Jew and his Judaism must be perpetuated and can be perpetuated only by their repatriation in the land of the fathers.

It is a miracle that, though we Zionists were not hitherto able to bring many to our way of thinking, nevertheless many in these days of stress think with pity of our little sanctuary. They have come to us and said: "Even if we do not see eye to eye with you, we are going to help you save the sanctuary you have established." Perhaps they feel that it will yield sanctuary, refuge, and protection in the days of readjustment soon to dawn, we hope.

If you succeed, in your appeal to the Federation of Temple Sisterhoods, in conveying to the Jewish women of America the need of such a sanctuary for the Jew, the need of a center from which Jewish culture and inspiration will flow, and if you can persuade them to set aside one day of the year as a Palestine Day, on which thoughts and means are to be consecrated to a great Jewish world-organizing purpose, you will have accomplished a result that will bring immediate blessing to those now in distress and in terror of life, and a blessing for all future times redounding to the benefit not only of those who will make use of their sanctuary rights in Palestine, but also those who like ourselves, remaining in a happy, prosperous country, will be free to draw spiritual nourishment from a center dominated wholly by Jewish traditions and the Jewish ideals of universal peace and universal brotherhood.

If you and they do not follow us Zionists so far, at least they will respond to the appeal for material help—at least they will recognize that for the sake of Jewish dignity and self-respect, even the purely philanthropic work in Palestine, for which so large a part of Jewry has long felt a keen responsibility, may never again be allowed to relapse into a pauperizing chaos. They may refuse to accept the whole Zionist ideal. But the wonderful vitality shown by the Zionist settlement in the Holy Land—the resourcefulness of the colonists, who could supply the cities with grain and food for months, and the usefulness of the Zionist bank in averting panic and the direst distress—they make of me a more confirmed and conscious Zionist than ever. I need not analyze the elements I have enumerated for you. You, who have been in the Holy Land, even if you do not—may I say, not yet?—agree with me, your mind will instinctively understand the leap mine makes in these troublous days to the Zionist conclusion.

Troublous days? I have often wondered during these months how many of us Jews here in America realize that we are living through times comparable only to the destruction of the second Temple and of our commonwealth by the Romans, and exceeding by far the horrors of the exodus from Spain and Portugal, and the abject misery and suffering of the pogrom years 1881, and 1903, and 1905 in Russia.

The Jew speaks of the first *Hurban*—the utter destruction of Solomon's Temple. He speaks of the second *Hurban*, the ruin of the second Temple by Titus. I feel that a future Graetz will speak of this war as the Jews' third *Hurban*.

There is only one hope in my heart—the effective aid being rendered to Palestine by all Jews without difference. In the first *Hurban* the Jews could not protect their sanctuary against the hordes of Nebuchadnezzar. In the second *Hurban* the Roman legions destroyed the Temple, leaving only the western wall, the last vestige of glory, now turned into a place of wailing. There is no third Temple on the hill of Zion to be destroyed in this third *Hurban;* but in Zion, nevertheless, there is a sanctuary, the refuge that has been established by Jewish pioneers, with the sweat, blood, and labor of those who believe. As American Jewesses they cannot possibly reject the centralized organization of Palestine, an endeavor for which Zionism stands first and last.

With cordial wishes for success, and, may I add this only once only, with Zion's greetings . . .

[TO JESSIE SAMPTER]
Mount Desert, Maine, September 6, 1915
Ko-ach [strength]—that should include everything, but one cannot help being specific and personal. So I wish for you—and it is a wish for all of us—that strength of body may be added to strength of mind and spirit, so that you may be able to grasp every opportunity, and miss none, to make your gifts available for the Jewish cause. I for my part am grateful that you and I were brought together. May the years cement the friendship and knit us firmly to each other for whatever the same developing years may show to be the good and the true. I owe you much; I want to owe you more. But if strength should not come in the measure in which I wish it for you, then at least husband what is vouchsafed you, for we need you. Much love.

[TO ELVIRA N. SOLIS]
Mount Desert, Maine, September 7, 1915
I know I have been neglecting you, but not in thought. Indeed you have been in my mind much and often as the echoes of the Congress-Conference controversy reach me.[2]

---

[2] A country-wide controversy over whether American Jews should express themselves on the problems arising from the war through a Conference of leaders or through a democratically elected Congress. The Zionists, including Miss Szold, favored the latter method.

I am not very desirous of leaving the quiet and beauty of Mount Desert—I expect to be back, nevertheless, by next Monday evening—and assuming a telephonic, tumultuous life in the dust and noise of the metropolis; but I *am* desirous of getting back and talking things over with my friends on both sides of the house. Meantime I am sick at heart about it—and of the same opinion still.

And the last week I have felt such blessed relief in the thought that our country was not being involved in the insensate struggle of the Old World.

The September days have been beautiful beyond compare—genially warm, sunny, the mountains standing out boldly in the clear atmosphere, and the peace of it! I realize that I have acquired a strong home feeling for the place. I am such a hidebound conservative that I love the old beyond the novel. Come to think of it, though, I am not on the conservative side these days!

IV

Two events now altered the tenor of her life. In recognition of her past services to the Jewish people, but, more than that, in the hope of liberating her for greater services in the future, a group of men, through the mediation of Judge Julian W. Mack, provided Miss Szold with a stipend that made her financially independent. She resigned from her secretarial post in the Jewish Publication Society. Thereafter she could work at what she pleased and for whom she pleased—not working, even at the age of fifty-five, being inconceivable to her. Years later she drew some keen conclusions from this happy status (see pages 197–8).

The other event was inexpressibly unhappy. After a long and painful illness her mother died in the summer of 1916.

[TO ALICE L. SELIGSBERG]

Mount Desert, Maine, September 8, 1915

A happy, happy New Year to you, to all of us!

Though I feel that I have need of special good fortune in the year to come, in which I contemplate making so revolutionary a change in my life (yes, I have practically decided in favor of the offer from the point of view of the work—it remains to be seen whether the business details can be arranged satisfactorily), still I am bound to say that my reflections at the turn of the year rise above the personal.

Was there ever a time when the individual counted for so little—ever a time when the right individual might have counted or might still count for so much? I have heard many say that, as the war dragged itself along, they were losing the sense of personal guilt and incrimination that obsessed them at first. Not my experience. The ache and the oppression grow in me.

[TO DR. CYRUS ADLER]   *New York, December 1, 1915*

Today I am mailing my letter of resignation to Mr. [Simon] Miller, and though Judge Mack has, as I know, told you all there is to say in regard to it, I feel that I want to communicate with you direct. Long as the interval is since I became secretary to the Publication Committee, I have as vivid a recollection as ever of the part you played in bringing it about, and I have not forgotten that you have always been ready to give me a hearing and advice concerning whatever affected my relations to the Society. If in this instance, when my official connection with the Society is to terminate, I did not as always before come to you first, you must attribute it to the peculiarity and the precipitateness of all the circumstances. I am still bewildered by what has happened—I feel as though I were reading in someone else's book of life, not my own. Judge Mack may have mentioned to you, however, that it was nevertheless my wish to speak to you and Judge [Mayer] Sulzberger first. He induced me to yield my judgment to his, and I did it without inquiring into his reasons.

I hope he also told you that I want the very first piece of work I do as a Jewish volunteer to be for the Publication Society, and I should like it to be the proofreading of the Bible, which I should have done if the tenor of my way had not been interrupted so strangely. Will this be acceptable to you?

Please give my love to Racie and my regards to your mother. My mother has gained somewhat in strength, but her progress is painfully slow.

[TO ELVIRA N. SOLIS]   *New York, August 22, 1916*

I need not tell you what the last two days since my return to New York have been—my return to an apartment that was a home. The pain of separation is keen, and the efforts at readjustment harrowing. But most harrowing is the insistence with which her suffering and her spiritual anguish of the last year push aside the picture of my dear mother with her rosy cheeks and blue eyes, her alert activities and equally alert interests, her never idle hands, her undaunted courage. Once I regain that picture of her, and all it implies of a beautiful rounded life, useful and happy in spite of its great trials, I shall have the courage to reshape my own life in her spirit. She was conscious to the end—spoke to me less than two minutes before her last breath was drawn, and a little while before bade me recite the *Shema*. I was alone with her, even the nurse was out of the room, and I closed her eyes. I am not sure that you are right—that I did the best

for her, but I am thankful I could do what I did, thankful
that I could be with her to the end. Often during this last
year I prayed that no accident might snatch me away before
she went.

[TO HAYM PERETZ]   *New York, September 16, 1916*

It is impossible for me to find words in which to tell you
how deeply I was touched by your offer to act as *"Kaddish"*
for my dear mother. I cannot even thank you—it is something that goes beyond thanks. It is beautiful, what you have
offered to do—I shall never forget it.

You will wonder, then, that I cannot accept your offer.
Perhaps it would be best for me not to try to explain to
you in writing, but to wait until I see you to tell you why
it is so. I know well, and appreciate what you say about,
the Jewish custom; and Jewish custom is very dear and sacred to me.[3] And yet I cannot ask you to say *Kaddish* after
my mother. The *Kaddish* means to me that the survivor
publicly and markedly manifests his wish and intention
to assume the relation to the Jewish community which his
parent had, and that so the chain of tradition remains un-
broken from generation to generation, each adding its own
link. You can do that for the generations of your family, I
must do that for the generations of my family.

I believe that the elimination of women from such duties
was never intended by our law and custom—women were
freed from positive duties when they could not perform
them, but not when they could. It was never intended that,
if they could perform them, their performance of them
should not be considered as valuable and valid as when

---

[3] The *Kaddish,* a sanctification of God, is recited by children in
mourning for their parents at synagogue services during one year.
By tradition, only male children recite the prayer. If there are no
male survivors, a stranger may act as a substitute.

one of the male sex performed them. And of the *Kaddish* I feel sure this is particularly true.

My mother had eight daughters and no son; and yet never did I hear a word of regret pass the lips of either my mother or my father that one of us was not a son. When my father died, my mother would not permit others to take her daughters' place in saying the *Kaddish,* and so I am sure I am acting in her spirit when I am moved to decline your offer. But beautiful your offer remains nevertheless, and, I repeat, I know full well that it is much more in consonance with the generally accepted Jewish tradition than is my or my family's conception. You understand me, don't you?

CHAPTER SEVEN

The World War Medical Unit

I

By the end of 1917 Hadassah had grown to be an organization with forty-seven chapters and about four thousand members. War conditions had forced its nurses to abandon Palestine in 1915; and one of them, Rose Kaplan, died at her post of duty in Alexandria, victim of a disease contracted while working for the Jewish refugees. As the war continued, Palestine was deprived of doctors and medicines. In July 1916, upon the request of the World Zionist Organization, Hadassah accepted the responsibility of organizing, financing, and dispatching a medical unit to Palestine. After extraordinary difficulties and painful delays—a "troublous period which left an indelible mark" on Miss Szold, who bore the executive weight of the task—the American Zionist Medical Unit reached its destination in the summer of 1918. Forty-four medical men, nurses, and administrators formed its staff; and ambulances, trucks, and automobiles as well as $50,000 worth of drugs and instruments comprised its equipment. Transportation and maintenance for one year was budgeted at $250,000. Part of this sum was given by the American Jewish Joint Distribution Committee; but, under the hand of Miss Szold, Hadassah raised a large amount of it and supplied the direction and organization to execute the entire undertaking.

The burden of organizing, financing, and dispatching the medical unit lies behind the following selection from her personal letters. In them Miss Szold is seen on the road and at her desk reacting to the larger issues of the period: the Russian Revolution, America's participation in the war, the beginnings of reconstruction, and American Jewish fragments of this world-wide drama.

[TO JESSIE SAMPTER]   *New York, March 8, 1917*

You are unspeakably good to me, and I am so glad to have you be good to me. Your note and the enclosure came when I longed to have someone stroke me and pet me and soothe me. Nothing has happened—nothing at all. But holiday times are so bare to me nowadays. So your note came just at the right moment. Your birthday gift to Hadassah has gone to the Medical Unit.

I had a fine evening with a group of Brownsville girls last night, about forty of them. I believe we are at last on the way to a real organization in Brooklyn. We ought to offer the group every help in our power. Somebody from here ought to be present at each one of its meetings until the chapter is rooted.

The earlier part of the evening was not so happy. I went to a synagogue in Brownsville to hear the *Megillah* read. Things were at their unloveliest, Jewishly speaking. It was a *Golus* scene and *Golus* sounds.[1]

Have the New Rochelle ladies reported our conversation to you? There are two good Zionists to your credit! But what can be done for the unregenerate in your smug suburb?

We had our propaganda class today for the last time for a long while. You know, don't you, that I am going away? On Sunday I go to Reading, Monday I speak in Philadelphia, Tuesday and Wednesday I shall be in New York,

---

[1] The *Megillah* is the Biblical Book of Esther. *Golus* is Hebrew for "Exile," and as used here connotes the distorted psychology of the Jews in the Diaspora.

Thursday Syracuse, then Rochester, Toronto, Detroit, Youngstown, and Cleveland, returning on April 1, a week or less here, and Passover in Baltimore. I wonder whether I shall be equal to it?

And what do you think of the news in this morning's paper? This evening the report is that Jerusalem and Baghdad have fallen into the hands of the English. If only America were not being drawn into the bloody maelstrom!

[TO HAYM PERETZ]   *Toronto, March 19, 1917*

I appreciate your gift, and that I do think it has value, the greatest value, derives from your kindly friendship for me and from its connection with the cause dear to both of us. It is in the interest of the same cause that I am now traveling from city to city. Whether I am doing any real propaganda I cannot judge. But this I know, that the feeling for Zionism and the understanding of it is growing apace in this country. A few years ago everybody would have been of the opinion that the miracle that has happened in Russia [2] would deal the death-blow to Zionism. Now its meaning is so well known that even non-Zionists realize that the liberalizing of Russia can only serve our cause. So may it be!

[TO ALICE L. SELIGSBERG]
                    Youngstown, Ohio, March 27, 1917

You would be pleased with me, I think. The trip, much to my own surprise, has done me good. I have had varied and stimulating experiences. The upshot is that Hadassah may be an instrument for great good, but there is a mountain of work before us to make it effective; that Zionism is worth working for, but the Jews who are to realize it are inefficient, spiritually poverty-stricken, uncouth, and un-

---

[2] The democratic revolution of 1917.

mannerly, yet with a marvelous something that will not let the faith in them perish. And now that the Russian miracle has removed the last vestige of the "charity" taint from Zionism, it ought to stand forth in its shining spiritual armor as a regenerative force in Jewish life, and in human life as well.

The Russian Revolution! I cannot believe that I have been privileged to live in its time. Perhaps we shall still rise up and bless this war. But no! Russia's gain is lessened through our loss. I am heart-sick over our own country. I don't know ourselves. We are falling over ourselves in our effort to demonstrate that we are full of hatred, suspicion, jealousy, and the whole brood of evil passions produced in less than three years. Can you believe that we are the same who at the outbreak of the war had a contemptuous smile for the chauvinistic vagaries on the other side?

[TO JESSIE SAMPTER]   *Youngstown, Ohio, March 27, 1917*

Ever since I left New York I have been wanting to send you a line to tell you that I think of you often and lovingly and wishfully as to your health. Otherwise I have nothing to wish for in you! Indeed, I may boast that I do more than think of you—I talk of you and I have done my utmost to utilize every opportunity to make known the value of your creation, the School of Zionism.[3] I am more than ever convinced that yours is our most important work. A nation cannot be remade by instinctive, vague, misty feeling, however fine the instinct may be. Feeling alone leads to some of the aberrations we are today witnesses of, and innocently enough in many cases parties to. We must bring emotion out of its obscurity into the clarification of thought. Else

_____

[3] This was part of the educational and propaganda work of Hadassah.

Zionism will remain forever an "ideal"—an amiable, *dolce-far-niente* fancy, making *batlonim* of its dreamy promoters, and unfitting them for the realities of life. I haven't said just these words to my audiences—of which I have had more than I can enumerate in the few moments I may devote to this letter—but I have said the plain equivalent absolutely every time I have had a chance.

[TO ELVIRA N. SOLIS]   *Baltimore, April 12, 1917*

I returned from Washington this morning, after two days of strenuous propagandizing. It tired me, not because my own part in it was busy, but because the atmosphere at the capital is thick with war talk, prognostications, and preparations. And Washington is so beautiful, particularly at this season! Most of the younger men with whom I came into contact are about to enlist. The unreality of the situation has disappeared for me—I realize all the sternness of our intentions.

[TO JESSIE SAMPTER]   *New York, August 23, 1917*

This morning I am going to pretend that there isn't a speck of dust in this apartment (there's a thick layer over everything in it), and by a main effort of the imagination I am going to believe that the various bits of work of all sorts that should have been delivered complete by me, some years, some months ago, are accomplished; because, even if I do not write a real, genuine letter to you, I want you to know that I appreciate yours as real and genuine.

There are too many drafts made upon my physical and my spiritual energy. I cannot possibly meet all the demands that seem to be legitimately made upon me. I wonder whether I call them legitimate because I haven't the stamina to turn them down? Or I don't turn them down because they are legitimate? If the former is the true diagnosis, then it only corroborates what I was going to add about my spiritual energy. Somehow or other I am a humbug. I seem to have won golden opinions which I have not earned. I am not what I seem to seem to others. I have told you this in other language before.

Then you retort—as my other friends do—modesty, diffidence, ignorance of her own powers! And having made the retort, you and my other friends go on expecting from me what I am not equal to. Don't you think I hate myself when I can't give the response to your mute and vocal appeals to me which you expect? But I can't and I can't. I also hate myself because I do not come up to my own modest expectations of what I might do. Because I must hold myself ready to meet a thousand claims from the outside, I have neglected my own little garden. I am not allowed to mature what is in me, because I must do all the time— morning, noon, and night—what others impose upon me. Some years ago I resigned myself to my fate, I no longer kick against the traces. I accept the task life seems to have set me, but even so I can accept it only to the extent of my physical powers—else there will be invalidism in another sense for me.

Deep down in the bottom of my heart I have always held that I should have had children, many children. It is only in rearing children that minute service piled on minute service counts. In my life, details have confused the issue; they have not gone to make a harmonious and productive whole. In a mother's life, ability to lose one's identity in details is the great thing for the future of mankind.

I should like to write you about the Provisional Zionist Executive Committee. But I can't. The situation is too involved, and in my own mind it is complicated with my atti-

tude toward the war and my consequent inaction as an
American citizen.[4] Your letter on the subject of the Medical
Unit does not help me. I am bound to confess that I do not
understand it. I envy Miss Sophia Berger her robustness—
she sails for France in a few days to do canteen work under
the Red Cross. I feel all sicklied o'er with the pale hue of
thought.

II

During a propaganda tour through Texas, her pacifist
convictions changed. And her Zionist convictions were
deepened as she related the ideals of Zionism to the larger
purposes of the war—freedom for all nationalities.

[TO ALICE L. SELIGSBERG]
Kansas City, December 26, 1917

No, life has not been mean to me, since you are my friend.
Indeed, it has not been mean to me at all. When it has appeared not to treat me well, in big and little things, it has
been because I didn't know how to handle it. That lesson
becomes clear and clearer to me as birthday anniversary
after birthday anniversary slips by with the swiftness of an
avalanche.

Speaking of birthday anniversaries, I celebrated one
yesterday—my mother's. Was life mean to me when it endowed me with my mother and my father? And it wasn't
mean to me when it made me capable of embracing a cause
and made me strong enough to cling to it even in the moments, no, the hours and the days latterly, when I despaired
even of its value. As I go about, I become impressed all

---

[4] Like many leading women of the time, she was loath to surrender
her ingrained and often affirmed pacifist faith. As early as 1902 she
addressed the Maryland Federation of Women's Clubs on "The Science of Peace."

over again with the essential worth of the Jewish material,
but also with the ugliness with which it is overlaid as by
a deposit left by ages of untrueness to self; and all over again
I am impressed with the bitter need mankind has to let each
of its groups find itself for the good of the whole. We Zionists discerned that before the cry for the small nationalities
was heard abroad. And as we discerned a truth in that direction, so I am sure the belief of some of us nationalist inter-
nationalists, that internationalism cannot come about until
the vexations of all the nationalisms are in a fair way of
settlement, will soon justify itself.

Up to this point my tour has been anything but a howling
success, as far as my mission is concerned. I should love to
hear the result of your meetings about the Medical Unit.
The chief nurse *is* a problem. A thousand loves.

[TO MRS. ROSE JACOBS]
Fort Worth, Texas, January 3, 1918
My trip has been not unsatisfactory so far. But I have no
startling successes to record. I was going to say the times are
not propitious, but I cannot blame my own shortcomings as
a missionary on the times, however bad; and in reality the
badness of the times is a point in favor of Zionism. The real
difficulty lies in the fact that Zionism, like Judaism in general, implies or presupposes a high grade of intelligence and
mental discipline. Our people, used up by the struggle for
existence, do not possess that. And they are disorganized
besides.

[TO JESSIE SAMPTER]
San Antonio, Texas, January 14, 1918
Texas has been a liberal education to me along military
lines. I have seen soldiers upon soldiers—at Waco, at Fort

Worth, here. The population here has been increased by 105,000 through the cantonments. Among them are 4000 Jewish boys. Here and elsewhere many of the Jewish army men have attended the Zionist meetings.

For the rest, I have also learned all over again that rebuilding Zion is not an easy matter. The unconverted are stubborn, the converted unorganized, in part unorganizable, and hampered by the boastfulness and aggressive arrogance of the ignorant, partly prosperous immigrants. There is going to be some result from this tour of mine, but I cannot be sure that the result will be big enough to have warranted the expenditure of energy, time, and money.

The President's last address was a comforting word— almost all of it. Or are these cantonments and the khaki-ized streets making me hospitable to war ideals?

[TO ELVIRA N. SOLIS]
En route in Texas, January 18, 1918
My Jewish experiences have made a hardened Zionist of me. If I hadn't been a Zionist before, I should have become one in Texas. And whenever the elevating experiences happened, I wondered whether they would be arguments to you.

We in New York haven't a conception of Jewish laxity— the distance between the Jew and Judaism. It is not a question of reform and orthodoxy—it is Judaism and non-Judaism. Zionism is the only anchor in sight. Here is the problem in its nakedness. How is it to be solved? I say through Zionism. What other solution is offered?

I am learning so much—so much more than I am teaching. In the first place, many refuse to listen when I try to teach, and I have seen so many, many "boys" in the Texan cantonments and I have been thinking hard. And I thought of every son's mother. But I also digested the President's last message and I was in a measure comforted. We pacifists have not labored in vain.

[TO JESSIE SAMPTER]
Galveston, Texas, January 21, 1918

There is no one in Galveston who will listen to me talk Zionism, so I may indulge myself to the extent of writing to you.

Texas is not different from New Rochelle or New York. The British Declaration [5] passed over the heads of the Jews down here as an unseen airplane from one of the Texan aviation fields. They didn't know that something epoch-making had just happened. What an argument in favor of Zionism is such stolidity. Alas! they don't feel the force and validity of that argument, either. Down here I have learnt to say a dreadful thing: "Rather assimilation than this!" Not that the Texas "this" is worse than the New York "this." But the Texas background, by its unfamiliarity, brought out the forbidding contours of our calamity—our gypsy state. And yet there is less active hostility to Zionism here than I have met in most other sections. "If some Jews will have it, I'm satisfied to let them have it, and I'll help them get it—help them a little." That's their spiritual summit.

But the brotherhood of man is a current phrase in all mouths. Education stop? No, not by any manner of means. Please to remember that the task we are undertaking through the Palestine Restoration Fund is one that must last at least three generations. During that period, no matter

---

[5] The Balfour Declaration of November 2, 1917, committing the British government to the establishment of a Jewish "national home" in Palestine.

what happens later, the Diaspora must be spiritualized. Else they, the Texan Jews, will say: "If we came here to Texas as pioneers, let them go to Palestine as pioneers. Who assisted us?" And the more telling the chronicle you will write of Palestine, the more insistent their negative attitude. The more they talk of the spiritual mission of the Jew in the Diaspora, the less spiritual are they Jewishly. And they don't understand the economic interpretation of history at all—at all.

This missionarizing that we are doing through agitator-propagandist-orators ought to stop. Or we ought to have angels to do it. More of this when I return. I should be content to return tomorrow. I know now that *I* am neither angel, agitator, propagandist, orator, nor missionary.

[TO JESSIE SAMPTER]   *New York, March 16, 1918*

Do you know that for many weeks, in fact I can tell you exactly how many—since January 8—I had been looking forward to our meeting to tell you that I had ceased to be what you call an "orthodox pacifist"? The President's message containing his specific war aims produced the change in me.

As usual, I am neither so articulate nor so sure of myself as you are. I haven't enough time for thought, and I do not know how to think in the most favorable of circumstances. But this I know, the process of change has been endorsed and hastened by the President's greeting to the Pan-Soviet meeting. Wherefrom you may infer that it is Germany's action in Russia that prompts my new attitude. In other words, I am ready to fight for the people, though I could not fight for the kings. So it was not fighting in the abstract that I objected to, but the cause. That leaves me a shred of consistency to comfort myself with. Indeed, unless I am

mightily mistaken, our overseas allies are none too well
pleased with American single-mindedness. I cannot yet go
the length of a Liberty Loan bond—but that is because I
cannot approve that method of taxation. I shall give my
support otherwise.

I must hurry on to the rest of your letter—yourself and
the Medical Unit. Even if you were a Samson, I should not
approve of your going with it. You do not overstate your
value as a recorder and reporter. Your words would be
deeds. But if our Unit does deeds, they will speak for themselves. And if the pioneers left over there resuscitate themselves as heroically as they have suffered, their deeds too
will be winged and burning words. What your pen could
add would not, to my mind, be so valuable as to justify
changing what I conceive the character of the Unit should
be—a strictly professional undertaking. To my thinking,
not one single individual ought to be attached to it who
is not needed to make the expedition efficient for its main
purpose. No subsidiary purpose deserves consideration.

[TO JESSIE SAMPTER]   *New York, May 4, 1918*
I didn't give your poems a second reading. How could I,
when my mind was being switched from one to another of
the thousand things that lie between government permits
and fine combs and louse fluid? When you supplement my
elliptical statement, don't forget to put in the human reactions to all sorts of propositions which I have had to parry
—parry in the way you and Alice Seligsberg do not like. But
I don't like your way any better.

There is another point of war contact between us. I quote
from your letter: "While I know my position is inevitable,
I am not happier for having relinquished my pacifism." You
have described my frame of mind. And I a materialist—

the sort of materialist who takes refuge in Christian Science
when I find myself writhing with the pain of the wounded
soldier! I am so glad the uniforms have high collars. I cannot bear to look at the young strong necks—strong and soft
—of the marines. I see them mangled and gory. Have you
read Barbusse? Or *Men in War* by Andreas Latzko? Pain is
the ultimate thing. The sufferer is alone with it. Sympathy
cannot reach him. What right have I to let someone suffer
for me? That way lies madness.

The educational question comes up now and again. That
and all others wait upon the adoption of the reorganization
plan.[6] To attempt anything now will result in patchwork.
We must have an Educational Department co-ordinated
with a Propaganda Department, and a Women's Department, and other administrative bureaus. I wish I could see
you. There is little hope even after the Medical Unit goes.
So many things are waiting.

[TO ELVIRA N. SOLIS]   *New York, July 23, 1918*

I do wish I might be somewhat less hurried, so that I
might not have to cut myself off from my friends; but more
than that I wish that all my friends—that *you* might be
traveling along the same wonderful road with me.

I am confident you will not misinterpret my words. They
are not actuated by perverted missionary ardor. We have
held different opinions and yet loved each other and—still
more—respected each other too long for you to believe for
one moment that I should be satisfied with persuading you
to my way of thinking. But I cannot deny that I should be
happy to hear some day that you had convinced yourself
—not *been* convinced—of the value, the Jewish value, of
Zionism.

---

[6] Of the Zionist organization in America.

I have not spoken this way to you before so far as I can remember. And I know that this is not the opportune time for such speech, for I know how your whole mind, soul, and heart are absorbed by the tumultuous feelings roused by the war. I am writing long before dawn—after a completely sleepless night. I don't know why sleep refused to be wooed —for I am perfectly well. Perhaps the unusual circumstances, the quiet outside, the excitement of the news from the Western Front, have forced Zionism into these pages. Since the Pittsburgh [Zionist] convention—the biggest assemblage of which I have ever been a part, and I say that though, for Benjamin's sake,[7] I made myself a part of the Fourth of July nationalities parade and the Bastille celebration last week, and was stirred by both magnificent demonstrations—since the Pittsburgh convention I have had the feeling that it must be my fault that you not only have not accepted Zionism, but that it revolts you. No Zionist, I believe, has been so close to you as I have. I should have had the opportunity of making you banish from your mind the foibles of the Zionists whose leadership you deprecate, and bringing before you the bigness of the movement, its soul-satisfactions.

I don't think I'll read over this letter. I might decide not to send it to you. It is very different from what I set out to write.

III

The convention in Pittsburgh to which the preceding letter refers was the most exhilarating assemblage in American Zionist history. All the liberal forces released by the war to make the world safe for democracy found expression

---

[7] Her young nephew, Benjamin Levin.

in an enthusiastically adopted program—known thereafter
as the Pittsburgh Program—which proposed that the new
Palestine be developed as a co-operative commonwealth
with public ownership of the land and natural resources.
"I felt," Miss Szold writes a friend, "as though Isaiah and
Amos were with us." Its vision colored Zionist thought and
endeavor for years to come.

An immediate change effected by the convention was the
reorganization of American Zionist bodies into a united
Zionist Organization of America. Having successfully completed the assembly and dispatch of the Medical Unit, Miss
Szold was placed in charge of all Zionist educational and
propaganda work.

[TO ALICE L. SELIGSBERG]   *New York, August 4, 1918*
The cargo [of the Medical Unit] left about ten days ago.
May wind and weather favor it. It is precious far beyond the
money invested in it. Will you forgive me if I sometimes
wonder whether your closer contact with the individuals
of the Unit gives you an idea of what the four months previous to the departure of the Unit were for me? [8] Usually I
am very quick to forget the details connected with a troublous period. I don't think I shall ever forget the period of
my Unit troubles. They have left an indelible mark upon
my soul, and if I find it difficult to adjust myself to the new
situation in the office, I attribute it in no small degree to
the loss of physical power and mental spring caused by the
disappointments and the actual griefs connected with the
Unit.

Hadassah's educational activities, its School of Zionism,
its library, its choral union, its publication work, including

[8] Miss Seligsberg was en route to Palestine as the Hadassah representative accompanying the Medical Unit.

the *Bulletin,* are all assigned to the Department of Education of which your correspondent has the honor of having been designated as secretary.

And thereby hangs the tale—a tale that you will characterize as characteristic of me. This work was thrust upon me at twenty-four hours' notice. I spent the twenty-four hours in vain protest. I feel myself thoroughly unfitted for it. I haven't the physical strength for it. I am ashamed to head the department when I know a half-dozen persons who have fitted themselves for the position. Besides, the department is ill-defined. You will notice that I am to preside over a *gatherum omnium.* So far as the journalistic part of it goes, I have a perfect aversion to it. I have never taken to journalism. I acknowledge its supreme value, but I have no affinity for it. I am to have a great deal of help, it is true; but I find that the more help I have, the more I shall be reduced to doing routine work, and the routine work will be so enormous and the details so numerous that I shall probably, even with the best organization, spend all the hours of the day on them. My chief assistant will be Mr. Emanuel Neumann. I know he is going to do fine work.

The truth of the matter is, I need a two months' vacation this year, and you will recall how I planned with the Hadassah Central Committee to get it. Instead, I have this new work which involves adjustment with established agencies that have been independent of each other. However, I am not finding it difficult to deal with them, not because I am particularly tactful or diplomatic. On the contrary, because I am only truthful. I lay my cards on the table in all these cases, and I warn them that, so far as I am concerned, I am not fencing with words.

I am sure that matters will be adjusted satisfactorily with these bodies, which I think should be maintained intact in order that they may stand between an office that might tend to become bureaucratic and the large movement outside which is palpitating with life, and life is impatient.

As for the Hadassah *Bulletin,* one more issue will appear, a valedictory issue, explaining the new situation so far as Hadassah is concerned. For the idea is that, though the Central Committee goes out of existence as an executive body, the chapters are to be maintained. How this miracle is going to be brought about, Mr. Lipsky [9] understands. I do not.

[TO ALICE L. SELIGSBERG]   *New York, October 10, 1918*

Your article in the *Zionist Review* was admirable. I read it in manuscript, and again when a copy of the *Review* came to hand. That I was touched by your reference to me, I need not tell you; and that my comment upon it was that you are generous, not that I am meritorious, you will also guess. Your dear words, for the first time since I took the decision that I was not going to allow myself to be considered as a member of the Unit, awakened some envy in me that I was not identified with this wonderful undertaking at the very outset of our national existence. It doesn't matter how unworthy the individual instruments are, the Unit is a deed; and to think that the work of the Unit begins almost simultaneously with General Allenby's march northward! It would have been good to have been there with you in London, and in Paris, and in Rome, and—in Jerusalem; but please do not imagine that I am so bereft of all merit that envy reigned for long. I know that my decision was right, and I know it every day more clearly.

---

[9] Louis Lipsky, at that time secretary for the Zionist Organization of America.

[TO ALICE L. SELIGSBERG]

New York, November 7, 1918 [10]

The day—the day of peace! I am celebrating it by writing to you, the only celebration I can permit myself to have. From early morning until the peace news heralded by bells and whistles and joyous cries came, it was a day of checkered emotions, of envy aroused by thoughts of you.

Did I devour your letters? I could not believe that the woman who had written these calm, sensible, circumspect, and considerate letters was harassed, and worried, and bowed down under tasks too heavy for three persons to bear.

Just then came the ringing of the bells. Our girls—we have nearly 200 in our office now—stormed in, laughing, crying, dancing, jumping up and down, embracing each other; and from the street, all the way up to our office on the fifteenth floor, rose shout after shout of joy. It was impossible to get the girls to settle down. So we assembled in one of the rooms, and Rabbi Eugene Kohn addressed them on the meaning of peace—the world peace. An almost solemn hush fell upon them; tears ran down their cheeks, and from their eyes came an electric response. I never knew so clearly as at that moment what a horror and scourge the war had been.

The office closed at once for the day, and we surged down, to become part of a human torrent rolling up and down Fifth Avenue. The spontaneity of the demonstration was overwhelming. I walked and walked with the stream, partly carried along by it, until it landed me in the very midst of a Zionist group carrying Herzl's picture, an American flag, and singing "Hatikvah." [11] By my side was an old, long-

[10] This is the date of the "false" Armistice.
[11] The Zionist anthem.

bearded Jew. Suddenly he touched the girl who was carrying the Zionist flag in front of us on the shoulder, saying in Yiddish: "Please let me carry the flag, only a little while?"

And I thought of you, and wondered whether you, in the midst of your tribulations, on the soil of the land of *Shalom*,[12] could still meet this emotion with a responding emotion.

In our office applications are beginning to flow in from those who want to go to Palestine to settle there. Now our real work begins—the sort of work you are doing already, and we shall do it under the same strain and difficulty as you. Is it to be wondered at that the thing is not easy? The thing that has never been done before? I realize that such reflections come easy behind one's desk. Out in the field one knows and feels that the work is hard and that the means and instruments, human instruments as well as others, are inadequate. I wish I were with you.

[TO ALICE L. SELIGSBERG] *New York, December 21, 1918*

I heard today that Dr. Lowenstein is again to leave for Palestine. Lucky man! Indeed, I am beginning to envy all those who are receiving missions to go abroad. The unrest which has seized all of us during the war has not worn off, and in my case it has been increased by the desire to escape from the multitudinous details of my new department. I have many assistants; but as the number of assistants increases, so does the number of executive details and I now feel like Pooh-Bah. I am like a Chinese mandarin, shaking my head yes or no, and feeling like a humbug because instead of "yes and no," I might as well be saying "no and

---

[12] *Shalom*, the Hebrew word for "peace." Under the form Salem it was the original name of Jerusalem. *Shalom* in Palestine and everywhere else is the traditional greeting of Jews.

yes." So much for being an executive. I have no doubt that if I were sent on a European or Palestinian mission I should be equally distrustful of myself, but at least it would be different.

[TO ALICE L. SELIGSBERG]   *New York, January 24, 1919*

There is one thing in your personal letter to me that I want to talk about—your disappointment at what the situation over there reveals, but you realize that much of what you abhor is due to the unusual circumstances of life not only in Palestine but in the whole world. When one reduces our life here in the United States to its essentials—I don't mean its external essentials but its spiritual essentials—I assure you there is as much in it to make one's hair stand on end as there can be over there. The whole world was on fire. The scars cannot disappear so soon—perhaps they will not disappear in our lifetime.

I hear about the possibility of mass immigration into Palestine the minute our political status is defined. Mass immigration will need not a paltry three million dollars, but at least tens of millions. I am sure that nowhere in the world are we prepared for a mass immigration, neither in Palestine nor in any of the countries of the Diaspora, and neither materially nor spiritually. Take, for instance, the Hebrew language in Palestine. Will not the outposts which the small group of pioneers have captured be overwhelmed by the onrush of Yiddish-speaking masses? And wherein, then, will Palestine differ from the East Side of New York?

Are you noticing in Palestine the change that is taking place in the name of the Unit? Here Hadassah is fading out of sight and mind. The Unit is known only as the American Zionist Medical Unit. The *Palestine News,* I see, still refers to it as the Hadassah expedition. I should like to make a suggestion. Eventually the name Hadassah will have to disappear, but would it not be well and fitting if we could at least secure its attachment to the little hospital that Dr. Kagan established before the Unit came out? Am I right in understanding that it still exists? If you think well of this suggestion and if the little hospital still exists, will you propose its keeping the name Hadassah Hospital as a memorial to our pioneer medical undertakings in Palestine? Would it not be lovely if Hadassah were to be memorialized through a children's hospital?

For the rest, please remember that I appreciate your difficulties. I even understand the temptation you write about of turning non-Zionist. I understand what you write and what you don't write, and I predict that it will take you many months after you return to set things in order in your own mind. We have always known that when our hopes are realized, our responsibilities will weigh heavily upon us. Just now I must confess to you that I tremble most of the time when I look ahead, but I console myself with the thought that one does not dream for two thousand years steadily and then have the dream come true without having the strength to live in accordance with the high ideals that made the beauty of the dream.

[TO ALICE L. SELIGSBERG]

Boothbay Harbor, Maine, July 13, 1919

A three months' vacation in such times as these! And at the very moment when the Medical Unit personnel was to be renewed! I had not intended to let you or Dr. [I. M.] Rubinow [13] know that I was ordered away. But suddenly it occurred to me that Mr. [Jacob] de Haas would probably

---

[13] Dr. Rubinow was the director of the Medical Unit in Palestine.

mention it at any rate. So it's better you hear from me that I am a very robust patient.

The doctor wanted me to stop in the third week of May —"Quit tomorrow," was his verdict then. I begged him to give me a reprieve for an Education Conference scheduled for the end of May and in the hope that the definite needs of the Medical Unit for the second year would become known over here in time for me to give them my personal attention. Nevertheless, I began at once to whittle down my work, so that I have been on a semi-vacation for some time. And the relaxation has done me a tremendous amount of good.

What is it all about? The doctor says (and I have known it for over three years) that my heart is in bad condition. It needs rest. I need not tell you why it is in bad condition and why it needs rest. But, nevertheless, I am inclined to think that if the physical conditions at the office had been better, I might have gone on indefinitely with even the indescribably hard work I have been doing. Perhaps not! Perhaps the machinery is worn out. I hasten to say that the doctor is not alarmed, he only thinks I must treat myself somewhat more considerately.

IV

With delight and misgivings Miss Szold learned that she was to be sent to Palestine. An international Zionist Commission was already at work there laying plans for the up-building of the land. The Medical Unit, despite its excellent work, was suffering from endless difficulties in administration and personnel. Her duties in this tangle were ill defined, her health was still impaired, but she prepared for a two years' stay—little guessing that, aside from intervals of commuting between Jerusalem and New York, she would pass the remainder of her life at work in the new Land of Israel.

[TO ALICE L. SELIGSBERG] *New York, November 30, 1919*

I am playing "hooky" this morning from the office, primarily because I want to write to you. I have been longing to do it ever since it was decided, three weeks ago today, that I am to go to Palestine. I held back, not because I did not have the time—I might have made it—but because I wanted to tell you precisely in what capacity I was going. It is only since day before yesterday that the details have been settled.

The first purpose to be served by my going is that the American [Zionist] Organization may have a direct representative on the Executive Committee of the Unit, someone in whose mind and time the Unit will have the first and if need be the only place. In other words, I am to take your place, the place you held in relation to Hadassah.

Your experiences, the experiences of others, the composition of the [Zionist] Commission, above all, the attitude toward American Zionists, which by this time is almost traditional, lead me to believe that the meaning is nil. On the other hand, I myself do not see what else can be done. The American organization hasn't sufficient confidence in me to appoint me the member of the Commission which it has been asked to appoint. The main reason is they do not think me equal to the responsibility. I am far from disagreeing with them.

My vacation this summer has restored me to strength; I am to some degree my former self, especially if I take at least twice as much sleep as I have been accustomed to have all through my life. Even so, neither my physical strength

nor my mental and executive ability is such as to make me
fit to cope with the problems.

I should feel a *little bit* more confidence in myself if I
spoke Hebrew as I speak English. As it is, so far as spoken
Hebrew is concerned, I am in the same position as Dr.
Rubinow. When I first heard of the possibility of my going
to Palestine I determined to arrive in Jaffa and Jerusalem
incog., hasten to one of the colonies, stay there for a month
or six weeks, and devote myself to Hebrew conversation.
Dr. Rubinow's recent communications convince me that
such a course is fantastic.

You yourself say that I should often find myself impotent.
Often? No, always. From what I know of what is happening and of what is being planned, I should stand like one
turned into a pillar of salt, not for looking back but for
looking forward. You mention my "devoted life," my
"faith." But of what avail are they without Hebrew elo-
quence? If I had truly possessed the "wisdom" you attribute
to me, I should have made myself speak Hebrew against the
emergency. But all this is futile talk. We need not fool ourselves. The Commission will not consider seating a woman,
particularly not in view of the women's suffrage question
among the orthodox leaders in Jerusalem.

However, tomorrow I apply for a passport. During the
next two weeks I devote myself to the Education Department, the budget of which was accepted only last Sunday;
then I leave the office and begin to dressmake, pack, and
make last wills and testament, for I plan a two years' stay.

[TO ELVIRA N. SOLIS] *New York, December 9, 1919*
I don't mind difficulties and hardships and privations, if
I could be sure that my being in Palestine would contribute
even in the smallest measure to the resolving of the chaos

that now exists there as everywhere else in the world. What a stricken world it is! And how our people are suffering everywhere! As always they suffer with the rest and then above the rest. And Palestine seems to epitomize the general situation.

[TO ALICE L. SELIGSBERG]   *New York, January 7, 1920*

I have said to myself and aloud, again and again during the last few weeks, that it will take the gentleness of the dove and the wisdom of the serpent if the situation [in Palestine] is to be met in a constructive spirit. Had we a right to expect less chaos? I think we had, and I believe we might have had less if our going up into the land had not been coincident with the great war catastrophes. I wonder whether you hear of the horrors of Jewish, of all life, in Eastern Europe? The conditions there—one cannot but use hackneyed phrases—beggar description. In a world in conflagration, could the Palestinian group alone remain unseared? And yet—and yet. . . .

And then I ask myself, what am I going to effect in the seething caldron—I who have got much older—much more old than the year and a half you have been away—and, in spite of my remarkable improvement since the summer, physically much less resistant, who by reason of the language difficulty cannot hope to exercise even the kind of influence I have exerted here in my limited sphere? You see, I am full of apprehensions. But it is right, nevertheless, that I go—even if I fail utterly. I conceive that it may be valuable for such as I am simply to live there, without doing a specific thing, though of course I am expected to busy myself with the Unit. But I want to be as little as possible a "worker"—just a liver. I can also conceive that I am entirely wrong. So I am keeping my mind open.

We ought to show by our acts (as Dr. Rubinow has been showing, I think, by engaging physicians from all over) that we expect to drop "American" from our title as soon as may be; and then "Zionist," and then "Unit"—so transforming a purely American undertaking into a Palestinian Jewish Medical Department.

As the Palestinian center becomes self-dependent, in the same measure will the American work become more exclusively administrative. In the larger Jewish community there will be big work to do, provided the big leader appears. He is not in sight. The big work will be religious in the largest, most inclusive sense—so large that it will inaugurate the interaction between Palestine and the Diaspora, in which Palestine will be the gainer as much as the Diaspora, and upon which, to my mind, the spiritual success of the Palestinian center will depend. Any notion that we are not part of Palestine Jewry, that Jewry the world over is not one continuous body, is barren and futile.

Isn't it curious how the Hadassah idea has taken hold of women? Here at home the sections absolutely refuse to go out of existence; and it is necessary to invent, actually invent, a specific Hadassah task to satisfy them. What we are doing is a miserable makeshift—it doesn't meet their heart hunger, nor even their longing for discipline.

Am I, oh, am I going to see you in Palestine? I expect to sail early in February. I am now in the throes of getting ready. You know what that means. Add to your preparations of a year and a half ago the annihilation of my household—no, my mother's household—and you will have a picture of my excitement and busy-ness. And I am such a cat—attached to the place!

CHAPTER EIGHT

Between Two Worlds

Henrietta Szold was in her sixtieth year when she set sail—February 1920—for the great adventure of her life. What with post-war difficulties in procuring visas and transportation, the journey from New York to Jerusalem consumed a little more than two months. The greater part of this prelude to her Palestinian career was spent in Naples and Florence. Something of her mood is caught in these fragments from lengthy letters written to her sisters: Rachel (Mrs. Joseph Jastrow) in Madison, Wisconsin; Bertha (Mrs. Louis H. Levin) in Baltimore; and Adele (Mrs. Thomas Seltzer) in New York.

S.S. Giuseppe Verdi, *March 3, 1920*

I can see that I shall not be writing anything but greetings to many outside of the family. My circle is too large. Mere greetings together with letters to the Zionist officials in the nature of reports are going to take up all the time I have for letter-writing. I expect Rachel to keep my letters for me as my record of the trip. I am trying to keep a diary, but I am sure the diary is not going to touch upon the things I am prompted to write to you about.

Immigration—and emigration—migration—is horrible. Its effects are writ as large in the face and manners of the Italian young matron from Chicago as even in those of the Washington Heights and Bronx matrons I know among the Jews.

In the second cabin there are some evidences of folk life.

It is filled with Italians returning home for good. Some are
actors, some street-workers, some farmers. Every evening
there is singing and dancing, and piano and clarinet playing. The most attractive figure there is a countess's maid—
the most exquisite piece of femininity I have seen in many
a long day.

There is only one non-Italian in the whole cabin, a Mrs.
Garry, who is going to Palestine to join her husband Dr.
Garry, now a member of the Medical Unit. He went to
Palestine as a member of the [Jewish] Legion. Figuratively
as well as literally Mrs. Garry is in the same boat with me:
she, like myself, hasn't her British permit. We both hope
to find what we need to go on with our journey at the British
Consul's office in Naples. We shall make a bee-line for his
office as soon as we land, which probably will be next Monday.

I am wondering what awaits us in Naples—a British permit that will enable us to go right on to Alexandria? When
is the boat to sail from Brindisi on the Lloyd Triestino?
Can we exchange our reservation on the Lloyd Triestino
for a place on the new line from Naples to Alexandria only
recently opened, which is said to have wonderfully fast
boats? Or must we stay in Naples to wait for permit or accommodations or both? And in that case see Capri, Amalfi,
the blue grotto, and Pompeii, *and* the Museum!

Naples, March 23, 1920

Today it is exactly a month since the *Giuseppe Verdi* set
sail from New York, and yesterday completed two weeks at
Naples. Last Thursday the Trieste boat with which I should
have gone eastward, on which a reservation actually was
made for me, left Brindisi, and so my last hope of getting
to Palestine before Passover was crushed. I am stranded—

not exactly on a desert island.[1] If I hadn't known the rich
feast spread before me to while away the interval of waiting, the last five days of pretty intensive sight-seeing would
have brought it home to me.

Thursday morning I woke up to find the bluest of blue
skies, and the bay at my window shimmering and dancing.
So I danced downstairs to the concierge, and had him summon a guide, Emanuele Bellati, a man nearly seventy years
old, to take me to Pozzuoli. I don't mind going to the Museum and the Aquarium and trotting through the city
alone; but when it comes to an excursion out of town, I
can hardly bring myself to taking it without a companion.
I have done it. On Sunday I went to Capri. But I had to
fight myself before I could achieve it. And now that I have
achieved it, I am not exactly enamored of the method—I
never did like solitaire as a game, however much I may have
liked my own company otherwise.

I can't tell you how sorry I am that I put my botany in
the box that is, I hope, on its way to Jerusalem. Of course,
I don't mean to imply that Grey's *Botany* (this takes me to
something way back) would help me identify the species
here. But it would be something if I could make sure of
first and second cousins to Grey's various families. It is impossible for me to describe the yellows, the purples, the
blues, the infinite variety with which the earth is carpeted
here. Do you remember how Papa used to complain of our
poor flora in America? I understand him now. But to think
that red tape is preventing me right now from seeing in
Palestine what, I am told, exceeds Italy in brilliance, variety, and perfume, as much as Italy exceeds America!

Again back to Pozzuoli. It was all interesting—the ruins,

---

[1] Delays in securing visa and transportation prevented her leaving
Italy for another full month.

the views, the volcanic, sulphurous phenomena, and the people. Pozzuoli once was Saracen. The countenances and the manners of the people still bear traces of the Saracen strain. And the Saracen-Italians are tremendously strong. I made the descent of Avernus, and was carried through the waters that have flowed in from the lake and the sea on the shoulders of the keeper, who told me that the same shoulders had borne the Queen of Italy and the King of England. The consolation I derived therefrom was that I was a lighter burden than either. There was a humorous little incident connected with my "descent." Just before I entered the Cave I stooped to pick up two flowers. One was a violet, the other a delicate cluster of white bells on a green spathe. I didn't have time to look at it closely. As I stood in the dark waiting for the torches to be lighted, I noticed a heavy odor. I asked the guide about it, and he suggested I might be smelling the resin of the torches. But I said it was more like garlic. That was impossible, he said, for Italians no longer used garlic—it was too expensive. All the way through Avernus, up the Styx and back again, always there was that garlic smell, and I came to the conclusion that hell had a torture the poets had not known of. When I got back into daylight, I saw that my delicate white bells were—allium.

Today I made my arrangements for going to Florence one week from today. I shall live at the Hotel Cavour, and take my meals at the Pensione della Pergola. How glad I'll be not to have to pick and choose, and to get a few substantial meals.

I wonder whether you realize how isolated I feel. Sometimes I am almost paralyzed with the fear that something has happened to one of you, and you haven't known how to reach me. I know you all will be saying that I have no right to complain. To have to wait in Italy is no mean good fortune. And I am trying to get all I can out of it. But I must confess that my trying is almost a duty. I like the duty. But try as I may, I cannot put my whole heart and soul into Italy. I am cut off from you, I don't know anything about what is happening at the [New York] office or in Jerusalem; and the affairs of the Unit are beyond my ken. There is not a soul to talk to—it is such a silly business, too.

Florence, April 7, 1920

The boarding-house isn't so bad as I thought it would be. The woman who keeps it is kind and lovable. The first *Seder* night at the rabbi's was most satisfying; at a table set for 21, six languages were spoken! Italian, French, German, English, Hebrew, and Polish. It was in every respect homey. About the second *Seder* night at the boarding-house, the less said the better. I'd as soon take part in a gypsy rendition. It was horrible.

Among the guests at Rabbi Margulies's table were Mrs. Herbert Samuel and her son, who were awaiting the arrival here of Mr. Samuel, on his return from Palestine, whither he had been sent three months ago by the British government. Since *Seder* night Mr. Samuel has arrived. He gave me the impression that his experiences in Palestine justified an optimistic view of the future, but he admitted that the Arab situation was serious and was held by the British military authorities to be serious.

I have come in contact with others who bring Palestine close. There are three boys here from Galicia. They are eighteen years of age; for the last four or five years they have been preparing to go to Palestine and settle there as agricultural laborers; they are traveling on their own means; they can't get farther because they can't secure the English visa of their passports. Meantime they are working

on a farm near Florence. They are fine-looking youths, at
least two of them are, healthy, intelligent, earnest, imbued
with social ideals of the most forward-looking type. And
they are the advance guard of a band of 20,000 more or less
like them in Galicia—this band itself being only one of the
series of groups of halutzim [pioneers], young men and
young women, in Russia, Germany, Austria, and Rumania,
who are training to become laborers and to speak Hebrew.

On the last day of my stay in Naples, when I was sending
off a cable to America in the post office, I was accosted by
three youths, who spoke a queer sort of English and who
appealed to me for help when they found that the telegraph
operator knew no English. They were from the island of
Malta, and they wanted to cable home for money to proceed on their way to America. They were spirited, hopeful,
and I have no doubt fine, but what a contrast to this Florence trio (which by the way is in the city this week to celebrate Passover). If they succeed in America, they will be
successful—that is not tautology. If they fail materially,
they'll have no resources to fall back upon within themselves. These Jewish boys can't fail, because they will always be themselves.

Naples, April 23, 1920

Here I am back at Naples, preparing at last to embark
for Alexandria. Cook's the suave assure me the *Umbria* will
sail as scheduled, on Monday, April 26, in the afternoon.

On my arrival here I found at Cook's office a package of
mail matter from the office which at once re-established my
connection with the world of living, palpitating beings, and
incidentally explained some mysteries. It was one of Miss
[Ida] Flatow's characteristic and charming epistles that de-
lighted and enlightened me. When Adele's letter was fol-

lowed by no others [from the family], I again began to be possessed, in a subconscious way, of the feeling one must have who lives in a court enclosed by high stone walls and covered with a heavy ivy except for one window high up admitting light but no sounds.

In my communions with myself—for which I naturally have abundant opportunity—I began to look upon my former existence as a sort of myth, a delusion. You all had reality, more than I had myself. I knew you were living hard, working, struggling, thinking (perhaps even of me); but I was simply existing—a charming existence, but also a charmed existence, the bonds of which I was powerless to tear off. Don't imagine I was actively unhappy; but I was aimless, stupefied, severed from my former life, my purposes, myself. Indeed, Florence is altogether too charming and too suggestive for anyone to love living in it.

I must confess I did not see all Mamma and myself had managed to put in ten years ago. It amazed me to see what Mamma had been able to do at seventy. But what I saw again, I think I looked at with more instructed, more seeing eyes. There was a keener edge to my intellectual enjoyment. One reason for my not seeing so much as before was my Hebrew studies, to which I devoted six hours daily. I cannot say that I feel a great accession of Hebrew power in consequence of my zeal and my teacher's passive help. I may have repaired the ravages of the neglect of ten Zionist years—that is all, I am afraid, the three intensive weeks have done. Jerusalem two weeks hence will reveal the truth. Just now I find that when I want to summon my little store of Italian to my aid, nothing but Hebrew will come.

When I am not writing and not thinking but am—for instance—ascending Vesuvius, as I did yesterday afternoon under as blue an Italian sky as I have yet had, though even it was not the traditionally fleckless sky the poets rave about, my alarms do not press upon me. These Italian adventures are like drink to a toper. If it were any other country I don't think I could have stood it.

S.S. Umbria, April 29, 1920
En route to Alexandria

I don't know how hard fate tried to keep me from getting on this vessel, but she's foiled, for I *am* here, and we are making good progress. In about twenty-four hours from now, at ten o'clock Friday morning, we ought to dock at Alexandria. Thence I hasten on to Cairo for what I hope will be the final passport hustle, and then by train, Sunday night, to Jerusalem.

Don't imagine all went smoothly at the end. Cook did his best, by means of a series of inaccurate statements, to make my last day the occasion for an apoplectic stroke. All he succeeded in doing was to make me spend a big sum (at least it looks big in lire) in tips to counterbalance his misstatements. You have no idea how courteously and suavely and fluently Cook can tell what is not so. I think I have proof that it is not misinformation, but real lack of information. He draws on his imagination.

However, Cook's office served a good purpose that last day in Naples. He had said that the steamship company was not permitted to issue tickets to passengers until the very last moment, so I had to go there early Monday morning only to find that they didn't have my ticket yet (others had theirs) and that the boat was to sail, not at four in the afternoon, but at noon. However, blandly he said he would telephone, if I'd have the goodness to wait, and see whether a change had occurred. So I amused myself by looking at the foreigners about me—English, Americans, French, Germans, and a sprinkling of Italians.

Suddenly I caught sight of a face that made me stand up straight and collect my thoughts. I'm never wholly sure of my memory of faces. I said softly: "Professor Schatz?" [2] The response was immediate and affirmative. We were still occupied with the exchange of introductory banalities, when he in turn started up and across the room to greet Dr. [M. D.] Eder, a member of the Zionist Commission, on his way back from San Remo [3] to Palestine. I was introduced and we discovered at once that he was to sail on the same boat with me.

Dr. Eder has been the very traveling companion I needed. He has told me scores of things I have been wondering about, especially the very serious Arab situation in Palestine, of which the powers that be are, it seems, not to be held wholly guiltless.[4] He had to leave San Remo before the Zionist question was wholly settled, but he carried away with him the impression that the negotiations were proceeding favorably for us. He thinks we may have a definitive report when we reach Alexandria. Perhaps, even while I am writing still doubtfully, you know from the papers that the mandate has been awarded, and that the military occupation of Palestine has to yield to a civil government.

From what Dr. Eder tells me of conditions in Palestine, economic and social, it is high time for the change to have come. Dr. Eder is a non-taxing companion. He talks Eng-

---

[2] Boris Schatz, founder of the Bezalel Art Institute in Jerusalem.
[3] The San Remo Peace Conference, which conferred upon Great Britain the mandate for Palestine.
[4] In April an Arab uprising against the Jews left sixty dead in Jerusalem; and in the Galilean outpost of Tel Hai, Captain Trumpeldor and nine of his men were killed.

lish, the real article. After the mélange of languages I have
been hearing and attempting to talk, that is soothing. It's
more than language, it is frame of mind, attitude, tradition.
Not only may I use the words I am accustomed to, but I
don't have to use so many of them. I can afford to leave
many things unsaid, without fearing that I shall be mis-
understood. And to think that I am in for two years of such
linguistic potpourri. Take our table companions on this
boat, from Constantinople, Alexandria, and a Greek-
American. They bandy French, Italian, Spanish, Greek,
Arabic, and occasionally Turkish, slipping from one to the
other with a gay facility that is almost annoying to the
heavy Anglo-Saxon trained mind.

Day before yesterday we took on a cargo at Syracuse. The
sight-seeing fever fostered by Italy had not left me. I rowed
across to shore, took a cab, and saw the old Greek theater
and the Ear of Dionysius. Incidentally, I saw also the luxuriant flora. Spring had reached its purple stage, and the
whole air was impregnated with the perfume of the orange
blossoms. It was worth while having gone to the trouble of
getting off, even though my heart did thump several times
at the thought that the boat might go without me. I have
been almost superstitious about my actually getting to
Jerusalem. With Dr. Eder's help I hope to have no trouble
about my passport at Cairo, though he tells me very strin-
gent regulations have been framed since my permit was
issued.

CHAPTER NINE

A Land in the Making

I

Palestine in 1920 was a poor, hard land rendered poorer and harder by the World War. A sizable Jewish immigration had barely got under way, and the ring of pick and crow-bar was beginning to be heard on the stony hillsides and the scrunch of shovels in the swamps. Life in Jerusalem, the only large city, was down at the heels. The pre-war agricultural colonies had hardly recovered from army depredations, disruption of transportation, and the long absence of markets. An impoverished land, bare, empty, disease-ridden, yet—and only seeing is believing—beautiful!

Should a Palestinian of today read the letters that follow, he would smile with wonder. If he were a newcomer he would be tempted to believe they must have been written a century ago. If he were an old-timer he could hardly trust his own memory that the land was once so desolate. For only in modern America, against much smaller odds and with infinitely greater resources, have similar changes been wrought in two decades. During that interval the Jewish population of Palestine mounted from 80,000 to 550,000. In 1920 Tel Aviv was a suburban townlet, and its mayor, Mr. Dizengoff, boasted of its 3000 inhabitants; the mayor lived to admire and govern a Tel Aviv of 200,000 Jewish citizens. In half that length of time Miss Szold would herself boast that "all Americans insist that Palestine is much more comfortable than the United States."

A contemporary Palestinian would particularly wonder at the prevalence of malaria and the absence of sanitation, hospitals, and medical service in the far-away days of 1920. Today it is a subject of antiquarian wonder because the American Zionist Medical Unit and its successors accomplished the healing of a people.

The least of the Medical Unit's difficulties was disease. As the reader will learn from Miss Szold's letters, the local doctors, midwives, and other dispensers of medical treatment, who had returned to Palestine after the war, hated the American "intruders" because they held comparatively lucrative posts, their standards were higher, they gave their services without fee, and not a little because they could not speak Hebrew. In addition, the "intruders," with a jealous eye on preferment, promotion, and their personal future, wrangled among themselves. Finally there was the perennial shortage of funds.

The letters will carry the reader through a cycle of the year from the end of the rains and oranges to their return —a cycle which for Miss Szold brought new and vivid experiences, each, as the Hebrew prayer goes, "in due season."

Jerusalem, May 11, 1920 [1]

In the morning we crossed into Palestine. Of course I was too late for the real spring here. But what is left of it was enough to make my heart leap and bound. It's useless for me to try to describe the transition from the desert to arable land or the weird beauty of the desert, or the joyous beauty of the flowery fields. Even the desert was not bloomless at this season, to my great surprise. But the most glorious sight of all was when we came in sight of the Mediterranean,

---

[1] All letters reproduced in this chapter and the remainder of the book are addressed to Miss Szold's family, unless otherwise indicated.

edged with sand dunes, the dunes merging here into the desert sand, and there being conquered by the rich, blossoming soil.

At Ludd I was met by the auto from Jerusalem. And in the auto were Dr. Rubinow, Alice Seligsberg, and Nellie Straus, now Mrs. Mochenson. Ludd presents a scene of confusion, military and civil; it is hot; the baggage question is shriekingly acute; but amid all the chaos I felt serene, because at last I was face to face with someone who represented home. I can't tell you what it felt like to see Alice face to face. At once this whole adventure of mine seemed right and normal, and I forgot all about the silly delay in Italy.

The ride up to Jerusalem from Ludd—up, up, and again up—is impressive. I have been struggling all week to put the impressions into words. It would be easy to enumerate the defects of the land and the people, and the enumeration would make a long, long list. It is impossible to enumerate the beauties, and yet the beauty is the final and conclusive element. Each day has added to the sense of charm. What is the use of writing about the magic of the moonlight, or the brilliance of the stars, or the perfumed, clear air, or the unearthly mixture of races with their pet fanaticisms expressed in face, hair, and costume? The charm lies not in them, certainly not in any of them separately. But the charm is there, and it is compelling and subduing.

It appears that I must have an "establishment" and not just hide myself away in a single room with a family, as I had expected to do. If I tell you that I failed to bring with me the only important utensil needed in Palestine and that the utensil is a samovar, you will understand all I mean by setting up an "establishment." Why, people come in every afternoon and expect to find a cup of tea awaiting them.

When we entered my room a tea was set forth: samovar, cakes, bread and butter and biscuits, and the table decorated with flowers, marmalade in a bit of pottery given to me by Alice, and the cake in a basket given to me by Libbie Oppenheim. Presently in came Alex[ander] Dushkin, and then Major [Norman] Bentwich, and the next day I saw Jessie Sampter and—I was going to say hundreds more whom I knew either from America or from my previous trip to Palestine. Rivkah Cohen, the maid, waits on me and mends and does my modest marketing. She is a girl of seventeen, a most useful acquisition. I am learning my Hebrew from her. Can you picture me in my Jerusalem surroundings?

What you cannot picture and what I cannot convey is the atmosphere. It is hot, that is, the sun is hot, the air isn't. Most of the time there is a cool breeze, even in the middle of the day. You can judge that it isn't hot as with our heat from the fact that the birds are active and vocal all day long. It is now high noon, and they are acting almost as though it was four in the morning.

On the spiritual atmosphere? I should have started with that, for it is a long chapter. I arrived a month, exactly to a day, after the attack upon the Jews—"pogrom" it is called here. It appears that the occurrence had all the familiar features of a pogrom—featherbeds ripped up, scrolls of the law torn, and hundreds of persons beaten up. The people who tell you about the riot still speak of it with tears in their voices. The victims here are all still unnerved. Some of the hospital beds are still occupied by beaten-up, battered individuals. One hundred and eighty Jews had suffered in life, limb, and property. I don't remember how many actually died of their injuries. An English court martial tried the Jewish Self-Defense members who had, with the consent of the military authorities, I have been told, provided themselves with arms; and twenty-four were condemned to prison for varying terms, their leader [Vladimir] Jabotinsky, to 15 years with labor! Five have since been released. A court of inquiry is now being held.

There have been two by-products. The Hadassah organization did magnificent work. At present, no dog is allowed to wag its tail against it. Even our battered automobiles, the subject of incessant vituperation in the newspapers formerly (not because they are battered, but because they are here—too American, you know), are looked upon with touching affection. The fact that we are an American organization counted for a good deal on the outside. It permitted our doctors and nurses to pass the cordons and bring help. I am told the garden of the hospital was filled with patients for three days, and any emergency space within was claimed. For the present, at least, we are in the ascendant.

The other by-product, the wiseacres say, was the unexpectedly swift action taken at San Remo. I don't want to expatiate on this aspect—else this letter will never reach you.

The work of the Unit here, there can be no question, has been—I do not hesitate to say—great. I have the well-remembered standards of ten years ago to compare with. But there are glaring defects in organization and execution. The director [2] has been working against great odds, chiefly because he has never received the full amount of his budget. He has had to keep his nose to the financial grindstone, and so he has laid himself open to the reproach that he prefers statistics to medical actuality, etc. etc. The pressure from without, from the colonies, has been irresistible; as a result

[2] Dr. I. M. Rubinow.

we have spun ourselves thin. To intensify the work we have already undertaken to do, we need two and a half times as much as we have, that is, a million dollars.

I am now seeing every last doctor in Jerusalem. I may have to give everyone in the whole country a chance to unload. We have forty-five physicians. If they hadn't sent ultimata and resignations pell-mell (a strike of the pupil nurses—seventeen walking out of the wards at one fell swoop—was another one of the incidents to make the first week of my stay in Jerusalem memorable), they would have had the opportunity of speaking to me personally and privately on the morning of the third day. But their excitement—and mine, for that matter—was unallayable for the time. I have gone to the [Zionist] Commission and asked for time, for I cannot think of treating with the Commission until the Unit has at least the semblance of unification.

Our American graduate nurses are the only body within the Unit that is calm, collected, and steady. The student nurses are young Palestinian girls being trained for a profession in a country in which a professional school was never established before. Fancy, the school must be run without the ghost of a text-book. Oh! these beginnings here are terribly hard. It would all be a little easier if the political conditions would be settled, and if the people were less political-minded. Besides, it requires a larger population to produce normal relations. The Palestinians form a huge teapot. And that is no joke. At least for me it's none, as you may know from what I said before. On Saturday, Miss [Julia] Aronson [now Mrs. Alexander Dushkin] is going to come and help me with my afternoon visitors. We've made a hit with her. Improvements follow in her footsteps, in the kitchen, the pantry, the dining-room, the hospital, and the boarding-place.

I am sure I never will be able to convey to you what is happening here. It is baffling.

[TO IDA FLATOW]   *Jerusalem, May 25, 1920*

My radicalism is unchanged, but more than ever I realize that radicalism may degenerate into logic-chopping. The people in Palestine do not understand that. For the present, suffice it to say that the logic-chopping of the members of the Medical Unit is just as I had expected.

However, I do not share your gratitude that I was not here at the time of the troubles. I can tell you that all those who lived through the stirring days of Passover of this year in Palestine have been enriched by experiences in an unforgettable way. They still speak of them with awe in their voices. So far as I can make out, the Jews have nothing to be ashamed of in what happened; all the intrigue and cruelty lay elsewhere; the Jews were courageous.

You would revel in the Jews here! It is traditional to make a pilgrimage to the Grave of David Mosque on Shabuot; I joined the pilgrims, both Jews and Christians. It was a wonderful sight, not an altogether happy one, but the interest was stirring.

One sees no conventional people here. Everybody dresses and acts—always excepting our Americans—as though there were no standard to conform to. Nobody wears ready-made clothes, for example, everybody is fanciful about the way he dresses—especially those who one suspects never take off their clothes even at night.

Still, I cannot write you a letter today. Don't imagine that New York is the only busy place in the world. I am finding it as impossible to keep up with things here as I did there. One owes letters here, one owes visits, one is besieged, one is beset, people believe that one is almighty—it is all as it was in New York.

Jerusalem, May 26, 1920

In the interval this has also happened—I dreaded it from the moment I knew I was coming to Palestine—Dr. Rubinow is leaving for America on a vacation. When I asked him whether he is going with the intention of returning, his answer was: "I am not going with the intention of returning, nor am I going with the intention of not returning." He is a tired, nervous man. The work here has been trying and in a sense ungrateful. Only in a sense, for he has the satisfaction of knowing that the American Zionist Medical Unit is the only piece of large organized work done in the country during the last few years. But he achieved the result amid criticism from without and from within which only an unusual person could have stood without flinching.

But how I am going to run the Unit—a huge, complicated machinery, with economic, social, professional, and truly political questions bobbing up every day and throwing the machinery out of gear—is more than I can prophesy. The tangled situation partly, and my long trip firstly, deprive me of what I had looked forward to—going to the *Jahres Conferenz* [3] at London. Dr. Rubinow is going instead. I cannot say that I am very hopeful about his return.

It's a pity! I don't know whether ever before a piece of work like this has been done. I have never heard of it. It isn't an expedition for a limited time; it isn't establishing a hospital—it is country-wide constructive institutional

[3] World Zionist Executive Conference, held bi-annually between the Zionist Congresses.

medical service, which would soon lead to public sanitation.

Jerusalem, June 3, 1920

I went down to Jaffa to inspect the Medical Unit work there. It hasn't anything like the compass and extent of the undertaking in Jerusalem, but it is well done. We have a small hospital with beds for children and for surgical cases, and in another building we have a clinic for general complaints, eye trouble, and dental work. Never is there a bed in the hospital vacant, and every day the clinics are full to overflowing. Our force is excellent—a first-class surgeon, an equally good oculist, and a fine staff of nurses. It's all ship-shape. Even our little laboratory is sought by all sorts of institutions, government and others.

Meantime I cannot report any progress as to my negotiations.[4] Every time the thought crosses my mind that in a few weeks I shall have to grapple with the intricate problems of the adjustment of a delicate piece of machinery whose parts are 400 human beings, and whose lubrication —that is, financial support—is inadequate, my heart contracts painfully. If Dr. Rubinow stays away three months, I may have time enough to wreck the whole thing.

And what am I to say about my homeward trip "up" to Jerusalem, from five-thirty to eight, between sunset and moonrise! Such coloring never was on land or sea. The hills, the sky, the Arabs behind or on their donkeys or on camels, or on top of a hay wagon, the fields yellow and green, the moon rising over the hills as large as a wagon wheel—it must be seen. And the wonderful coolness of these summer evenings. I have not yet found the heat unendurable, and I go out in the sun daily for my midday meal. But however

---

[4] With the Zionist Commission.

hot it may be during the day, a wrap is never uncomfortable in the evening.

Jerusalem, June 21, 1920

For one week I was on an automobile trip to all our Medical Unit stations north of Jerusalem; the second week I was endeavoring to get the hang of our complicated machinery at the desk by way of preparing for Dr. Rubinow's departure; and the third week—a hot, hot week—I have been the acting director of the Unit—*Menahelet Zemanit* is my official title.

I have always, in my thoughts at least, compared Palestine to a monastery. Its inhabitants claim a living from the outside world. That is bad enough, but the responsibilities of its inhabitants—those who assume any—are worse; they have no life of their own. One belongs wholly and completely to a protean public. Whosoever will claims your time, your strength, and your means too. It's a hard life here in any case; but what I have undertaken, or had to undertake, is appalling.

The Unit now has 400 employees, not one of whom is satisfied with his salary; one physician maintains that our present maximum (£60 monthly) ought to be our minimum, and that in the face of a £10,000 deficit. While half of Jewish Palestine is streaming into our office and demanding a place from us as the biggest employers of "labor" in the country, the employees are cursing us because we haven't merged ourselves completely with the Zionist Commission. While from every quarter, colony, city, and settlement, demands come that we take over the medical service and furnish physicians, nurses, druggists, and automobiles, we are sneered at because we have automobiles. In short, we are damned if we do, and we are damned if we don't. As a matter of fact we have bitten off more than we can chew.

My first reaction when I saw our hospital in Tiberias was to close it up. It is in a private house, and not a large or commodious one at that. And as for the clinic, the situation is hopeless. But when I saw the crowds and shoals of help-seekers, and when I heard the description of what there was before Hadassah came, I repented of my reaction. Only I refuse to remember the scene, and I refuse to think that the Safed hospital, fairly good on the whole, has a kitchen and a pantry and a laundry that ought to be condemned, and that the pupil nurses there are living as miserably in the home we have provided for them as in their own homes.

The whole of Palestine has been starved of medical aid. Everybody is in need of repairs. And what shall I say of the dire need our school work reveals?

In spite of all our shortcomings, it is a big piece of work we are doing. But will a single member of my family succeed in answering the question: Why am *I* doing it? Isn't it ridiculous that I should be directing hospitals, nurses' training-schools, laboratories, clinics, school hygiene, and most medical service? And isn't it sad that I should be fighting forty-five doctors?

Jerusalem, June 21, 1920

After all I can't give you a telling characterization of what I am living through. The curious thing about it all is that hope is not blighted by all these responsibilities. Just as the stoniness of the soil doesn't kill one's confidence in the fertility.

As I traveled all the way up from Jerusalem to Nablus, Samaria, Jenin, Nazareth, Tiberias, and Safed, and panorama after panorama unfolded itself before my eyes, I was almost overpowered by emotion. That's not sentimentality. It's being choked with sensations that are painful because while one feels them, one feels at the same time that one cannot convey them to others—never will be able to convey them.

The land is treeless, largely waterless, at this season the green has largely disappeared, and the dry thornbushes almost crackle under the hot sun—and yet it is beautiful, so beautiful that I almost resent our intention to make it blossom and bear fruit. The stones are soft with colorfulness, and between them spring up blossoms so curiously adapted to the peculiarity of the land that one cannot wonder enough. If I were forced to pick out one spot as the most beautiful I think I should, with apologies to all others, designate the Sea of Tiberias.

All the time I was straining my eyes to take in what I now understand shaped Jewish sentiment during the thousands of years Jewish eyes did not rest upon it, my side was strained by contact with a revolver in Dr. Rubinow's pocket. That is the way we had to travel. Indeed for three days we had to have the protection of an armed gendarme. At least they said we had to. Wherever we came, the Jewish colonists in the fields were armed. Their little settlements were surrounded by trenches and protected by sandbags. Earth walls were thrown up even on the inside of the walls of their wooden houses. The fear of the Bedouin is upon the whole land. In several colonies there has been violence, loss of life, and loss of all movable property.

Here in Jerusalem every morning I watch the soldiers drilling under the domes and turrets of the handsome creamy church in the Russian Compound. Last week there was another scare. It was the event of Ramadan, the great Moslem festal month. It was feared that it would be marked by excesses, because again handbills had been distributed with "Down with the Jews" as the heading. Next week the civil government takes possession under Herbert Samuel. Then we shall see what we shall see.

On my return trip we stopped at Haifa, and after inspecting the clinic work there, drove along the Mediterranean shore, following its blue windings, to Accho, where, in the old medieval crusaders' fortress (in the walls of which Napoleon's bombs are still lodged) we visited Jabotinsky and his twenty associates, imprisoned for leading and participating in the Self-Defense organized during the Arab demonstrations and excesses in April.

We got there immediately after the prisoners had been informed that General Allenby had refused to revise the decision of the court martial. They were debating the propriety of a hunger strike. Which did not prevent the mild little botanist among them from pressing his specimens gathered on his last walk outside the rickety prison, which, it seemed to me, was hardly more than an invitation to escape. Jabotinsky himself is a whole man, and a fascinating one. I have never sympathized with his ideas—he is militant and aggressive—but when one listens to him, they assume charm as well as cogency. My visit to him will be a memory I shall always want to recur to.

The second day at [Zichron Jacob] was spent with the Aaronsohns going over the remains of Aaron's life.[5] Such a handful of ruins! A few vestiges of his incessant work are left; and over these hovers his old father, broken-hearted but proudly resigned. His one prayer is that what is left may be preserved as a memorial of the son who was his pride.

---

[5] Aaron Aaronsohn, founder of an agricultural experiment station near Zichron Jacob, and discoverer of wild wheat. See page 69.

Jerusalem, July 4, 1920

As I wrote the date I saw justice in the crowded calendar that made me skip my regular letter day and gave me at least a semblance of leisure on the Fourth. Though the *Nation* robs one of all illusions about its gloriousness, it was with me all day. Just now, when I was freshening up a bit and putting on a lighter dress than I use at the office, I found myself singing and humming all the patriotic songs, from "The Star-Spangled Banner" to "My Maryland," I had ever heard. I hasten to reassure you—there wasn't anyone within hearing distance.[6] The celebration was strictly a game of solitaire.

The past week was notable. Sir Herbert Samuel, the twentieth-century Nehemiah, entered Jerusalem. All the way up from Jaffa, along the whole road, and within the city on all the main streets, lines and lines of soldiers were drawn up, Tommy Atkins side by side with the stately Sikh, to guard the new governor, for there had been disquieting rumors about disturbances to break out among the Arabs. At all events, nothing happened.

The next night, exactly at full moon, I gave a picnic on Mount Scopus, the site of the Hebrew University, to thirty-five pupil nurses and their beaux. Miss Aronson provided the lunch, and the girls the merriment. From the top of the hill one looked down upon the Dead Sea, fifteen miles distant as the crow flies, and yet so distinct that you felt you could run across for a bath and back before the company had time to miss you.

A week ago the Jewish community gave a farewell dinner

---

[6] Her singing was always off-key. At seventy she took singing lessons and cured the defect—merely to satisfy her scientific belief that it could be done.

to [the American] Consul Glazebrook. It was the jolliest testimonial dinner I have ever attended, and the regret at parting from "the Consul of the Jews," as the Arabs call him, was thoroughly sincere. We had American songs and of course speeches. I spoke myself. What left the strongest impression on my mind was the fact that I had to stand up and drink a toast to the—King! It's a funny world—Sikhs in Palestine, tents on every hilltop, a king!

I have reserved the most astonishing bit of news for the last. I am about to become a householder. Sophie Berger and myself are going to rent a little house on the outskirts of Jerusalem, surrounded by a big garden, with olive trees, figs, oranges, and vines, not to mention flowers.

[TO IDA FLATOW]   *Jerusalem, July 23, 1920*

The attitude toward the Unit is changed. It is, however, my conviction that so far as the large strata of the population were concerned, there never was any but the kindliest feeling.

The excitement was caused, first, by the outside physicians; second, by inside physicians; third, by newspaper critics who are insatiable in the matter of good stories. That the Unit was imperfect—that it is imperfect now—no one knows better than I do; but when all its imperfections are summed up, there remains an achievement, attained in a period of less than two years, which, in my judgment, will be one of the bright spots in the history of the early reconstruction movement in Palestine. I am not very conversant with medical literature, but I have no hesitation in expressing my doubt whether any such big piece of constructive medical work has ever been done in a "colony" even by the greatest imperialistic colonizing powers.

A few days ago I was in the government hospital in Jaffa.

I was sorry I was there alone, I wish some of the critics could have contrasted it with our little box of a hospital, a stone's throw away. Besides, I have the standard of Palestine ten years ago; contrasted with what existed then, our Unit is an Aladdin's lamp wonder.

I have no doubt of the need of the Unit here; on the contrary, I believe every nerve ought to be strained to give us a bigger budget. When I think of the coming immigration and look at our inadequate preparations for receiving it, I shudder! But whether I ought to be here is what perplexes me still, as it has perplexed me since I have been here and as it perplexed me while I was in America. You will recall that I was very uncertain about the wisdom of my coming here. If anyone comes with the intention of settling here, that's another matter.

II

Hardy young pioneers were spreading through the country a new watchword, *kebush,* which somehow escaped Miss Szold's pen. *Kebush* means "to subdue"; and the word will be found in the times of Joshua when "the land was subdued" by the armies of Israel. In 1920 the enemies and weapons were different, but the spirit of conquest remained the same. By draining swamps and building roads and clearing a stony soil the pioneers subdued a wilderness; but they sickened and fell under the assault of the anopheles mosquito, which had long since driven the Arabs from large tracts of the land. Then, in turn, the Medical Unit set out to subdue malaria.

Jerusalem, September 14, 1920

A journey of 7000 miles across seas has made no difference. Nor will it make any difference for me to admit the truth of what A. says in one of her letters: that the mending of the world will depend not on my solving my difficulties inside the Unit or making economies sufficient to cover the deficit, but upon Lenin and Trotsky. Bertrand Russell's articles in the *Nation* go far toward making one believe that they will not or may not succeed brilliantly.

However that may be, and however whole-heartedly I may assent to A.'s disbelief in my powers, I yet find it impossible not to yield to the insistence of circumstances. And circumstances here, chiefly in the form of suffering human beings, and planning and scheming human beings, and fine, bold, adventurous human beings—these circumstances are an army wielding *force majeure*. I at least cannot stand up against them. So long as I can keep my eyes open, I must work for amelioration. It's my eyes, not my brain.

The two things that prevented me from writing to you all this time were immigrants and malaria—not my malaria, for up to now I have remained unscathed, but almost everybody has it. A terrible scourge! As I go through the country, I feel as though every stone (and this country is full of them, God knows) were vocal with suffering. The immigrants, who are coming in at the rate of 300 a week through the port of Jaffa, fall a prey to it before they are here a week. They go off to their places of employment in the open country, and in a jiffy they are back in the cities claiming hospital space—which is non-existent. Daily we turn away dozens of patients with 103 degrees of fever. And the worst of the situation is that with prudent planning and not an excessive sum of money the country might be cleaned up in less than nine months.

Now at last you have the background of my new tasks. I have been organizing the immigration work at the posts— medical, sanitary, and prophylactic. And I have organized a prophylactic and sanitary campaign in the hinterland, in Galilee, where most of the workingmen's groups are stationed. Concurrently I have been dictating to our one Public Health man popular educational leaflets on the diseases of the country and their prevention. Isn't it absurd for me to be doing this sort of thing when I am approaching sixty?

Tomorrow I go to Haifa with an engineer to see what can be done about opening a small hospital. It won't in the least meet the need that exists. Not hospitals are needed, but preventive, educational, sanitary, and prophylactic work, begun now for next year. If we had all the money in the world, these first immigrants would be bound to serve as dung to this land. Our task must demand the sacrifice of young lives. It is *war* with nature. I still believe it worth while. But it is hard—awfully hard.

Haifa, September 18, 1920

I investigated the British preparations here for the Jewish immigrants, and I have also spoken to the British officials and inspected the government hospitals. I believe it is my business, if I may do so as the representative of an American voluntary organization now partially disavowed by the Zionist International, to urge a larger participation of Jewish medical and other official personages in the immigration work.

Probably I have already been remiss in not pushing myself and our work upon the notice of the British authorities. You know how stupid I am about politics. I still am naïve enough to believe that if one will go ahead and do one's work well, merit will count. I am learning that in colonial government such simplicity is a crime. So I return to Jerusalem with the resolve to let people in authority know in words what they know very, very well in print, that the Medical Unit is on the map.

On the same trip I went to visit a group of 400 immigrants, who are breaking stones on the road between Haifa and Nazareth—men and women. I went with the doctor from Haifa. We found a number of malaria patients. Many of the doctors stationed in the Galilean colonies insist that the prevalence and violence of malaria this year have been much less than before, while in Jerusalem and in Judea it has been a worse season than since many a year. The reason assigned in both cases is the Medical Unit sanitary work, which is being done in the northern colonies but has been forbidden by the British civil government in the cities. The prohibition would be just and proper provided the government fulfilled its functions. [But] it has a corps of Arab, low-class inspectors, who are charged with practicing graft. They sell the petrol entrusted to them for wells, cisterns, and puddles, and accept bakshish from householders who desire not to have to drink petrolized water.

To return to the immigrants. They are under a £30,000 contract with the government. The contract was taken over by one of the Jewish labor parties, the *Ha-Poel Ha-Zair*. Out of a certain percentage of the contract money they are supposed to meet administrative expenses—tools, tents, etc. Medical care ought to be included. But it isn't. So Hadassah is appealed to. Of course it is out of the question. We have no funds to care intensively for thousands of immigrants. There are now 52 such groups working at swamps and on roads.

While we are in the midst of the malaria madness, nobody can be made to think. Everyone is hectic and impulsive. The physicians beset me like bees, and they sting. Send a nurse here—a doctor there—medicine here—bed linens there—quinine—you must!—you don't dare refuse?—until I am almost beside myself. My response: "No money," is met with: "Then America must send some!" Beset as I am, I still see clearly that medical care must be rendered automatically as part of the living arrangements of every group, whether temporary or permanent. I have written to the American organization, and have offered to carry on an educational campaign in the rural districts on the subject of malaria, after Dr. Rubinow returns.

We went to the camp of the road-builders in an auto, had two accidents on the way, had to finish the journey in a springless wagon drawn by mules. By the time we were ready to return, the auto was repaired. We got in, and five minutes later it telescoped into a wagon, and was smashed. We had to return to Haifa in a wagon, drawn by two mules, and toting the battered auto after us. We arrived hours and hours after we were expected, and the town was aroused about our safety. An auto here is no convenience, because there are no real chauffeurs.

It is true I am working hard, very hard. The job Dr. Rubinow left me was difficult enough in all conscience, the office staff he had gathered are mostly new at the work, they couldn't give me help automatically; new as I was, I had to go into every detail, and in most instances had to look back into the files to acquaint myself with every new situation; and above all life refused to let one carry out the modest program I had set myself when Dr. Rubinow went away— simply to keep the machinery of the Unit going. Many new undertakings had to be inaugurated. This week was the first time I felt the strain—not of work, but of a moral question badly handled. I am still too close to it to write about it. Then, for the first time, my heart reverted to its state previous to Boothbay Harbor days. So I stayed in bed all day today.

Jerusalem, October 26, 1920

I may as well confess, since you read it between the lines, that the life here does not make me happy. What else was to have been expected? Again there is a generation of the desert which will have to perish in order to fructify the soil.

First a synthesis of the Jews gathering here from everywhere will have to be brought about, and then we may expect the life here to have some gracious aspects. To what extent the life in Palestine is of a piece with what the whole world is, I don't pretend to be able to tell. To judge from the *Nation,* America is not a marvel of comeliness these days either. Nevertheless, there is no gainsaying the fact that Palestine now is a bundle of problems, and problems are not conducive to happiness. And it isn't conducive to happiness if we keep thinking of the hundreds and hundreds of immigrants in tents while the more fortunate are tightening up every rift and seam to protect themselves against the rains now almost due.

And yet things are not so bad that you must insist upon my coming home. If a woman, asked to guess my age, insists on thirty-eight for me, as happened today, I am not yet a *nebbich.*[7]

You ask me to make a promise to ease up when Dr. Rubinow comes. I make the promise, and I make it all the more readily as I must do just that if I want to be useful here in Palestine. By the way, you are right when you say

---

[7] The sort of person about whom people wag the head and say: *"Nebbich!"*—that is, "Alas, poor thing!"

that the field for me is America and not Palestine. Palestine is for the young.

And the glory of these days before the rainy season! It is now full moon. This evening we had our supper on our little terrace overlooking our garden of olive trees, oranges, lemons, figs, and almonds, and we ate by the light of the moon. A man came with a note, which I read by the moon-light. And the walk in the early morning to the office is a joy.

Haifa, November 7, 1920

I am on my last inspection tour both before Dr. Rubinow arrives and before the rains arrive. In this region some rain has already fallen. Since I have been on the way—five days —I have encountered none, but in the distance several times I saw it descend in sheets. The hillsides are green, there are patches of turf everywhere, and flowers are begin-ning to blossom forth. And if I thought the birds numerous and interesting before, while the earth was crusted and dry and the roads and trees were enveloped in a coat of dust, I don't know what to say about them now. They are vocal. I even heard the bulbul in Tiberias. If I had never read the Song of Songs, I should have said, had I been plunged into the country suddenly at this season, that this is the Palestinian spring. The coloring of the sky and hills is more entrancing than ever, on account of the clouds promising rain.

But the interest of my trip is human. I must have written to you before that immigration medical work was thrust upon Hadassah, but those who flung it at us forgot to throw the appropriation along with it. There are now some 60 labor groups in the country clamoring for doctors, nurses, drugs. Among those groups there are five large ones, from 300 to 500 men and women in each. They live in tent colonies. I have been telling their leaders right straight through the summer that they must devise a sick insurance policy that will make funds for medical care grow out of the wages and the contract. At best, Hadassah can give administrative supervision. But they won't stop to think, and delegations come daily to the office and insist: "Only this one thing more. This need is *so* great."

In this way it came about that a field hospital was planned for the largest group, near Tiberias. The contractor was to furnish certain things: tents, beds, etc. By means of the peculiar Palestinian wireless telegraphy I learned that the workingmen had not kept their part of the arrangement, and I flew up there to find my worst fears confirmed.

Incidentally, I had a better opportunity than ever before to come close to the "pioneers." And for the first time I saw one of my hopes connected with Zionism realized. It is not an objective realization—it is not an achievement. We are far removed from any sort of achievement. It is this: I faced a human problem in which Jews are concerned, and alone concerned, and I forgot wholly that they are Jews. And so did they. These "pioneers," a war-bred generation, are living a primitive life, and are grappling with elementary, basic problems of living. I have a strong desire to join them.

Of course, I can't break stones as they do, but I may be able to organize them so that their living conditions are improved. The East European Jew has idealism and persistence; what he lacks utterly is system and grace. His good qualities are permeated with a stolidity that keeps him from sitting down and thinking out the method whereby his paper plans might be realized bit by bit; or when he lives in communities, he doesn't know that a modicum of social courtesy acts like oil on machinery.

We have at least five hard years of this primitive struggle ahead of us here.

Jerusalem, November 13, 1920

Meantime the immigrants are pouring into Palestine and no preparations are made for them. How they are going to weather the rainy season in their tent homes, I can't understand. I suppose there will be influenza and pneumonia, as there was malaria and typhoid in the summer. But what they are suffering here is not nearly so bad as what they ran away from in Central and Eastern Europe.

Our colonial life goes on merrily nevertheless—with the announcement of the formation of a Sports Club which I am enclosing as an illustration of what I call the Kiplingesque atmosphere. Your own sister found it necessary, pressure having been brought on her as the acting director of the Medical Unit, to join the "Jerusalem Ladies' Club"! And tomorrow I take tea (being hot water) [8] with Lady Samuel, who has just arrived and established herself at Government House on the Mount of Olives.

Jerusalem, November 22, 1920

Mr. Pincus Ruttenberg was our guest tonight at dinner. He is the Ruttenberg who was the Kerensky mayor of St. Petersburg; and after all sorts of vicissitudes in and out of prison, he became the engineer who has drawn up the big plan for harnessing the upper sources of the Jordan for hydro-electric power and the conservation of the water supply. He is also the founder of the first *kvuzot*, that is the

---

[8] Miss Szold detested tea—and found herself in a land full of Russian Jews and Englishmen!

road-building gangs for the halutzim—the "pioneers."

He is a real personage, a little too optimistic for my taste, but nevertheless interesting and spirited. I object more than ever to optimism.[9] It's good enough if one looks ahead to cycles of Cathay. But with real problems facing one nakedly, I want some wholesale pessimism that devises ways and means—particularly means.

III

The return of Dr. Rubinow to assume direction of the Unit enabled Miss Szold to relax a bit, and her letters now dwell a little more on the amenities of her new life.

Jerusalem, December 1, 1920

Dr. Rubinow arrived just a week ago. I feel like a bird with the door of its cage open. It doesn't fly out, but it knows it can. I am still at the office for five or six hours daily, to give Dr. Rubinow a chance to deal with certain fundamental questions—*Prinzipenfragen*. There are a number of them and of course there is the eternal financial problem. Poor Dr. Rubinow comes with the strictest sort of injunctions from America not to roll up any more deficits, for they will not be met. So retrenchment is the order of the day. You know, without my telling you, that retrenchment is hard work anywhere, but nowhere so bitterly hard as in Palestine, where no one can be dismissed because there is no other position to go to.

The weather after four days of wild downpour is glorious. Such sunrises and sunsets, such delicious golden sunshine!

---

[9] In this case optimism was justified. Mr. Ruttenberg lived to build his dam, and in 1940 the Palestine Electric Corporation sold 93,873,482 kilowatt hours of electricity.

And after the rains one can see the grass growing. Our oranges and lemons are ripening fast in our garden. Daily we have a dish of our own olives on the table, and the market still yields delicious grapes. The succession of fruits here, where transportation facilities are not such as to bring the products of distant regions within reach, is remarkable. Since the day I arrived, fruit has never failed—I began with the last of the oranges, then came apricots, peaches, pears, bananas, grapes, and figs, all in rich abundance, and now we are back to oranges again. The other day an acquaintance from Egypt brought apples—real apples, said to have been imported from France. My first bite into one of them caused me the acutest homesickness I have yet experienced.

If I pass on to larger subjects, I can only repeat the jeremiads which the whole world is composing. The other day I received a copy of the New York *Times,* the issue of the day after the elections, sent to me by my faithful friend, Rose Zeitlin. What a world to live in!

Our problems out here are huge in inverse proportion to the size of this little land. Turn where you will and you are met by utter impotence. The immigration continues to increase, and the only opportunity for work is at road-building while living in tents. The food is only Australian bully-beef, which creates gastric disturbances and utter disgust. The contractors have no capital for beds, tents, and machinery; nor have they experience in tent-pitching and bivouacking. But would you believe it—the "pioneers" are not asking for pity. What they left behind in Central and Eastern Europe is much worse!

Many are going away, nevertheless. That is because they see no future ahead. For the moment it looks as though the Jews are not able to grasp the opportunity that has come after so many years of waiting. The movement has not

failed; the idealism is still there in full force; but circumstances are too stubborn. The organization is breaking
down. In Central and Eastern Europe there are said to be
enormous sums of money for Zionist purposes. They will
have to remain there for years and years, until a more normal exchange situation evolves. At present, it takes 1,500,-
000 rubles to pay the traveling expenses of a man and his
wife from Russia to Palestine.

Jerusalem, December 8, 1920

This morning I stayed away from the office—my first indulgence due to Dr. Rubinow's return. For what? Oh! you
know what one does when one has had no time for femi-
ninities for months and months. First of all a hair wash,
under the douches [shower-baths] which I have learned to
love in spite of the cold, the bitter cold, on the top of the
mountain called Jerusalem. It was a delight to dry my hair
in my sunny, sunny room, with its two large south windows.
I could hardly remain sitting in the broad shaft of sunlight
while it dried—so hot it was, when you have the contrasts
one enjoys here. Once the sun is up, genial warmth; once it
goes down, and the minute it's down, bitter cold.

This morning for the first time I knew how charming
our house set in its dear garden is. It's the first time, not ex-
cluding Sabbath days, that I've been able to know it at all
hours. The Arab proprietor left wonderful window plants
with us; and through the leaves, touching them with delicious gleams of color, streams the sunshine. You see how
I always get back to the sun. Can't help it. It is the domi-
nant fact in Palestine. In the interval between the first rains
and those bound to come some time or other soon, we are
having golden days. What's the use—I can't describe them.

Then, after the hair wash (oh! so badly needed), there

were buttons, and rents, and darns, and search for commodities that had slipped out of sight in all the journeyings and movings, and now letter-writing.

I must tell you about the wedding of Sir Herbert Samuel's son, Edwin, to a Palestinian girl, Hadassah Grasovsky. Probably I wrote to you about the engagement from Florence, last spring, when I met the whole Samuel family at Passover time. The engagement had not been announced at that time, but Mrs. Samuel told me the secret, probably because I had known her future daughter-in-law eleven years ago, when I first visited Palestine.

Everybody was invited. It was a most interesting pilgrimage up the slope of the Mount of Olives. I am sure every house in Palestine was mobilized. Indeed the whole of Jerusalem was on the *qui vive*. The magnificent hall of the German building, which is used as the government's, was filled from door to door with as varied a throng as eye ever beheld: sheiks and Dominican priests and Chacham Bashis and Russian popes and Abyssinian clergy and military men, all cheerily jovial with ordinary plain citizens like myself. The canopy was in the center, the audience was disposed on all four sides. It took three rabbis in the gayest regalia to tie the knot. It nearly didn't get tied, because the master of ceremonies had forgotten the [sacramental] wine. The vast audience was on its feet, and the whole bridal party under the canopy, when the omission was discovered. For minutes without end we all stood in spellbound silence. I had visions of a horseman having to gallop down to Jerusalem to fetch the wine, so long it took for the messenger to return. Poor Sir Herbert! And dignified Sir Herbert. To look at him as he stood there one would have inferred that omitting to prepare wine for the Jewish ceremony was the only proper way to conduct the wedding.

The congratulations were offered and received in another large hall. The whole huge crowd shook hands with the bridal party. You should have seen the Bedouin sheiks in the throng. Then the bridegroom was made an honorary sheik under the open sky in the court of the building. While his bride stood next to him, he was clothed in a sheik's costume.

The wedding gifts were of truly Oriental splendor—carpets, and wines, and silver, and embroideries, and daggers, and chased revolvers. But the best and most Oriental of them were not displayed: thirty horses presented to the bride by the sheiks, and a whole village—houses, men, women, and children, and all their belongings. And then I rode down the hill to a meeting to discuss cutting down the budget.

[TO ALICE L. SELIGSBERG]   *Jerusalem, January 3, 1921*

Even you, who witnessed my early struggles with the Unit work, cannot picture to yourself what it became in the late summer and the fall. Malaria was more than the usual scourge. The most experienced agree that such a summer has never been. The office of the Unit was besieged by emissaries from everywhere—from every workingmen's group north and south. And when the immigration began to pour in the situation became unbearable.

I know you want to hear about myself. Well, I am not so acutely unhappy as I was at first. That is partly due to the lovely duo-life Sophia [Berger] and myself are leading in our darling home. Sophia mothers me—as much as I allow her to. She would, if I let her, make me a truly old woman sitting back in an easy chair and letting others do for me. I may be old enough for that, but not yet meek enough. Indeed, I feel so well and so spry that I resist her coddling of me rather strenuously.

Our home is really charming. I think people like to come to it. Sophia shuns no trouble to have them come here. And she is really a good cook. Her "little" dinners are becoming famous. The distance from the center of the city I have not yet found objectionable, even in the heavy rains, which we are now having. But, oh, such glorious days in between! My only complaint is that I am not properly prepared for the severity of the weather. By now I have managed to equip myself for the cold inside, but not yet for the wet outside. I dress not unlike the Arabs, who strut about in miscellaneous rags. When I was preparing for Palestine Sophia told me two things: take warm clothes with you, and you'll have lots of time for reading. I let my mind dwell only on the second point. What has happened is that I have neither the warm clothes nor the time to read.

Coming to Palestine has not changed my fate. I still stand about, as it were, waiting for things to come along to be done. I haven't long to wait. They come in shoals and my days are as disunified as ever and as crowded. But after all it is the Unit that still keeps me busy. When Dr. Rubinow returned I felt it would be unjust to leave him to flounder in a sea of details. I go to the office daily. I believe I am doing the right thing. The Unit, with all its faults, and it is riddled with faults, is a big piece of organized work. With Dr. Rubinow back, it has again become a storm center. At once he had to face difficult problems on his return—as of old a deficit, the swallowing of the Health Bureau, the opposition of all medical forces inside and outside of the Unit. I see now that by some hocus-pocus of which I am guilty, though not consciously a sinner—some trick of manner, perhaps, rather than sterling quality—I kept the Unit quiet all summer.

The turmoil now is almost as great as it was when I arrived in May. In order to economize, physicians will have to be dismissed. Though, at my urgence, the doctors are now organized and have their representatives in the Executive Committee, we can't get their effective co-operation. I have reached one incontrovertible conclusion—doctors are unorganizable. Our need for economizing comes at a time when the Joint Distribution Committee too is shutting down. The whole country is groaning. Unless some plans are devised soon and money is forthcoming to execute them, there will be a shameful moral collapse, with the immigrant as the victim in the tragedy.

You ask about our Saturday morning meetings—no progress. We are still holding on—all of us, Jessie, Leah, Dushkin, Sophia, Norman Bentwich, and his two sisters. But we are not creating even the smallest germ of anything vital. At present we are reading the Mosaic lesson, the prophetical portion, and we are studying Jeremiah. You see how we are back at the intellectual, and as far as ever away from edification.

Perhaps you are right—it is a Felix Adler who is needed here. Perhaps—but perhaps an even greater is needed, a real prophet, one who can scourge and console, refine and stimulate, urge forward but yet keep the people—stiffnecked and wayward—attached to the truths hardly won in the past. I am happier than I was, but I am of the same opinion still of the life here. I am happier because I have conquered my disappointment at our people. We are still on the lowest rung of the ladder—we had thought ourselves near the top! When one recognizes that the whole climb is

still ahead, one cannot be disappointed; one simply has to
resolve to work harder.

My birthday—they made a public celebration of it. I
don't know myself who *they* were. Some say that Dr. Rubinow, the most forgetful of men as a rule, brought the date
with him from Miss Flatow and Mrs. Danziger, my two
steadies. However that may be, I was a public personage,
and ever since I have been receiving birthday wishes from
all over Palestine.

IV

Miss Szold's sixtieth birthday was celebrated in gala style.
After a dinner given by the doctors and nurses, with the
High Commissioner and Lady Samuel among the guests,
more than one hundred and fifty workers and friends ten-
dered her a reception at the Hotel de France. Something of
what Palestine thought of Miss Szold after less than a year's
acquaintance may be read in the following contemporary
account:

"All the employees of Hadassah had Miss Szold's name
inscribed in the Golden Book of the Jewish National Fund.
One of them, the statistical expert, made the presentation.
He said: 'We have done this not because you were the temporary director of Hadassah, not because you are a great
Zionist or a well-known writer, but because you are a fellow-
worker, a human being whom we love and honor.'

"He spoke of her devoted work, sixteen and more hours
a day, of her painstaking kindness to each person that approached her, no matter on what errand, of those who
would otherwise have gone away disconsolate, having come
for work and found none, but who having spoken with

Miss Szold went away comforted if not satisfied. A woman, he related, left the office saying: 'I have not found work for my daughter, but I have found a human being!' And then, when Dr. Rubinow returned, she left her place in the main office, and took up her work at a little table in the same room with the other employees. Love and honor in proportion to her greatness and her modesty!

"The tone, the expression said even more than the words, and I found myself moved to tears. There is poetic justice in life, after all!

"The room was cleared of chairs, and the guests joined in the Palestinian rondo, which is danced to the singing of Hebrew songs. Miss Szold wound in and out among the other dancers, rosy and brisk as a girl of sixteen. Then there were waltzes and other round dancing, and not one dance was allowed to go by without Miss Szold participating. And so it went on until after midnight."

CHAPTER TEN

Naked Realities

I

ON the threshold of her second year in Palestine Miss Szold was in the mood to marshal her impressions and experiences, even if they could not merge into a unified picture. She was brought, as she says, face to face with naked realities. Where the Jews were struggling against the hard soil, an inimical government, a hostile population, and their own temperamental and financial handicaps, the realities were grim and baffling. In an old, quiet, and settled village like Rehobot the realities were gracious. Pervading all was a magic beauty which made the land worth suffering for, and suffering there was to be.

[TO MRS. LEON M. SOLIS-COHEN]

Jerusalem, March 13, 1921

I am on the great adventure of my life. In a sense it is rejuvenating me, in another it is aging me. My sisters used to call me "stick in the mud" because I was "set" in my ways, loath to change my habits. I was homekeeping like a cat. I think even they—sisters are proverbially hard critics—would concede my adaptability if they saw me adjust myself to new work and new conditions. Is it not enough that in these latter days of mine I should have had to undertake a piece of medical reconstruction work? How does that comport with proofreading, index-making, and editing—and of what? Jewish books. Sometimes when I am alone—it doesn't happen frequently—I laugh out loud. It seems downright funny for me to be doing medical organization in Jerusalem. That's one evidence of adaptability. But what do you think of my riding up one of the steepest mountains strewn with stones, donkeyback, sitting astride? I am so proud of that feat that I can't stop talking about it. Usually I forget to mention the fact that the donkey was a dear, intelligent beasty, who needed no guiding.

But, after all, the doctors in the American Zionist Medical Unit at one end and the donkey picking his way between boulders, rocks, and pebbles, at the other end (sometimes I indulge in the blasphemous thought that if the popular conception of donkeys were correct—it isn't—there wouldn't be an enormous difference between the two ends), are only externals. The real thing is the gamut of human emotions and reactions that lie in between. And that is hard to describe. There are so many aspects of life that go to make up the whole: the British government, the inner workings of the Jewish community, its relation to the government and the other communities, the immigration movement, the religious situation, the political parties, and many others.

After all these months my impressions have not yet combined themselves into a whole picture. One reason for this sloth may be that I have lost touch with general standards. Would you believe that since I left America I have not read a daily newspaper? So I can't judge what is peculiarly Palestinian, what mandate-governmental, what Jewish, and what is part of the general reaction to the war.

I do know that the struggle is fierce, naked and undisguised. There are no horrors as in Eastern Europe. But so far from being Pittsburgh-Platformian,[1] so to say, life is typically colonial in its developments. The Sikh soldiers

---

[1] See pages 107–8.

are not the only element that makes one think of India and
Kipling. If *über hundert und zwanzig Jahren* the Jews possess a homeland, conquered for themselves by work, physical and intellectual, what a testimony it will be to their
finer qualities! And I still believe the conquest is possible,
though it will be after the long interval implied in the
phrase *über hundert und zwanzig Jahren.*

The Jews are ready to work—they are working. Among
all my new, vitalizing experiences, none can compare in
stupendousness with what I saw and learned in the Jewish
road-builders' camps, the labor squads of the halutzim, the
pioneers, young men and women from Central and Eastern
Europe, who have been preparing themselves for years in
language and manual work, for Palestine development.
The camps are full of faults of organization, the campers
full of faults of temperament, but the movement as a whole
is a phenomenon equivalent to a miracle.

And the country? It too is a miracle. Full of faults, like
the camp and the campers, but so beautiful. It too must be
conquered, its stones, its climate, its swamps, but it is worth,
oh! so worth the struggle. I was sent to Galilee on business
four weeks ago. It was raining, raining all the week I was
away. Neither clouds, nor mist, nor downpour of abundant
waters, nor bad roads could obscure the beauty of the land
in its spring garb.

The Medical Unit is doing superb work. It too is full of
faults and imperfections, and the people, who resent its
Americanism, criticize it pitilessly, but it is worth while.

And myself? I am comfortable. Sophia Berger took a
house on the outskirts of Jerusalem, its olive-tree garden,
with almond trees interspersed, facing the Mount of Olives.
Our little house is a dear home. It would be perfect in my
eyes if it could be fitted up with steam heat. At a distance

one forgets that Jerusalem is perched on the top of a mountain and is cold. Our little kerosene stove has to be hugged if it's to make any change in one's sensations on a winter night in a house with high ceilings and stone floors. No wonder rugs come from the Orient. My only wonder is they ever allow a single one to leave the country—they are so badly needed here.

[TO MRS. EMIL WEINHEIM] *Jerusalem, March 2, 1921*

It took some time to transfer the whole complex, involved, intricate business of the Unit to Dr. Rubinow. In the process of handing things over to him it became apparent that I could not carry out my intention, cherished all the long weary months of waiting for him, of getting out of the Unit work and devoting myself to other interests. Interests lie around loose here—in fact, they are heaped up at every corner and turn! I realized that it was my business to stick to it. In the first place, there is too much administrative work for one man. In the second place, the situation here is so delicate that I felt that the moral support I could give him by being constantly at his side would be a source of comfort and a real support. I therefore took over two administrative departments, the school hygiene work and the Nurses' Training School. By no means do they take up my whole time. But as a member of the Executive Committee of the Unit, and by reason of my being at the office during business hours regularly, I am drawn into many, many other concerns in our busy Unit world.

In brief, I may say that I am at this late day undergoing what I may without exaggeration call the biggest experience of my life. Here one is brought face to face with naked realities. Elsewhere they are disguised by the complexities of civilization. The grooves and ruts are drawn for one living in New York. Here you are bound to think out every step. It won't do to say that you will act as you always acted before. To be sure, that attitude has its dangers. For, after all, human nature is the same the world over. If I may say so, here human nature is more so than elsewhere.

In the first place, there are the varieties of human nature. There are the Jews from everywhere. So long as they are everywhere, in America, in Russia, in Austria, in England, they think of each other as Jews primarily. It's their likenesses that count. Here it's their traits as Americans, Russians, Hungarians, etc., that obtrude themselves. Jewish growing pains are very painful in consequence. Facing this complex Jewish community are a number of diverse and to some extent equally complex communities: the Arab world, and its two divisions, the Christians and Moslems— or its two other divisions, according to social rather than religious cleavages, the fellaheen and the effendi; [2] the Western Christian communities; the British officialdom, guarded by its military establishment of Tommy Atkins and the Sikh regiments; and all the cranks that gather in Palestine for no one knows what reason.

This variegated world has had the agelong habit of looking to the outside for its life blood. Not only the Jews here, but all classes except the land-working fellaheen have gotten their subsistence from the West. In the new era they are faced with the demand that they become a self-sufficient, independent political group. Again growing pains. You can see how here one is running up against all sorts of deep, elementary problems all the time. And so life is intensely interesting.

The adjustment is difficult even in the matter of climate. With all my knowledge of Palestine, I have been completely

---

[2] Fellaheen are Arab peasants; effendis are Arab landlords.

surprised by the rigor of the winter in Jerusalem—I say
Jerusalem, not Palestine. I suppose what one forgets is that
Jerusalem crowns the summit of a fairly high mountain.
That makes its exquisite beauty, and it accounts equally
for its severe weather. There is wind and rain, and hail, and
snow, and yet all the time what the calendar calls winter is
really exquisite spring. Immediately after the first rainfall
comes a great transformation. Out of dryness comes suc-
culent green, and soon thereafter blossoms and color, and
abundance. Each night, when I go to bed shivering, I mourn
to think that the cold will kill the rosebuds ready to burst
into bloom, and freeze the orange and almond blossoms,
and wilt the calendulas and violets and anemones, and
silence the birds. And the next morning there is glorious
brilliant sunshine and nature continues in its unsullied
bridal attire. I'd like to tell you about my recent trip to
Galilee, where the climate is gentler than here. But it's
useless to try. Its beauties beggar description. The land is
worth suffering for—and there will be suffering before it is
won.

Fortunately none of the pioneers deceive themselves on
this subject. The immigrants come prepared to work, to
endure, to be patient. They also come with the assured
hope that the end will be what they hoped for. It is a pity
that up to this time we organized Zionists have put into
practice none of those wonderfully logical plans which we
put down on paper so prolifically. I am in hopes that Weizmann's visit to America will clinch the matter.

[TO DR. HARRY FRIEDENWALD]
Jerusalem, March 16, 1921
Your letter of birthday greetings shamed me as much as
it pleased me. After my long neglect of you, I didn't deserve

it. The things one does not deserve are those one likes best, and I felt confident that you, having been in Palestine and knowing the problems of the Unit besides, understood all along why you were not having a direct word from me. I was the loser. To you I might have written with the least effort. You could have supplied the atmosphere for every problem of the multitudinous problems that beset me from the hour I set foot on the stones of Jerusalem—problems as hard as its stones.

My long delay in reaching Palestine had created a state of tension, to which my arrival added intensity. I came modestly in my private, personal capacity. I had received no mandate from the American organization. Here it was expected that a word of mine would decide long-standing disputes between the Unit and the community, and still more aggravated disputes between the members of the Unit, and between its physicians and its director.

At the end of two weeks I was a wreck. I was ready to flee back to America, I wondered bitterly whether I had devoted twenty years of my life to an ideal that had turned out to be a will-o'-the-wisp. For what is a Zionist who no longer believes in the Jewish people? In those first days after my arrival a voice kept shouting inside of myself: "These are not your people. You have no part and parcel in them."

That period has passed. The halutzim have done much to restore my balance. But even before they came, the situation even in the Unit quieted down. Still, truth demands that I confess to you that I still find the moral atmosphere here stifling, whether among the orthodox or in the new Yishub.[3] The education of the children is false. We are

---

[3] The modern Jewish settlements, in town and countryside, taken as a whole.

raising an arrogant, self-sufficient generation. My hope again lies with the halutzim, a fresh stream that may carry away on its swift current all the deposits of decay that impest the air.

The Unit faces two dangers according to my analysis of the situation: its isolation from the Zionist government and its ability to turn about face and make of itself wholly a piece of medical machinery for the needs of the immigrants. In spite of all, the Unit has done a great piece of work in Palestine, in some respects the greatest that the Zionists have accomplished. I make the superlative statement in view of my disappointment at the educational system. In one respect the two systems, the medical and the educational, have the same requirements to insure their perfection—buildings. We, the Unit, shall never reach the heights to which for other reasons we might aspire, unless we have modern hospital buildings. So with the schools. Yet I repeat my satisfaction with the Unit in another form: I doubt whether a voluntary association anywhere has achieved such results in the short space of thirty months.

April 27, 1921

I wish I had the power of putting into words the storm and stress of my life here. And I wish this thing had happened to me in my youth, when there might have been time to elaborate upon my experiences and turn them into the fabric of character and action. The new people—a war-created generation—who are coming here are wonderful. But I cannot, cannot accept them. I want to—and I cannot. I love order. Disorder nauseates me. And they are systemless. They hate efficiency—almost because it is efficient. I hope I don't worship efficiency. I hope I don't love it to the exclusion or detriment of other qualities. But I want to be

efficient, and I want life to be ordered efficiently. Yet *they*
are heroic, not I. If indeed I am fine and aristocratic as you
say I am, why do I not embrace them?

What is the use of going on? I can't make you see things
as they are. I can't make myself see them as they are. I suppose I must be satisfied to pursue my own narrow beaten
track in the way I am fitted to do it, and let the new generation go its way without doubting criticism.

The older one gets, the more complex life becomes to
the vision. One is drawn to the cowardice of pretending to
see it simple by keeping to the path with the signpost
"Duty." And then, alas! one is assailed by doubts whether
one has read the word aright or followed the path to which
it pointed.

Storm and stress should come in one's teens and not in
one's sixties!

Rehobot, April 27, 1921

The little hotel at which we are staying is clean and comfortable. We actually have running water in our room, in
the fashion of the staterooms on board a boat. In a little
outhouse, not too far from the main building, is a douche
and other acceptable arrangements. As for the food, it is
the best prepared and best balanced I have yet had in Palestine. There are all sorts of Passover goodies, though not the
ones that awaken home reminiscences.

The life in the colony is equally well balanced. One gets
the feeling here of "arrival"—achievement. Thirty years are
more than thirty months.[4] There is a measure of co-operation, with the result that there is good water, the unpaved
streets are clean, and the far-stretching fields are beautifully
cultivated. Recently the women, who from the first have

---

[4] Rehobot was founded in 1890.

had the right to vote, have also been made eligible to offices. The little town even has its "character," a scientist, the only man in Palestine who knows its birds and insects, truly a scientist, one who is recognized by the German universities as the expert authority.

Best of all is the social life among the young people. There is that touch of grace about it which I have missed elsewhere. At sunset every evening everybody streams up to the top of a hill on one side of the village, and there is singing and gentle talking while they watch the sun sink behind the dunes.

On the opposite hill stands the synagogue, almost a feature in the landscape. Between the two hills, the shining white and red-roofed homes lie in actual groves of trees in a long crescent, at one tip of which is a group of Yemenite houses. The first of these was in process of construction when Mamma and I were here eleven years ago. Now they comprise a minor village, with a life of its own. Sophia took occasion to look into the home conditions of the half-orphans to whose mothers the Joint Distribution Committee is paying a subvention. In this way we got into the houses—most of them spotless, though bare of what we consider the first necessaries of life. On the other hand, the women all wear heavy silver ornaments on arm, neck, and head. The courtesy everywhere is delightful. We stopped on the road to ask the way of a man and his three young girl companions. We got the information, and one of the girls, who was carrying flowers, stretched out her roses to us for us to take. And in the Yemenite houses they insisted upon our filling our pockets with their roasted sesame, which seems to be a Passover treat.

All this is so different from the Galilean *kvuzot,* in which social experiments rather than life are carried on. That's what one feels in Palestine chiefly—a strenuous stirring, a reaching out for something that eludes. Perhaps if the truth, the whole and detailed truth, about Russia gets out, now that trade treaties are at last being made with her, our people here will have better guidance in their muddled aspirations. At present, loads and loads of money are sunk in the experiments, and all my eyes have seen is a disorder that keeps one uncomfortable in mind and body.

To be sure, the outward harmony here in Rehobot is purchased by the employment of Arab labor! There, of course, my sympathy is enlisted by the Galilean system. Not that I believe Arab labor should not be employed. Such a course would increase the political menace which, it cannot be denied, hangs over us. The crux is the terms and the manner of employment. It is interesting that the little Arab boys and girls here speak an exquisite Hebrew. Some of them know how to read and write it, while they know their Arabic only as a spoken language.

Talking of political menace, last Friday, just before Passover came in, I saw the religious demonstration that caused the great trouble a year ago—the so-called pogrom. I have never seen anything more wonderful, in a way more overwhelming, than this Nebi Musa celebration.

Between Jerusalem and Jericho is a great building, which, among the Moslems, is reported to be the tomb of Moses, in spite of the Biblical statement that the place of his sepulcher is not known. Once a year there is a great pilgrimage to this tomb, for the purpose of having the flags blessed. From all Palestine the Moslems come to Jerusalem for the departure of the flags, which are carried down by a religious procession headed by the Mufti. The celebration coincides (at least it has the last two years) with Passover, being the Feast of the Prophet Moses, the hero of Passover.

Sophie and I, the only women in the crowd, and two of the very few Jews who dared mingle with it, accompanied the procession from the Mosque through the gate of the city, up along the road by Gethsemane, to an eminence on which a huge tent was pitched. Both sides of the road, marked off by the stone walls of the gardens and terraces, were packed with throngs of the faithful, the women on one side, the men on the other, with no choice between them for richness of color and variety of costume.

The interest centered in the dancing. Every group of dancers was surrounded by a dense mob excited to the wildest pitch. The dancers themselves seemed to have lost all sense of their surroundings. They abandoned themselves to their ecstasy, while their followers clapped their hands rhythmically. Can't you understand how a pogrom might arise? A single word might inflame such a multitude.

At the tent a great crowd was assembled, brilliant and varied as all assemblages are in the East. I discovered an old friend there—did I write to you about the sheik of the Mosque of Omar who came to me and begged me to save his five daughters from starvation, and when I asked him who told him to come to me, said with head thrown back and eyes turned heavenward: "Allah!" Such having been his guide I could not but help his daughters substantially, and he kissed the "hem of my garment." Well, the sheik offered up the prayer (for the Sultan!) in the presence of the mounted Mufti, amid the acclaim and solemn "Amens" of the faithful. The young Mufti—the old one had died only a few weeks before—sat on his white horse, a most dignified figure with palms upturned in prayer. The contrast with the religious dancers in their frenzy was something never to be forgotten.

You will wonder that Sophie and I dared mingle with

the crowd. Indeed, Jewish Jerusalem was in great fear. But we knew nothing would happen. The defensive preparations were complete. Even the Medical Unit, which last year saved the situation for the Jews, had had its place assigned to it by the authorities. Machine guns were displayed on all the hills.

II

But something did happen. The "single word" to inflame a multitude was given two days later, not in Jerusalem but in Jaffa. Miss Szold met not only naked realities but tortured and bleeding.

Jerusalem, May 18, 1921

It's no use waiting any longer—some time I shall have to write to you about this dreadful thing that has happened here. I thought I'd understand it and write to you about it, intelligently. But as the days go by, I understand it less and less. Only this I know—it is a very different thing from what it seems when you read a three-line cable in our papers at home about it.

And I walked right into it. It caught me on the way from my happy vacation in Rehobot to Jerusalem. We left Rehobot early Sunday morning [May 1]—we being Mrs. [Mary] Fels, Sophie, and I, and a young friend of Mrs. Fels's. At half-past eleven we got to Jaffa. There we were going to have dinner at Moscowitz's, where we always stay. It is, by the way, a Hungarian family of beautiful cultivation, with cooking precisely like Mamma's. For my sake she had *matzoh-klös,* the only ones that tasted like ours in the whole of Palestine. That was all we were going to do in Jaffa—eat dinner, and at two we were going to go up to Jerusalem.

The auto was ordered for that time. In the half-hour be-
tween arriving and dinner I ran out to get a glimpse of
Nellie Straus, who lives in Tel Aviv. On my way to Nellie's
I met a procession with red flags—it was May Day.

.While we were seated at the table we heard shots. Sophie
and Mrs. Fels, who had gone shopping while I ordered the
dinner, told us that they had come upon a procession in
trouble with the police. Their driver had taken a circuitous
route. The men at our table insisted that the shots we heard
were being fired into the air only as a display of authority
—a warning. Somehow or other their explanation, given
in good faith, didn't satisfy us. Though Tel Aviv is at some
distance from Jaffa, from the spot at which the disturbances
were taking place, we had felt a tenseness that is indescribable.

Then came two o'clock, but no auto. Mr. Blumenfeld
went to see about the auto. He didn't return. And the tenseness grew. I ran to our hospital, telling Sophie to call for
me there if the auto came.

When I got a few blocks, I knew a war was on. And when
I reached the hospital I saw the victims of the battle.
Eighteen wounded were already inside, outside was a long
line of stretchers with wounded and dead, in the yard the
dead were lying, the operating-room was jammed with
wounded waiting to be bound up.

Of course I stayed and tried to make myself useful. Sophie
came too, and together we took charge of the arrivals and
of the crowds of relatives looking for their people. We were
there until night, and body after body was brought in. And
in what a state! The little hospital looked like a shambles.
The floor was strewn with the wounded. And we had only
the worst cases. Other hundreds were at the Gymnasium

near by, at the Immigrants' Reception House, at the French Hospital in the city, and in private houses.

I can't give you any statistics. There must have been at least forty dead among the Jews, and half a dozen or so among the Arabs. We telephoned to Jerusalem for supplies and for nurses and doctors. By chance some of our doctors and nurses came down late in the afternoon on a little holiday trip. They had had difficulty on the road, but had been protected by a lorryful of troops that had been summoned from one of the military stations near by.

The next morning we had to telephone to Jerusalem again for bread and eggs. There was nothing in the city to eat. All the shops were closed—Jews and Arabs alike were terrified. Everybody was armed with sticks bristling with nails. The wounded in our hospital showed bullet wounds, knife wounds, and wounds from clubs and iron utensils. Some were actually battered.

Then the rumors began to fly around about the origin of the trouble. They are still flying around. No explanation but the fundamental one of racial hatred suffices—none but the opposition of a certain class of the Arabs to Zionist interpenetration of the land. The inquiries that have been made by Jews have elicited the facts that early in the morning of May Day a number of Jews were warned by Arab friends that something was brewing, and that they had better take measures of protection. There are other indications that the massacre was planned.

A massacre it was. Eye-witnesses told me of what had happened in the Bet Halutzim, the reception house for immigrants, in the city. It was full of new arrivals. A vessel had come in a couple of days before. The gendarmes rushed into it, first having pulled off the shields with their numbers, and with knives and revolvers hewed into the helpless crowds. In our hospital a boy of twelve came with his mother, both wounded, and they were looking for the father. They had been in Palestine two days, in the Bet Halutzim.

The next morning there was shooting again in the outskirts. A young Jew who was guarding an orange grove right off the house we were living in was shot down by an Arab—unprovoked. The scenes on the streets of Tel Aviv beggar description—the crowds of Jewish young men and women armed with fence rails and clubs.

At noon Dr. Rubinow arrived with supplies, and Sophie and I determined to go back to Jerusalem. When we got out on the road, we saw signs of suppressed excitement. There were troops of Arabs, all armed with clubs. Later we heard there had been murdering done in the Jewish houses between Jaffa and Mikveh Israel. In one of them the poet Joseph Chaim Brenner with the whole family whom he was visiting was hacked down. I suppose we did a foolhardy thing. Later in the week all who traveled on the road carried cocked pistols. Closer to Jerusalem, we came across a group of Arabs dancing to their own music. They seemed to be jeering at us. We did not stop to find out their meaning, I assure you.

That experience was horrible. But you know that in a sense what I experienced in Jerusalem was worse? Here I saw what a panic means. I went out on the street to go to a meeting and found our own clerks, a dozen of them, standing at the door excited; a few steps down the street the merchants were putting up their shutters (I forgot to say there was nasty looting at Jaffa—some people were cleaned out of all their belongings), and they looked pale with fright. I begged them to open their stores again and not evoke an assault. Their very fear seemed to me to be a suggestion to the Arabs who were standing in the street in groups talking to each other. Some of the Jewish merchants followed my advice. The farther I proceeded on the street, the worse the signs of panic. I kept assuring the people that they were victims of their imagination. They were, but it turned out that there was some basis for their fears. I was told that a handbill had been distributed, calling upon the Arabs of Jerusalem to imitate the example of their brave brethren in Jaffa and Haifa (where there had been an assault upon the Jews a few weeks ago—a baby assault compared with the Jaffa incident). But the immediate cause of the panic was the chasing of a thief by a policeman. The thief ran from his pursuer—and the whole street was alarmed.

Then your mother's daughter went to the office of the Zionist Commission to give advice. It seemed to me the proper thing to do was to organize a band of young men and let them keep up the courage of the Jews in the different parts of the city. None of the heads of departments were there. The young man to whom I spoke asked me about my business—he would transmit it. By that time I had cooled off, and I entered into a conversation with him about what I had seen. I used some strong language about the Jews being chicken-hearted. I got my lesson. He asked me—he was a stranger to me—"Madam, how many pogroms have you been through?" Of course I said, none. Answer: "I have been through twelve." Do you understand that I was silenced?

All week the news came in of outbreaks in the Jewish villages against the Jews, some of them disastrous.[5] Even

---

[5] Petach Tikvah was attacked by thousands of armed peasants; Kfar Saba was destroyed, and Hedera and Rehobot badly damaged. The most conservative estimate of the total casualties in these May riots was 95 killed and 290 wounded.

peaceful Rehobot saw blood. But by then the Jewish young men had organized their self-defense, and they sold their lives dearly. In Jerusalem too there is a self-defense movement. And by the side of it almost paralysis.

Our friends wanted Sophie and me to go into town, to the Hotel de France, the home of the American nurses and doctors. We refused and persisted in our refusal even when there had been a disturbance in our neighborhood due to looters, who of course might have become murderers if there had not been the self-defense guards, who quickly secured help. We have been careful about getting home after dark—that is all. Our Arab next-door neighbor, on the second morning after the Jaffa outrage, came to our window with a bouquet of roses and said sadly: "Jaffa, Jaffa!"

Immigration has been stopped. It is said that 1800 men were on the way from various ports. They are being returned. The newspapers are censored. Their editorial pages are for the most part absolutely white. We don't understand. We didn't understand why the excesses broke out, we don't understand what the policy is now. The common impression is that the Arabs are armed. The Jews certainly are not. Do you see why I couldn't write to you? I feel utterly perplexed. I feel soiled.

Jerusalem, June 22, 1921

I am still paralyzed by events here. The political situation is worse than if the Balfour Declaration had never been heard of. We are told that Churchill endorsed the interpretation of the Balfour Declaration given by Sir Herbert Samuel on the King's birthday, on June 3, though only a few weeks earlier he had delivered a vigorous address to an Arab deputation which waited on him to secure the re-

pudiation of the Balfour Declaration from him. His address acknowledged the Declaration as the fundamental
principle of the mandate government. Its interpretation by
Sir Herbert nullifies it completely as a Jewish document.
Sir Herbert told me personally that unless he had spoken
and acted as he did, there would have been a massacre of
every Jew in the country. Thereby he acknowledged what
is known to be a fact, that all the Arabs are provided with
arms and ammunition, while every Jew who was found
with a revolver and using it in self-defense without a permit
was put under arrest.

This actually happened in Petach Tikvah, which was set
upon by an armed force of 4000 Arabs. The whole colony
would have been wiped out if a few of the Jews had not had
"concealed" weapons, and if by chance a Hindu regiment
had not been passing and come to the rescue of the attacked.
Sixty Arabs lost their lives and four Jews. On the persons
of the dead Arabs were found gauze bandages and other
material for binding wounds, leaving no doubt of their
complete preparation.

Meantime the judicial murdering has been going on at
the legal inquiries into the Jaffa excesses. I think I wrote to
you of the onslaught on the Immigrants' House by the
police, who had torn off their numbers from their breasts.
The Arab lawyers maintain that no evidence, clear and un-
mistakable, can be adduced against any individual police
officer. So they are going free. And yet 38 Jews were killed!
On the other hand, Sir Herbert, in his address, almost in
the same breath in which he adjured us not to prejudge the
Jaffa cases, himself put the blame on the Bolsheviki.[6] But

[6] For some years after the last World War it was a fashion on the
part of private individuals and governments to blame the "Bolsheviki"
for everything that menaced or perplexed them. There was only a
handful of communists in Palestine.

there are very, very few who honestly believe that their pressure or their parade had any real connection with the massacre.

The whole policy—stopping immigration, promising a representative assembly at this moment, apprehending the Bolsheviki, arresting the Jews who bore "concealed" arms and defended themselves, while the Arab assailants go scot free because no convincing evidence can be found against them—it is all a policy of cowardice. There isn't one of us who would not rather fall in a general massacre than be saved by such methods. Of course, I admit that Sir Herbert cannot say for me that I should prefer to be killed to being saved—by him. But he could have resigned.

And it isn't the Arabs! The agitators against Zionism among them are really few in number, plus a few Britishers, whose work and machinations are insidious. They are government employees, who to my thinking should have resigned their posts if they could not make up their minds to accept the Balfour Declaration as the fundamental principle of the mandate government. I have long felt, since last summer, that they were lying in wait to trip up the High Commissioner. Meantime they were instrumental in forming the Moslem-Christian Club, the combination that ran the infamous Haifa Congress at which probably the attack upon the Jews was planned—the same Haifa Congress which has now sent a mission to Europe to agitate against Zionism, and which has already formed branches in many European cities.

Did you notice that I wrote: "We are *told* that Churchill, etc."? We don't read it, for the Hebrew press is severely censored. Some days the editorial and no less the news columns are almost entirely white. The following, for example, has happened. The [Hebrew] editor wrote: "The following are comments in the Arab press on the situation in Jaffa," and all the rest was deleted. The Arabs were permitted to read the comments, the Jews not! Do you wonder that the Arab children in my neighborhood lie in wait and throw showers of stones after me as I pass? The gentle sheik next door to us, the one who brought us the bouquet of roses as a propitiatory offering, went to see their parents about it, and they have stopped. And do you wonder that the Jews are nervous and overwrought? Another outbreak is bound to come.

Of course, behind it all are two vital, dominating facts. The Jews have been recreant to their duty. They have not created the economic opportunities which would have satisfied the Jewish immigrant and the Arab inhabitant. The agitators might have produced the Jaffa excesses even if the Jews had brought work and money into the land, but they would have been of an entirely different character. They would have been localized. In many sections the lowest of the fellaheen refuse to join the effendis because they know that their well-being materially depends upon the proximity of the Jews.

The other vital fact is that we owe the Balfour Declaration to the sword. We'll never get away from that taint. The shadow of imperialism is upon us, and it is a pall. You may think that with such views I ought logically to renounce the Balfour Declaration altogether, in fact and in principle. I don't. Palestine is an empty land. The Jew need not and will not rob the handful of Arabs of their rights or their property. Palestine could be made a land of immigration for the Jews if the Christian and Moslem agitators were not thinking of their own advantage.

If our cause is just, wholly just and righteous, we are bound to find just and righteous and peaceful means of conciliation. We shall ally ourselves with the best of our Arab fellows, to cure what is diseased in us and in them. *Arukat bat ammi* and also *Arukat ha-goyim*—the healing of the daughter of our people and the healing of the nations! [7]

III

Once again Miss Szold was in full charge of the Medical Unit. The struggle against doctors as well as malaria, and a growing sense of victory over both, were the workaday background for kaleidoscopic glimpses of Palestinian life.

Jerusalem, July 13, 1921

In the stagnant East time flies faster than elsewhere. Yet there is more time. I almost have the 26 hours a day one always wishes for, because one sleeps less than elsewhere. My day extends from 4:30 in the morning until 12 at night, and I am kept busy all the hours inbetweentimes. I am actually at the office, or at least at work, from 7:30 until 6:30.

The past week was spent partly in an interesting mission to Jaffa and Rehobot to interview the new candidates for our Nurses' Training School. We have had only 135 applicants. Miss Kaplan, the supervising nurse, and myself are now going to different parts of the country, and are having the applicants come to us at given convenient centers. We are trying to raise the standard, both in respect to general education and Hebrew knowledge. That makes the list melt away like snow under sunshine. I liked meeting the young women. Such broken lives as theirs already are. In almost all cases their education shows serious flaws on account of the war.

---

[7] This final paragraph is taken from *Familiar Letters from Palestine* (No. 4, May 3, 1921), lengthy accounts written from time to time for publication by Hadassah.

Jerusalem, July 31, 1921

I am writing on the eve of the anniversary of Papa's death. Nineteen years ago!—over half a generation. It is hard to believe. Out here my recollection of him, his views, and his attitude toward all sorts of questions has become more vivid rather than less. As problem after problem comes up —and life here bristles with them—I involuntarily ask myself how he would have met them; he seems to me a modern of moderns. At all events, summoning back to my mind his way of dealing with social human perplexities helps me to serenity better than anything else.

One problem I have solved: I am not going to the Zionist Congress at Carlsbad. With most forces arrayed against me, and with logic, at least abstract logic (not the logic of Palestinian events) on their side, I should be a dear little old lady—so devoted! so idealistic!—come to plead for a cause to which she has devoted so many years of her life. Poor dear! It's a shame, they'd say, but there is nothing else to do—she must be swept aside. The Medical Unit must be swallowed up by the Keren Hayesod; [8] and the organization Hadassah in America, the best-disciplined and most-competent Zionist body, must be fitted into the same Procrustean bed. And there's an end on it.

So I am going to stay here and take Dr. Rubinow's place as the director of the Unit, while he gives figures and facts concerning medical work at Carlsbad. I do not look forward to the task blithely. Last summer I was the fool that rushed in; this year, I may not be an angel, but I am at least wise enough to know that I ought to fear to tread. One satisfaction I have enjoyed. The other day the executive committee of the Hadassah doctors' association had a meeting

---

[8] The Palestine Foundation Fund for colonization, collected and administered by the Zionist Organization.

for the purpose of discussing the medical situation with reference to the Carlsbad Congress. They invited me to be present. They wanted to memorialize the Congress to let Hadassah exist! *That*—after two years' agitation against the separate status of Hadassah and constant insistence that the medical work must come under the central Zionist political body.

In two weeks it will be three years that the Unit arrived in Palestine. I expect to have a moonlight garden party in our lovely garden—never lovelier than under moonlight— to celebrate the anniversary.

The Christians are much slower than the Arabs themselves to recognize the folly of the May riots. A considerable portion of the Arab press has already begun to denounce the agitators who are responsible for them. These writers deprecate the sending of Arab delegates to England by the so-called Moslem-Christian Committee which organized the notorious Haifa Congress, the real author of the whole mischief. I believe even the High Commissioner [Samuel] is beginning to understand that he was fooled by his Christian-British advisers. Meantime the Hebrew papers continue to wear the appearance of the copy I mailed to you—ghastly white. The censor is still as active as ever, and the bars are still down against the immigrants.

However, if the *Nation* tells the truth, your American world is as queer as our Kiplingesque world.

Jerusalem, August 4, 1921

I had lunch a few days ago with Governor Storrs—Ronald Storrs, a typical "younger son" of the English novel.[9] He is said to be Sir Herbert Samuel's evil genius, the one who

---

[9] Sir Ronald Storrs was governor of Jerusalem.

inspired the policy of mistrust and deference to Arab wishes. He is a dilettante—littérateur, archaeologist, excellent music critic, above all he handles the English language as a virtuoso does his fondled instrument. He knows personally all the prominent men and women, and their descent, and their expectations upon peerages, etc. My head whirled— my poor democratic, uncolonial head, which never was good on genealogies.

And he despises the Jews. They are materialists. Else why don't they now come crowding into Palestine, no matter at what cost, no matter if the mandate has not yet been given, no matter if they run the risk of butchery by the Arabs, no matter if he, Mr. Ronald Storrs, insults them through the censorship he orders? The pioneers? Oh! that is Zionism for the poor brother Jew. The Jewish government employ- ees, that is not pioneering. And so on and on. The dilettante idealist's demands, as he sits on soft Oriental cushions and looks upon brasses and rugs and rich hangings gathered in all parts of the East. The truth of the matter is that the Jew is not a "native"; the Arab is. Kiplingesque!

Nevertheless, I forced him to have a kosher lunch for me.

Jerusalem, August 18, 1921

The most recent American mail has brought me letters, documents, newspaper clippings, that have made my hair stand on end. Hadassah, of course, the well-disciplined re- sult of ten years' work, is disrupted. Whatever happens, the achievements of the Unit cannot be gainsaid. They speak for themselves. I fully expect to hear its former detractors, once they have divided the spoils among themselves, boast of its efficiency—boast that never before, in any country, except in wartime, has such a complete and extensive medical establishment been erected in three years, raising the standard of medical work from practically nil to the American height. If only they don't completely destroy that Nurses' Training School for which we all have sweated and bled. Whatever else they destroy will recover after the lapse of years. But the Training School is something they don't understand. It is thoroughly American and therefore at once incomprehensible and reprehensible to the Russian-Jewish mind.

The thing that matters most, that hurts most, is the disruption of Hadassah. They have been writing to me that things would not have come to such a pass if I had been in America. I don't believe it. No one person could have prevented what happened. I can't enter into an analysis of all the forces which at this distance I see at work—foiled personal ambition, foolish doctrinairism, ignorance of what good organization means, love of a political game, lack of respect for patient, loving work. I am heart-sick.

Nevertheless, I issued 162 invitations to the Unit employees—doctors, nurses, druggists, clerks, chauffeurs, etc., in Jerusalem—to celebrate the third anniversary of the Hadassah Unit's arrival in Palestine. If I had invited all the lesser employees it would have made a party of 275—they and their wives or husbands, as the case might be. The moonlit garden would have held the larger party easily. It was a question of punch-glasses, ladles, and chairs. It was a lovely party. The pupil nurses were there almost in complete force, and their spirit was beautiful. I believe I have won them over—not on account of the party, but the party showed I had conquered. Six months ago they wouldn't have come to any party of mine or any other person in authority. . . . We had music too. Some twanging thin mandolins from the Blind Asylum, three selections by an

almost real violinist, and, best of all, singing by the pupil
nurses. *And* we had the Palestinian moonlight!

Jerusalem, September 2, 1921

Dr. Rubinow, when he left for the Congress, had been
at it not quite nine months since his long vacation in
America, and he was almost in a state of collapse. He welcomed the Congress as the opportunity of escape from the
Unit, though he was probably flying into the arms of unknown ills.

For my case the Unit duties are augmented by those which
have accumulated on my individual shoulders during the
year, inside and outside the Unit. The most difficult aspect
remains the unorganizability of the physicians. Their utter
medievalism is beyond belief. The question of precedence
in rank absorbs their whole thought. Ten days ago, I had
to be fetched out of a meeting of ladies, not connected with
the Unit, to settle a quarrel between two doctors who had
been charged with submitting a report on their respective
departments in the school hygiene work. Naturally the report was to have some sort of unified form. It took me three
hours to compose the differences. Meantime I, who had had
no lunch on account of press of business, kept Sophie waiting for supper until all hours. The two doctors are now
mortal enemies, and the report is in such shape that it cannot be sent to the Public Health Department. A pity, too,
because we have done admirable work in the schools, far
beyond anything the government attempts in its schools.

On the way back—a glorious ride—our Ford suddenly
became as medieval and unorganized as the doctors, and
I had to walk toward Jerusalem—please remember, one
always walks *up* to Jerusalem—until an Arab auto picked
me up.

Mencken's article was a joy—a delicious walk through Maryland woods. If I rave about the beauty of "us here," that does not mean that I do not love, still love, my Maryland. There is nothing like it.

Jerusalem, September 17, 1921

If I am needed here, I'd rather stay my self-assigned term out, and then go home for good; but home I must go, if not now, then in the not too distant future. And spry as I am, I am not going to forgo the privileges of sixty-one. Adele thinks I never tasted all the privileges of youth. I don't intend to waste the opportunities of old age similarly. For a week I have been plucking daisy petals, figuratively speaking: should I, should I not? Tomorrow I decide. Otherwise I may not be able to secure visas and a place on the steamer to Trieste. I'll go across the Continent to Cherbourg and thence home.

I speak of myself as spry. What do you think of my going on a donkey ride of two hours one way and nearly three hours back? We left, a cavalcade of twelve, all on donkeys, large ones and small ones, at about five-thirty, for Nebi Samuel, an Arab village on the top of one of the high hills, the reputed burial place of the Prophet Samuel.

The whole road from Jerusalem to the village—it isn't a road at all—it isn't even a path—nobody but a wise, patient donkey could find a foothold among the rolling stones—goes up and up, through the silent Judean country. The sun was well down on the horizon when we started; and for an hour we could watch, as we jogged along, the melting of a brilliant day into a moonlit night. Arrived at the top we had supper and returned through the magic moonlight to Jerusalem, reaching home at half-past midnight.

The next morning I was at my desk at seven, while my

"young" companions hobbled to the hospital at nine for their day's work. They all asked with a peculiar smile after my comfort, and I think were distinctly disappointed when, in comparing notes, they found themselves a good deal worse off as to soreness and stiffness than I was. But I must admit I found the long ride a little hard on my nerves. The tension was too great. It's the way to get acquainted with the Palestinian country.

I had another diversion this week, and it was a real joy. Our first girl at the Nurses' Training School completed her three years' service. Before she left the institution her companions gave her a farewell party. All the way through, it was a demonstration of my having won out with the girls. I made my first impromptu speech in Hebrew, rather haltingly, but I managed to get a few ideas into Hebrew form. Simultaneously the cable arrived from Carlsbad with the announcement that the Unit had been definitely given over to the World Organization. I keep wondering whether by staying here I could save it. It is our realest achievement, a real boon to an immigrant country. And it has a future and I am at least *persona grata*. It's galling. I wish somebody would not only tell me what to do but command me to do it.

Jerusalem, October 7, 1921

I can give you no idea of the bigness of the Unit work in the field and in the office—actually and administratively. For the administration of the work we have an inadequate personnel, inadequate in number and in efficiency. The result is that everyone in the head office must work at a constant high pressure. Please picture me sitting from morning until night inside of a mountain of letters and notes which I myself create. I cast them out faster than they can be picked up and executed and carried to their destination. For one removed, I vomit forth a dozen.

But I'd rather tell you of my days away from the office. There were nine of them, during a tour of inspection through Upper and Lower Galilee. I touched at thirty-one points in which the Unit has some interest, either a doctor, or a nurse, or a sanitary inspector. That gives you an idea of the extent of our undertaking. I hasten to admit that it is not so intensive as extensive. I have been oscillating between these two poles, without being able to decide which should have been sacrificed to which. We cannot have both without a budget out of all proportion to the financial powers of the Zionist world. What the extent of our work should indicate to you is that the criticism made against it very freely before the Congress at Carlsbad, that we are doing nothing for the halutzim and workingmen in general, the "productive" Jewish population, is false. Most of the thirty-one points are camps, workingmen's groups, colonies, etc.

Some of our critics went to the Congress with the intention of proposing that our hospitals be given up and all our available funds be devoted to the immigrants, the proper charge of the Zionist Organization. There is logic in this contention. Indeed, from my point of view, which is that everything of a public character ought to be thrown on the shoulders of the mandate government, the Medical Unit ought to cease to exist. Unless we make the government concern itself with us, it will never be our government in any sense of the word. The Zionist Organization pledged itself to take care of every immigrant for one year after his arrival. This, then, should be the extent of its medical task —logically.

But the course of Zionist development has not been any

more logical than the rest of life has the habit of being. By
force of circumstances, the Zionists have evolved a medical
service which has served, and for some time to come will
continue to serve, as a standard to the government itself.
The government establishments cannot compare with ours.
And Jews being Jews, with a very proper regard for their
bodies, must have a better service than the Palestinian government can now give them. Then it is folly to think of
abridging the Unit work—or to think of caring for the
immigrant at the front without good, modern hospitals
behind the lines. I should urge the Zionist Organization
to make one magnificent effort and secure a great sanitary
fund. The malaria-sanitary problem in Palestine is so well
defined that it can be solved without residue in a short time
and with not too much money.

First I'd like to tell you more about my trip, especially
about the malaria-sanitary work, which, in a way, is the
best we are doing. Most interesting of all is the anti-malaria
experiment carried on since last March, by means of a
fund of $10,000, the special gift for the purpose made by
Mr. [Louis D.] Brandeis. The settlements at the north and
south end of the Sea of Tiberias were chosen as the scene
of the experiment. They comprise some of the well-known
pest-holes of malaria. At Migdal Farm, for instance, a para-
dise—oranges, lemons, palms, bananas, almonds, and what
not—with the anopheles mosquito playing the part of serpent—there were seventy-eight victims of malaria last summer, out of a possible eighty employees and laborers. You
must consider what that means—on the average two attacks a season for each victim. Can you calculate the economic loss? This summer, so far—the malaria season ends
only in December—the record is reversed: only two cases
of malaria! In the whole region, comprising a population

of about 1000 to 1200, there have been only five cases of malaria.

The results are all the more interesting because part of the population is shifting. It includes two road-builders' camps to which new forces from malaria-ridden sections are constantly being brought, and also it includes a few Arab villages which have been treated along with the Jewish settlements. The whole paraphernalia developed in Panama and Arkansas, etc., has been applied: petrolization of swamps, canalization and regulation, treatment of carriers, quinine prophylaxis under strict supervision, mosquito-nets, clearing of grassy spots that serve as breeding-places, etc. There is a microscopist on the spot, the doctors are enlisted for the therapeutic treatment, and a small corps of sanitary inspectors watch the swamps, execute the works, administer the quinine, look out for dripping faucets, etc. Result: the men sleep in the open, without nets, and remain unstung! It is a miracle.

When the money arrived in the spring for the purpose, we called a little conference of the physicians who had been in the country for more years than our Unit and who consider themselves malaria experts. The conference was to work out a plan of prevention within the limits of the budget. The best known among the physicians was rather contemptuous when he heard that the conference was expected to plan on a $10,000 basis. The Palestinians are very magnificent in their notions. Six ciphers is the minimum they are willing to manipulate with, especially when malaria is to be handled.

The experiment has proved conclusively that for three-fourths of Palestine the malaria problem is not a million-dollar engineering enterprise at all. In all but a few remote spots, it is a "thou-art-the-man" problem. The individual or rather the community of individuals can grapple with it. To be sure, there must be supervision, propaganda, education. I wish I could find time to write to Mr. Brandeis and give him a description of what has been done with his $10,000—which, by the way, has not been used up by a long shot.

It is such a pity I haven't time to keep in touch by correspondence with people in America. I have much material stored up, some of which would stimulate the interest of certain groups, and some of other groups. Do you know that in addition to the snug sum I carried with me from friends in America when I came here—it amounted to about $1300 —to be applied as I saw fit, I have received $4150 since I am here for all sorts of purposes, named and to be named by me? Most of the sums came in response to letters of mine containing a bit of description of something or other out here. I never asked for money, never even thought of it. Isn't it a pity that I always get entangled in a multitude of administrative details?

You asked whether I have made friends with any of the Arab neighbors. Alas! the language difficulty. Three or four months ago a huge family took possession of the home next to us, which the head of the household has been building who knows how long. Since we have been here he has been working assiduously, but practically single-handed, laying stone upon stone, patiently. The whole harem down to the third generation visited us time and again. We—that is, Sophia—talked to them with the aid of the glossary in Baedeker. Sophia has some Arabic from her Red Cross days here. The trouble began when they talked back. Baedeker does not provide for the second half of the conversation. A week ago they invited us to a betrothal party. I am charitable to surmise that the men's part was interesting. In the women's apartment it was deadly dull. My only emotion was aroused by the sight of the sick babies nursing at their mothers' breasts—eternally. I wanted to pick them up— oh, but they were so dirty!—and carry them to my hospital.

I V

On the second of November the Arabs went on the war-path again. The accumulation of realities led Miss Szold to make penetrating observations not only on British politics and officialdom and on the state of the world at large, but on the "secret" of her personal position as well.

[TO MRS. EMIL WEINHEIM]

Jerusalem, November 9, 1921

I want sympathy too—not for myself personally, for in spite of constant, unremitting hard work, I keep perfectly well—but for the Jews here and for the Unit. And yet, when I come to think carefully, I am wrong to claim sympathy for the Jews on account of the excesses we have just passed through in Jerusalem—the occasion or pretext having been Balfour Day.

When the balance is carefully calculated, we have more to record on the credit than on the debit side. Five killed outright and some twenty wounded is bad enough, not to mention the excitement and all the other concomitants of a riot. But the Jews have nevertheless come out triumphant. They have behaved beautifully. They defended themselves, but even in their righteous indignation they did not indulge in vengefulness. They obeyed orders. They never gave the slightest occasion for a demonstration against them. The funeral of the victims was held under such conditions that it would have been almost natural for them to go beyond bounds. But the funeral turned out to be a most remarkable display of self-control.

Above all, the Jews have come out boldly and demanded the removal of the official who showed his incompetence in not meeting a situation for which he had every reason to be prepared. Governor Storrs has been reputed an adversary of the Jews and of the policies involved in the Balfour Declaration. But the indictment against him on the part of the Jews is [that of] sheer incompetence. The case against him is to my mind proved. Nevertheless, in spite of the popular clamor, I am persuaded he will remain. However, the moral effect of the Jewish denunciation of his course of conduct has been tonic.

Jerusalem, December 3, 1921

One of Adele's letters relates the gist of Mrs. [Rose] Jacobs's interview with Mr. Brandeis concerning my return to America, and the flattering things he said about me. Here is the whole secret of my success here. It is not character, it is not wisdom, it is nothing more nor less than the fact that my monthly check comes to me from no one knows where. The important point is that, so far as everybody here knows, it does not imply a subtraction from any fund collected for Palestinian purposes or invested in a Palestinian undertaking.

Do not jump to the conclusion that "colonial" life has made a cynic of me. But I may say that I have never before witnessed the economic struggle in its nakedness as here. The more idealistic men are in profession (in all sincerity), the more realistic is their rivalry in their chase after necessaries and luxuries. Now, here am I, one person who can stand by quietly and without envy while all the rest crowd and jostle each other.

I repeat I am not a cynic. I am simply an observer and a recorder in this instance. I am not a saint, I *am* an American; and there is no reason for excepting me when American characteristics are censured. I can simply afford not to enter the competition. To the outsider it seems or it may seem that my withdrawal from the conflict is self-abnegation; in point of fact, it is luck, chance. I might be as devoted as I am to my task; but if the doing of it granted me a salary, my devotion would at best go unnoted and at worst might be interpreted as a trick to ingratiate myself with my employers. I don't deny that I have some character. But I don't deserve what Mrs. Jacobs and Mr. Brandeis say about me in comparison with others.

I wouldn't have dwelt at such length upon this personal matter if it had not occurred to me that my estimate of it is the best way of conveying the quality of life here. I must have made many attempts to do it before. I don't know whether I ever succeeded in making you understand the mixture of idealism and materialism which, to my mind, is the chief characteristic of Palestine life—of Jewish Palestine life. So far as I have the opportunity of judging, British life is compounded wholly of materialism.

The British officials, I fancy, would hardly deny that they are here for a career. And as for the Arabs, they hardly know what public spirit means. Zionism has opened political vistas to them. Their political aspirations are the only manifestations of public spirit which I have noted. They have no voluntary associations of any kind for public purposes —no libraries, no hospitals, no schools of their own that amount to anything. They have only clubs, which, ostensibly social, serve political ends.

Jerusalem, December 3, 1921

The second of November excitement has not yet sub-
sided. The trials of the offenders and supposed offenders are
going on. The legal point is that bomb-throwing [on the
part of Jewish defenders] is not self-defense. My mind works
twistedly on the business of bomb-throwing. I consider it
the finest form of preparation for self-defense—the form
least likely to lead to indulgence in assaults. Granted, as the
government has demonstrated in Jerusalem in 1920 and in
Jaffa in 1921, that it cannot protect the Jewish community,
and the Jews must stand for their own lives—then preparing
a bomb is safer than constantly carrying firearms and concealed knives, which may be plucked out of inside pockets
on the slightest provocation. Bombs are not carried around;
they are kept at strategic points.

Last night we were making a catalogue of nasty conflicts
throughout the world: Ireland, India, Egypt, Galicia, An-
gora, the Ukraine, and I can't remember all the other places.
We had to come to the conclusion that Palestine is perhaps
the peacefullest of all. Does the second of November loom
so large in our eyes because we are in Palestine, or is there
something particularly tragic in the circumstances that the
Jews thought they were coming home to security—and
leaving persecution outside?

CHAPTER ELEVEN

A Year of Troubles and Tourists

I

THE post-war depression in America threatened to snuff out the Medical Unit. While Miss Szold sat tight, wondering what would happen next, she ruminated on the topsy-turviness of the world and she detected signs of an approach to "normalcy" in Palestine.

Jerusalem, January 11, 1922

At present the Medical Unit is again hanging in the balance. That means primarily that we are not getting our budget money regularly or fully. Daily Dr. Rubinow and I ask each other: what are we going to do? I am in mortal terror that Dr. Rubinow is going to throw up the job and leave me to grapple with the problems of the break-up. So I ask myself day in and day out: will the Unit live, will it die? As soon as that question is settled, and no matter which way it is settled, I shall begin to make my preparations for homegoing.

It's time for me to be going back, spiritually and physically. I want to get back to you all, I need the atmosphere in which I am taken for granted among those whom I take for granted. And I am in tatters! You will remember that I equipped myself at a time when everything was frightfully expensive, and as shabby in quality as it was expensive in price. Sometimes, lately, I have given my imagination freedom to shape my life when I get home. What am I going to do? How am I going to live?

Jerusalem, January 23, 1922

Only one assertion: it was not due to forgetfulness that you didn't get your birthday letter in time. I am sensitive on that point. Forgetfulness would be a reflection on my age, and the older I get the less do I want to be old. There is so much to be done in this topsy-turvy world of ours that I want to be doing. Especially here in Palestine the young have so many chances to show their prowess and will that I envy them. I'd like to start out upon life this moment. Of course, I'd want to make the condition that I must not give up my memory of all that happened to me in my first life. I wouldn't have a second chance if I were not permitted to remember.

One of my friends has been keeping me supplied with copies of the New York *Times* lately. That keeps me in touch with America's peculiar topsy-turviness. If I were there, I suppose I should be just as eager to be young all over again and try my hand at getting things to run as they should —or as I think they should. Probably there is a great difference between the two ideas.

The idea of being in America is not a stranger to my mind these days. If I had only a mind, or if I had a mind without a conscience, I'd be there in less time than it takes to say Jack Robinson.

But there is that conscience to be reckoned with. That conscience insists that I stay here until things are settled.

[TO THOMAS SELTZER]   *Jerusalem, January 25, 1922*

The world we are living in *is* wretched beyond anything my imagination, nurtured in a mid-Victorian atmosphere, could have conceived of in the idyllic days before the war. So far as I can make out, the war has produced only one of the many beneficent results attributed to it by our whatever-is-is-right optimists: a very much larger circle of men and women than ever before is thinking thoughts that may bear acts in the generations to come. Do not conclude that this result justifies the war in my eyes or even makes the thought of it bearable. As the days of peace multiply I learn to hate its memory more and more. For the very minds which it has stimulated to think, it has at the same time crippled in other respects. The flotsam and jetsam of East European Jewry which is washed up on these Palestinian shores is my argument and evidence. Doubtless by the same token my own mind is lame and halt. Sometimes when I sit at the office trying to meet problem after problem, little personal problems all of them, I feel as though I had abandoned every central, unifying principle of true living on which I formerly prided myself, either as a heritage or as the outcome of my own feeble grappling with the problems of life.

I might, however, give some joy to you, even from this distance, if I could put into words the beauty of these winter days in Palestine, when nature celebrates its springtime, all the more surprising because of its long repression. Here there is seven months of dryness against five months of juicy revival. I don't mean to imply that the dry months are without beauty. It's a sterner sort of beauty. Now the insistent rocks are clothed with green and soon they will be wreathed with color. In the dry season, one thinks of Elijah and Job and Amos. Now it is Ruth as Botticelli might have painted her, and the Psalmist in his non-militant mood, and a little bit Jeremiah at his tenderest.

The economic situation here is not rosy. And yet I must admit that day by day life grows closer to normality. Daily, settlers are coming in with capital and experience and the good-will that belongs of right to their Zionist idealism. Of course, long ago all ideas of a centralized doctrinaire development according to the Pittsburgh Program have been abandoned. I am in the unhappy position of being able to say: "I told you so!" Between the Balfour Declaration date and the formulation of the mandate, I repeated and repeated the admonition to get the Pittsburgh Program economic system into the mandate. Meantime, the mandate has not been endorsed and the "colonials" have had their chance to put their dirty paws all over the paper. And "colonials" are Jewish as well as British.

II

American sight-seers began their post-war invasion of the Old World, and Palestine became an imperative three-day diversion for every purchaser of a Mediterranean tour.

Meanwhile, in July, the League of Nations ratified the British mandate for Palestine. The British government adopted as its Palestinian policy the principles formulated in the Churchill White Paper, the nub of which was that the terms of the Balfour Declaration "do not contemplate that Palestine as a whole should be converted into a Jewish national home, but that such a home should be founded *in* Palestine." The immigration policy set forth in the White Paper made it clear that even this home would be created only if room could be found for it without disturbing any of the inhabitants of the land.

Miss Szold's letters at this period deal with the tourists and the mandate.

Jerusalem, March 2, 1922

When I was held up in Naples on my way to Palestine and saw the flunkyism produced by tourists, I feared for Palestine. And now I am a flunky myself. There are only

two days of the week on which I can call my soul my own
—Tuesday and Wednesday. By Tuesday the tourists of the
previous Thursday must hurry off to catch the boat at Alexandria; by Thursday the new consignment is in. I shouldn't
mind showing around those who bring letters of introduction to me, if only they didn't know more about the Arab,
Jewish, and British question, and about the possibilities of
the land and its products and needs, on the second day than
I know after two years of aching head and heart.

This afternoon I had a funny experience with a couple
from Cleveland, owning to about one hundred and twenty
years between them. They came with Clarke's Tour, six
hundred strong. My couple might have belonged to that
Oheb Shalom Congregation in Baltimore in Papa's time—
stodgy and stolid, wondering what ever did make them take
the hard trip to Palestine. They wanted to know where—
they are living in a Catholic hospice—they could get a
good Jewish meal. Not that they cared about kosher; they
were beyond that. But they wanted to taste Jewish food in
Jerusalem. And they wanted me to know—especially the
man did—that they were not orthodox and had nothing to
do with Zionism. And what was the language I spoke? Hebrew? Why, he didn't know any Hebrew but *Shema Yisroel!*
And when his wife remonstrated, he asked her what was the
good of lying about it. Whereupon she meekly admitted
that in Cleveland they spoke only English—sometimes a
little German. The last shot was: "What can you show us
tonight after six?" I vowed there was nothing to be seen in
Jerusalem after dark. Which they found so different from
Constantinople; there, life began at night.

The Adolph Ochses were here. Immediately upon their
arrival they put themselves in touch with me. Only I was

away in Jaffa (such anemones as starred the whole road!)
interviewing candidates for the Nurses' Training School.
On my return they came at once to see me at my office. Mr.
Ochs met me with the poser: "When did we see each other
last?" I didn't confess to him that I had no recollection of
our having met before. But he was right. As soon as he mentioned the time, I remembered vividly every incident connected with his and his bride's visit to our house in Baltimore on their wedding trip. One of the few days he spent
in Jerusalem happened to be the anniversary of their wedding day, which they celebrated by giving me a check for
$1000 for a supplementary X-ray apparatus for therapeutic
purposes, in memory of Isaac M. Wise of Cincinnati, Mrs.
Ochs's father. Another impossible combination—Cincinnati, Jerusalem, Isaac M. Wise. But Mr. Ochs made the
impossible possible, for one of his chief topics of conversation was whether a reform synagogue with pews, organ,
mixed choir, *and* English prayers and services minus hats
could be developed in Jerusalem! He is going back as unregenerate an anti-Zionist as when he came, but deeply
interested in spite of himself. His chief concern was to know
whether we realized the danger we were in from the Arabs.

The Arabs, indeed, are most active at this tourist season.
They are distributing propaganda literature on the "Zionist
Aggression" among the American travelers. And the Christians are helping them efficiently. The Christians! There
are some here who are reputed not to be missionaries. I have
been sitting on all sorts of boards and committees with them
since I have been here. Recently the fiat has gone forth that
I am to be boycotted! I am somewhat in the position of
Alice Seligsberg, against whom Mrs. Z. warned some of her
friends with the caution: "She is too intelligent."

Jerusalem, March 24, 1922

I should tell you of the dinner at Norman Bentwich's to which I was invited to meet Lord and Lady Milner. I want to tell you about it because in a way it was a repetition of my experience in meeting Ramsay MacDonald. Again an English gentleman (again I sat next to the guest of the evening) with manner, diction, and convictions, coupled with the frank open-mindedness that banishes every vestige of self-consciousness from conversation.

Like Ramsay MacDonald, Lord Milner is most sympathetic with the Zionist undertaking. And he understands its inwardness and its difficulties. Above all he realizes the character of the Arab relations to the Jews. To me it seemed that, in spite of his administrative past, his attitude was untinged by the colonial-mindedness which offends me in Governor Storrs and the other British officials in Palestine. Lady Milner, whose first husband was Edward Cecil, is as sympathetic and open-minded as Lord Milner.

Lord Milner and Ramsay MacDonald are in one class of tourists. Those who came with Cook, Clarke, the American Express Company, or Raymond-Whitcomb are in another class. The second class are to be blamed for my neglect of you all these weeks. Scores have come with letters of introduction to me, scores without such open-sesames. I have felt sorry for and mad at all of them alike. They allot three days for the whole of Palestine and then weep because they haven't seen anything but churches and Holy Places. Those whom we have succeeded in detaching from their Arab guides have been profuse in enthusiasm and gratitude. At least they are not going back with completely but immaturely made-up minds on all our problems. I can't recall how much I have written to you about the Jewish unpreparedness for tourists and of the well-prepared discrimination against Jewish shopkeepers, carriage drivers, and guides, not to mention sites, sights, and institutions.

Jerusalem, July 1, 1922

The Arabs are making great preparations—so the rumors flying thick and fast say—for demonstrations at the time of the discussion of the mandate at the League of Nations. There are two days of voting, a general strike, all shops closed—and when shops are closed there is no telling what mischief will be found for the idle hands. I feel no personal fear, but in the light of my personal experiences with such men as Keith Roach [1] and Governor Storrs, my eighteenth-century-rights-of-man soul is in revolt. You have no idea how we are hated and how baselessly. If you were to see, as I have just seen at Haifa, a campful of Ukrainian refugees, helpless, degraded, hungry, you'd know how baselessly. And I come home from Haifa, open the *Nation*, and read the attitude of Harvard toward Jewish students. America and Harvard, exactly like Hungary and Palestine?

The next two weeks will be decisive, I fancy. I have already heard that the mandate will be emasculated, so far as the Jews are concerned. The British government has adopted Sir Herbert Samuel's notorious June 3 speech as its policy. That speech "interprets" the Balfour Declaration— away. And if the Balfour Declaration had been carried out, it simply would not have been an injustice to the Arabs. I took the trip to Haifa in an auto—it took five hours and a half. For five hours and a half we flew through an empty, deserted country. What harm to the Arabs if Jews develop it?

[1] Assistant to the Civil Secretary.

Jerusalem, July 22, 1922

Our maid and two of her companions have just burst in with the news that the mandate (all except Article 14 concerning the Holy Places) had been signed. They report great excitement among the Jews—the more fools they for betraying joy. All the more as the signing of the mandate has no immediate significance. Here and there it may encourage a well-to-do Jew to risk his life and property and establish himself here. It enables the Palestine government to launch a loan, which, if successful, will stifle the complaint of the British "taxpayers." The fact of the matter is that the Jews haven't even the ghost of a chance at political power. So far as I can see, the mandate makes Palestine more "colonial" than it was, and a still snugger berth for the British "careerist." The Jew, I am still confident, will win out in the end, but the end is far off. Far off is to be measured by generations, not years.

Jerusalem, July 29, 1922

My object in going to Haifa was to help in the organization of a Women's Society for public welfare work.[2]

It is just two years ago that I attempted to form such a society in Jerusalem. It has been uphill work, but we have arrived—not yet at the very top. But when I remember our early meetings, the Babel that was supposed to be a discussion of purpose and method, and contrast with it the parliamentary order that prevailed at the last public meeting with one hundred in attendance, I consider myself justified in making a similar attempt at Haifa and next week at Jaffa.

My intensest struggle was to get it out of the heads of the

---

[2] Miss Szold is already envisaging a country-wide system of social service; eight years later she will begin to make it her major business.

members that I was going to secure the money for the work from America. I insisted that I would have nothing to do with the organization unless the members themselves raised the money among themselves and unless they contented themselves with doing what they could pay for. The result is a society of 575 members, with receipts now amounting to £26 a month from the membership and the work being done by four sub-committees, whose records are modern to the last dot.

My triumph is that I do nothing—the committee must do everything, under my direction. But it's been like holding in wild horses. They have wanted to jump when they did not know how to crawl. And the chief lesson I have carried home is a co-operation with the agencies that actually exist. The spirit of rivalry has given way, I think permanently, to the spirit of friendly co-operation. Whether the two long-distance experiments in Haifa and Jaffa will succeed, I can't prophesy. It is interesting that the women of these two cities, having heard about the Jerusalem society, have asked me to come and help them do likewise.

[TO JESSIE SAMPTER]   *Jerusalem, July 29, 1922*

If the Palestine you knew when you left beckons to you to come back, the Palestine you'll find will give you comfort and satisfaction. In spite, or perhaps because, of the failure of America to provide the expected funds, life has become much more normal here. There has been an influx of settlers, most of the newcomers having come because members of their families were here. This in itself is normal, unstrained. Many of the others have learned to put behind them our surcharged, doctrinaire ideals. It is now understood that our overnight transformation of Palestine into the Utopia of the Zionist dreamer is a foolish expectation. We have armed ourselves with patience, which after all is more potent than the conjurer's swift tricks. With the growth in normal thought and action has come more gentleness and considerateness. I hasten to say that we are not yet angels, not yet even righteous and true; I still find many and many a reason for blazing indignation—you know my capacity for that.

The saner sobriety is illustrated by our conduct last week when the news of the ratification of the mandate was received. Such demonstrations of joy as we permitted ourselves were restrained. The most meticulous, fault-finding Arab nationalist could not have found anything objectionable in our expressions. To be sure, there was an inner reason for that as well as prudence. It is part of our more normal frame of mind that we recognize the close limitations of the mandate. Not to have secured it would have been a disaster. To have secured it gives us no advantage. Whatever is to be done, we, we alone, must do. No help is to be expected from anyone. The passage of the mandate will make Palestine more colonial and careerist than ever— that means, more selfishly British than ever. The Jew has an opportunity, provided he grasps it and grasps it hard.

You know probably that, upon orders from America, I go to the Carlsbad Conference.[8] I hope some sort of instructions will reach me, else I shall not know what my function will be there. Such a mess! All I want is to work quietly in Palestine or in America—yea, in the America of anti-Semitism. I cannot tell you how shocked I was at the Harvard revelations.

---

[8] The Carlsbad Conference was a *Jahres Conferenz,* that is, one of the bi-annual meetings of the central executive body held in the interval between the Zionist Congresses.

III

Miss Szold went to the Carlsbad Conference and proved to herself that she was a poor special-pleader. The Medical Unit's needs were desperate; and, contrary to a lifelong principle never to make a personal appeal for funds, she tried her hand at it in Paris with Baron Rothschild as her target—and tried in vain. Although her heart was set upon returning to America, she could not desert the Medical Unit in its direst hour.

[En route to Carlsbad], August 15, 1922

I may decide to take a look at Prague, and renew my impressions of thirty-nine (!) years ago. From there I shall go to Vienna for a two weeks' stay—one week for shopping and one week for family. I am really excited about getting back to a place in which "things" are to be had. Of course, I no sooner allow such a frivolous thought to pass through my mind than I have a correspondingly blacker vision of Vienna's plight. But you have no idea what it means, for instance, to be deprived of the possibility of getting shoe-laces for oxford ties for a period of twenty-seven months, when one is expected nevertheless to be civilized enough to wear oxfords instead of sandals or going barefoot.

If I am not prepared in the way of clothes for a day of Europe after a cycle of Cathay, what am I to say about my mind? I go to Carlsbad in obedience to a plea from America. But I don't know what I shall do there. Plead for more money, when there is less and less? Plead for the medical work in particular, when there are scant funds for education and colonization and immigration? I am still objective enough to see the whole of the Zionist undertaking. So I make a poor special-pleader. However, the Conference promises to be important. The question of the Jewish Agency is to come up—whether the Zionist Organization alone is to be the official representative of the Jewish people in matters Palestinian or whether it is to be expanded into a general Jewish representation.

The boat is full of Zionists returning home [to America] after a visit to Palestine, and I want to go with them. But the more ardent my longing to see you, the more clearly my conscience tells me that I have no right to desert at this time. Dr. Rubinow's resignation, the coming of a new man to take over his complex job, and the uncertainties of our budgeting future leave me no choice.

But it is the last emergency to which I shall allow my conscience to respond. After the new man is in his chair and has become acquainted with some of the ropes at least, I shall up and go. I ought to be home by the middle of September. Among the tourists on board are several Hadassah-ites, who corroborate the impression I have received from others that from the point of view of Hadassah, too, I might be usefully employed in America.

Carlsbad, August 27, 1922

I have traveled through a considerable portion of Europe, as you see by the dateline, and I have been charmed by all but man. . . .

The dejection of spirit as to the likelihood of our raising sufficient funds for Zionist purposes I have met here, and the consequent tendency to let things already established in Palestine slide, tumble, if they will, and turn to new projects in the hope that their novelty will stimulate the Zionist jaded forces—this makes me feel that I must not let go the Palestinian end until the new director is installed.

The likelihood is that even the Unit shall get only one-third of the needed moneys for the coming year. The sessions of the Conference have had a human interest, but Zionistically I am afraid we are simply marking time.

I wish I could carry my room and its furnishings with me. You have no idea how it affects me to find things being used for the purpose they were made for—no makeshifts. And so solid and beautiful. No chinks in the doors, locks tight, sufficient closet space, and all provisions for decency and cleanliness. I had forgotten what Western "bathroom civilization" is.

Max Löbl [4] did come to Carlsbad and we had an afternoon and evening together. I played hooky. I wonder whether you will find me aged as I found him. I warn you there are pathetic little puckers all around my lips, and my hearing is impaired, and I think a lot of my comfort, and my hair is whiter than it was—but I don't *feel* older.

The others [at the Conference] got vitally interested only when a political point came up. To me such questions seemed removed by an immeasurable distance from Palestine. The latest news is that there are again Arab outbreaks. They can be met not by politics, not even political thought, but by normal work and life. You see what an opportunist I have become. I feel as though I were—we all were—living in a sickroom in the after-the-war days. The only thing to do is to do. Rank materialism.

Paris, October 10, 1922

For five days now I have known that my trip to Paris is as futile as I had expected it to be, and still I am here. Baron Rothschild received me last Thursday in his *palais* or *hôtel*, in the rue du Faubourg Saint-Honoré. As one passes

---

[4] A European relative whom she had not seen in many years.

through the narrow, crowded street, lined with antique shops, dressmakers' establishments, and all sorts of less brilliant shops, one would never suspect that one is separated by only a few feet from a baronial residence, gardens, art treasures, and princely furnishings.

All the Baron needed to have done was to have waved his head nonchalantly toward one of the two paintings standing on easels in the salon in which the deaf old gentleman received me, and said: "There is a little thing of the school of Leonardo da Vinci (perhaps by the master himself)—take it," and the Unit's fortune would have been made. He didn't say it. On the contrary, my plea for the Unit gave him the opportunity for an assault upon American Jews in general and the Zionists in particular, who don't support even the little they start. My usual ability to see both sides made me a poor advocate. I could not but admit that it was impertinent of us to ask more of one who for forty years has steadily been executing a well-planned and expanding piece of work. And so we parted.

Don't infer from any expression I have used that the interview was in any way disagreeable or humiliating to me as a *schnorrer*.[5] He was every inch a gentleman in his manner toward me. A very presentable, attractive man, who bears his years beautifully. Even a little foppish in his exterior. It is difficult to gain access to his mind, he is so deep. This circumstance left me with an unfinished feeling. I am sure I did not reach him. I did not convey to him the peculiar situation the Unit is in. He was fulsome in his compliments upon the work we had done: the only Zionist work, etc. I have heard that too often now to be flattered. Fine words butter no parsnips and keep no hospitals going.

---

[5] Beggar.

One thing stuck in my mind—his advice to go to America. He was the last of a long series of advisers to say the same. Everybody, from Carlsbad through Berlin, Vienna, and Paris, has urged America upon me. As in the case of Rothschild, I have no faith that my going to America would produce results in clinking coin. The one result it *might* have would be to re-consolidate Hadassah and thus produce help for the future.

Paris, October 11, 1922

Immediately after I mailed my letter of yesterday to you, I received the cablegram from Dr. Rubinow which makes me turn my back on you and America. I think I wrote you that, in view of all that has happened to me in Europe, I cabled him for advice about going to America. Here is the reply:

"American trip desirable for Joint Distribution Committee negotiations, but you must return from America immediately unless my successor appointed. I cannot remain later than end of November. Zionist executive declines responsibility for Unit. Hadassah collections declining. London remittances uncertain. I cannot carry responsibility alone much longer. Ascertain American wishes."

I did not attempt to ascertain American wishes. In the first place, I know them—they want me to come to America. In the second place, I couldn't be back in Palestine by the end of November; and as for a successor, this is not the time to be choosing a successor in a hurry. If you read between the lines of the telegram as I do, you will know that a hopeless man indited it. And what sort of woman do you suppose is going back to Palestine to take hold—to take the helm of a sinking ship? Mr. Lipsky told me in Carlsbad that, if the

Palestinians had always spoken of the Unit work as they now do, there would not have been difficulty in collecting funds for it.

If you size up the situation at my end with any degree of precision, you will not be hard on me for not coming back now. Oh, dear, oh, dear, if you knew how hard it is on me not to go back!

By way of comforting myself, I ate a supper of brioches and roasted chestnuts in my room. And by way of penance for I don't know what, I now proceed to wash handkerchiefs. French laundresses are artists and must be paid like prima donnas, and colds consume handkerchiefs.

IV

For a third time she found herself in charge of the Medical Unit. It looked like the last time, for the Unit's days appeared to be nearing an end. Then a "miracle" happened.

S.S. Esperia, *October 22, 1922*

Somehow or other, or rather no way or other, I feel that I shall find some amelioration of conditions. Perhaps the Joint Distribution Committee has relented and will continue its subsidy another year. Perhaps a miracle has uncovered new resources for Hadassah to tap. Perhaps somebody has died and left his fortune for the upkeep of the medical work. So many things may have happened—or not. Curiously enough, it is home news that I am always least sanguine about. In anticipation I already feel the tremor running through me which always makes me hold a letter from one of you in my hand for a moment before I pluck up the courage to open it. You see, I am still as sentimental as before.

Well, one more confession. About the Unit I am cultivating optimism; about you I force myself to be calm—to pretend that I have no tremors, when I have heard nothing from you since August; but I have neither optimism nor calm to summon to my support when I think that Dr. Rubinow is going to leave Palestine in a short month from now; and that, it appears, the whole administration of the Unit will rest upon my shoulders. Admit: it is too much for a woman of my age and disposition to face. I am not ashamed to admit that I am a coward about it. Perhaps I may still have to do what I felt like doing in Paris—decamp to America and you.

Jerusalem, December 3, 1922

Two days ago Dr. Rubinow decided to take passage on a vessel leaving Jaffa on December 10. In seven days more I shall have to carry the Unit. The task seems insupportable. We are practically bankrupt. We have completely exhausted our credit. The Zionist Organization of America continues to send us cables bidding us not to lose courage. A cable today even says some hopeful words about Joint Distribution Committee possibilities. But can we hold on until the situation in America clears up? I cannot get it out of my head—we—that is, Hadassah here—shall be like the patient who dies after a successful operation. We have all but made up our minds that we must liquidate at once. But we haven't the money even to let go. We can't pay off salaries or tradesmen. It's appalling. And such a situation as once more I have to face with the doctors. Just as it was when I came out here two and a half years ago. They are out of bounds—at least their leaders are.

Jerusalem, December 2, 1922

I can't believe my record—that I haven't written to you for nearly four weeks. Probably it is correct, for during these four weeks Dr. Rubinow left. He fortunately could carry one bit of good news with him. By this time it has probably become known in America that Mr. Nathan Straus cabled me $20,000. In his message he said nothing about the use to which the princely sum was to be put. He simply said: "We have placed at your disposal for immediate use $20,000."

We are about £20,000 out. I know the agony of an honest bankruptcy. Hour by hour I sit in the office and count and calculate. To no purpose! I feel like a hunted animal. Can you imagine what Mr. Straus's generous cable meant? It may still save us—these $20,000 of his. If only we use them ourselves. The question is to pay salaries or to pay suppliers. Soon nobody will let us have drugs, bread, milk, and eggs on credit. And we can't even shut down any of our hospitals. Liquidation is more expensive than hanging on.

Besides Mr. Straus's cable, there is another ray of sunshine: Dr. Magnes. He has put himself entirely at my disposal. He is at the office daily, and with him I discuss every problem. He knows the Joint Distribution Committee inside out. He has a good head for figures and accounts. He has conceived for our work almost as much affection as we have ourselves. He is an excellent mediator.

Another ray of sunshine: the head office, the clerks, accountants, etc., are wonderfully loyal. They have rallied around me like an army devoted to its chiefs. And even a few of the doctors are coming out true blue in the crisis.

One of Rachel's wishes for me is: "I hope something pleasant will happen to make you happy on your birthday —a rich man leaving the million or so you need for the

Unit in his will." Mr. Straus's gift almost realizes the wish, doesn't it? At least in its unexpectedness, for I should tell you that it came wholly unsolicited. I had written the Strauses a long letter about the Unit—that events had proved me not a pessimist but a prophet: witness my interview with Baron Rothschild, which I described in detail.

My guess is that my letter produced the $20,000. At all events, I do know that I did not ask for the money; of this I can be sure, for I never do. I don't remember any more what *was* in the letter. If it really produced the result, I am sorry I haven't a copy of it. I'd like to try it on a few other millionaires.

CHAPTER TWELVE

A Commuting Executive

THE honeymoon with Palestine—for so those first fresh years must have seemed in retrospect—came abruptly to a close. In March 1923 Miss Szold received word that her sister Rachel (Mrs. Joseph Jastrow) was gravely ill. She returned at once to America. And then for eight years she commuted between the two lands—absorbed and as usual driven to the limits of her endurance by a succession of stupendous tasks. Personal griefs—the loss of Rachel in 1926 was the most poignant—added to her burden.

"I am so constituted," she wrote a friend at the beginning of this period of toil, "that I see no promise in any movement which is not built up slowly, bit by bit, each layer of stone and each trowelful of cement tested by every known principle of organization." Stone by stone she helped in the building of one structure after another. But none of them embodied a new creative phase in her life.

She presided over and advanced the growing fortunes of Hadassah for a number of years. Upon her return to America she had found it a sturdy body with 15,000 members, and by 1925 the number was nearly doubled. The old Zionist Medical Unit was transformed and enlarged into the Hadassah Medical Organization with an annual budget of about $500,000. In its behalf she made repeated trips to Palestine, and each time was amazed at the growth of the land and beset and worried by its problems. But all this was by then an old story. Moreover, her eventual withdrawal from the active direction of Hadassah meant that

under her inspiration and example new leaders had been
trained to carry on and carry even further the work she had
founded.

In 1927 she was elected one of the three members of the
Palestine Executive Committee of the World Zionist Organization—the first woman ever to serve in this capacity.
"I fought like a tigress," she said of her efforts to avoid the
office. "The most disconcerting feature," she felt, "is that
at this critical juncture the great Zionist movement had no
one else to turn to but a tired, worn-out old woman of sixty-
seven."

To serve as one of the three governors of all Zionist affairs in Palestine was indeed a new experience, but not one
calculated to give scope to her creative talents for organization. It meant—for two years—holding the fort against a
besieging army of difficulties: a severe economic crisis
largely due to a huge immigration; inadequate funds to
cope with the distress; a Jewish population torn with fac-
tionalism; a growing enmity on the part of the Arabs which
finally burst forth in the country-wide massacres of 1929;
and, throughout, the constant sabotage of all Jewish effort
by the British authorities. New or not—a work of creation
or merely stubborn maintenance—it left no time for other
than business letters.

One of her two colleagues on the Palestine Executive,
Harry Sacher, fills this gap in her correspondence with a
testimony to her work. "Courage is of many varieties," he
writes, "but I like to think of Miss Szold's as not the lowli-
est. For months at a time she was left in Jerusalem the solitary representative of the Executive. Upon her fell the burden of all departments normally entrusted to her colleagues
as well as her own [the departments of health and educa-
tion]; and upon her the burden of directing the political

work and conducting negotiations with the Palestine government, and adjusting relations with the Yishub.

"Palestine is still of the East. To the Palestine administration political discussion with a woman was strange and not unembarrassing; and the Yishub had to accustom itself to take guidance and instruction from a woman. Nobody saw more clearly than Miss Szold all the inevitable difficulties, but when the occasion demanded that her colleagues should leave Palestine, she was the first to approve and agree. She conquered her own diffidence, she squeezed forty-eight hours out of every day, and very soon she had won the respect and regard of all, official and non-official. Everybody speedily learned that she never spoke without knowing her subject and her mind; that she was utterly free from any thought or feeling of self; and that she was always ready to meet critic or opponent, and, if possible, to convince him, and that no calculation of party or person could divert her by one hair's breadth from that which she believed to be right.

"Dearest to Miss Szold's heart during those years were her own special departments of health and education. The reorganization of our health service involved differences with the Hadassah, which was far away, and with the Hebrew University, which was near. The recasting of an educational system brought her into conflict with what in this region is called religion; yet if there was among her opponents a more religious person than she, I have not the organ to detect him.

"Of Miss Szold's industry it is almost futile to speak. It is the despair as well as the admiration of those who know her. She read everything, she saw everybody that claimed an interview, she was a link with the Yishub and with peripatetic America, she traveled the country, she was always the first to volunteer for an address, she maintained an enormous correspondence, she kept in intimate touch with Zionism in America, she wrote the most admirable memoranda. Precise expression, delicate sensitiveness as to the meaning and quality of words, lucid marshaling of fact, steady logical persuasive development of argument, a tinge of emotional warmth—these are among the qualities of her style.

"Miss Szold's services as a member of the Executive found least understanding and appreciation in America. In Palestine she had more critics and opponents, but all had some estimation of her value. In America there seemed to me to be a chill isolation. Even in the early months, those who had urged her into the office forgot and fell away in the most difficult hours."

In 1929, when America was riding to an economic crash and Palestine to hideous massacres, a Jewish Agency was created, embracing Zionists and non-Zionists, to conduct all Jewish affairs concerned with the British mandate *vis-à-vis* the Palestinian government. The World Zionist Organization elected Miss Szold to serve as one of its representatives on this new body. Only her sense of duty to Palestine led her to accept again what was at bottom a purely political post. She soon regretted it. The number of her critics in America was thereby enlarged to include some prominent non-Zionists, and her resignation was requested. She told off her critics, especially for their incomprehension of democratic procedure and Zionist ideals, and finally resigned with a sense of the futility of politics.

She spent her seventieth birthday in America. Hadassah celebrated it with a flourish which had the effect of increasing her stature and its own membership and morale. But a life of adulation, meetings, and speech-making was intolerable. "I haven't done an honest hour's worth of work or thinking since I arrived here," she confessed; "it's dinners and banquets and luncheons and teas and meetings and messages and gossipings until I feel like a bubble filled, not even with gas, but with that 'inspirational' fluid I am expected to give out all the time. The worst of such a regime is that it unfits one for the real things."

Fortunately, a real thing loomed up across the ocean. The National Assembly of Palestine, theoretically the self-government of Palestine Jewry, offered her a seat on its executive committee. "In Palestine," she said, "they seem to think I can do a definite piece of organization work. So I go back."

The work promised to be the transference of her cherished departments of health and education to the control of the Jews of Palestine themselves, through their elected Assembly. It proved to be something quite different—the resurrection of her dream of a national social service. Once more she could begin at the bottom, laying stone on stone, journeyman's work; but the structure to be raised was new —and her own.

CHAPTER THIRTEEN

Before the Storm Breaks

Jerusalem, June 5, 1931

I HAVE been in Palestine eighteen days, as many days exactly as the passage across two oceans lasted, and I am only now finding a quiet moment in which to tell you that I have arrived.

I had what may be called a "Messianic" reception. My coming meant, according to some, the beginning of real work; according to others the completion of the work; some expected me to solve all public problems; others, to find a solution for their private woes and troubles. After subtracting all these "interested" parties, there remained, I cannot but say, a large group of friends who were just glad to welcome me back. Some of them came down from Jerusalem and all the way to the vessel lying at anchor outside Jaffa; some met me as I disembarked at Jaffa, many crowded into my room at the hotel when I reached Jerusalem, and there has been a steady flow of them since.

In spite of all these social and semi-social claims I had to plunge into the work I came for—the organization of the Keneset Israel.[1] Twenty-four hours after my arrival, I traveled to Tel Aviv for a meeting, and since then I have been there three times for the same purpose. The meetings in Tel Aviv do not exempt me from meetings in Jerusalem. Palestine is as meeting-beridden as the United States.

Teamwork! There's the rub. Here there is too much by far. One cannot budge—the step from talk to action cannot be taken. I keep asking myself: "How does anything

---

[1] The union of the Jewish communities of Palestine.

ever get done in this blessed country of ours?" The fact is, however, that much gets done. I am amazed at the progress during my absence made in spite of the economic depression. As a matter of fact, so far as I can judge, the depression has affected the official Zionist circles, the teachers, the nurses, the doctors, the members of the clerical staffs in the various institutions, and, of course, the institutions depend upon contributions from America. There is much individual suffering and need. That there has always been, and I don't know whether it is greater now than before. But in the circles composed of normal elements—businessmen, artisans, and even laborers—the situation is not such as to make the "economic depression" the constant subject of conversation as it is in America. Not even unemployment is so grievous as elsewhere.

Instead of economic depression, all the articulate talk politics. I don't. On that subject I am not of the articulate. The preoccupation with the government and MacDonald and Passfield and Hope Simpson and Sir John Chancellor and the lesser officials in Palestine—that is what is paralyzing the forces that should devote themselves to organization. My task was to be elaborating the method of transferring health and education from the [Zionist] Executive to the Keneset Israel.

But method is of no use unless there is money, and not a single step has been taken to establish the taxation apparatus which is to draw funds from the community. Just now everyone uses the Zionist Congress—to which the whole of Palestine is preparing to go—as the pretext for not coming to a decision. Meantime a degree of disintegration in the public work has set in that is to me appalling. I warn them that they are going to have the experience of those who refused the sibylline books at the first price. It looks to me as though I had come here to pursue a phantom. No sooner do I write down these words than I remember my own verdict that nevertheless things get done, and my hope revives.

You will, I think, be interested in one point of my situation here. I did not know until I got here that I owed my place in the Executive of the Vaad Leumi to the Workingmen's Party.[2] They gave up one of the seats to which they were entitled, in order that I might be assured of a place. Their intention was that I should be the seventh member of the Executive, the member holding the balance.

[TO ALICE L. SELIGSBERG]   *Jerusalem, September 10, 1931*

I do not know to what extent the structure of the Keneset Israel organization is known to you in its details. May I give you a sketch? The Keneset Israel is supposed to be constituted of *kehillot,* organized local communities, of which there could be about 120 in Palestine. The Vaad Leumi is only the Executive Committee. It is suspended in mid-air so long as the *kehillot* are not organized in such a manner as to levy taxes upon their constituencies and collect them. The process of organizing the *kehillot* is under way. It is not an easy undertaking. We butt up against tradition, vested interests, and, to a certain extent, also indifference, an indifference growing out of failure to realize that the Vaad Leumi has no existence without organized *kehillot.*

We Jews seem to have an unconquerable penchant for the political aspects of life. The Asefat Ha-Nivharim, the annual National Assembly of the Keneset Israel, arouses great interest; so does the choice of the members of the Vaad

---

[2] She makes a point of this because it was the same labor party, the strongest organized element in Jewish Palestine, which opposed her election to the Palestine Executive Committee in 1927. The nature of the Vaad Leumi is explained in the next letter.

Leumi. But when it comes to brick-laying, the enthusiasm wanes. Once the *kehillot* are organized, there will be budget making, budget approval by the government, government approval also of the rate of taxation; and only then, when the collection of taxes becomes a reality, will the Vaad Leumi, as the Executive Committee of the Keneset Israel, receive income to be applied to its administrative expenses. Only then will the department which I am attempting to organize be able to function.

This brings me to your last paragraph, in which you say that it would help you to help me if I could give you an idea of the various types of social service agencies functioning in Palestine today. I believe that roughly it may be said there is every sort of social service agency functioning in Palestine today except—and what a big exception it is! —family case work, ordinary relief. Relief of the destitute is still a matter of hysteria. People must beg. There is no center in any community to which to refer them with the assurance that their case will be lovingly investigated and dealt with. The result is that, as I am convinced, much money is spent and little is accomplished. To a certain extent this problem has not been tackled because there are too many persons still in the Palestinian community who consciously and subconsciously hold that charity must be spontaneous. In other words, the people who spurn the use of the word charity and talk much of justice have not yet come to realize that the organization of charity is the only approach we have yet found to justice.

I am convinced that unless we find means of employing a trained social worker for each one of the three large cities, we are not going to succeed. The greatest success, of course, would be attained if, in addition to these social service workers in the local communities, we could afford to have

a trained organizer in the department for social service attached to the Vaad Leumi, that is to say, someone to replace me. I have not the faintest notion that, within a
period of time measurable for me, funds will be found for
these purely administrative offices. You know the attitude
toward large salaries in Palestine. Trained social workers
must be paid adequate salaries. Over and above this, even
if funds could be found, the sentiment of the community
has not yet sufficiently developed on this aspect of the administration of social service.

Jerusalem, June 12, 1931

The outstanding event of the week from the public point
of view is the publication of the report of the Commission
on the Western Wall.[3] I must confess that I cannot follow
all its involutions intelligently. But I do know that the officials handling all such legislation, in Jerusalem and in
London as well, are violently opposed to Jewish aspirations.
Adele will wonder how I have the courage to persist. I
couldn't if I didn't think the opposition to us basely unjust.

And I persist not only in the face of opposition from outside forces. What I am learning on the inside about machinations and fanaticism is as bad. Since my arrival here
there has been raging a controversy—and carried on with
fists and stones as well as words—on the subject of football
games on the Sabbath. The Executive of the Vaad Leumi
—of which I am a member—is the court of appeal. You
should have seen me sit down with delegations of the Agudath Israel,[4] who picked me out as the last-comer and a

---

[3] The remnant of the Temple, before which devout Jews mourn
the destruction of ancient Jerusalem. An attempt of the Arabs to
prevent the Jews from praying before it occasioned the massacres of
1929.
[4] An extreme orthodox organization.

woman and a Sabbath observer to fight their battle of observations!

I myself should be glad if the sports clubs would guard
the sanctity of the Sabbath—if they did it of their own ac-
cord and as an outflow of their feelings and convictions.
The alternative is to force my convictions and feelings on
them. The result was the result of all extremism—I was far
more in sympathy with the Sabbath breakers than the Sabbath observers. The demand made by one of the Agudath
Israel was that I go to the government and get them to use
police force to prevent the game! I let them know my defi-
nition of traitor and treason.

That's the sort of quiet old age I am enjoying in the Holy
City.

Jerusalem, July 3, 1931

I've been reading systematically, the first time in at least
thirty years. I get up early, breakfast early, and read, read,
read intensively from seven until nine. What? First the paper, then history. Someone gave me a huge—600-page—
history of modern times, and I keep at it day after day. Unless there is an influx of visitors tomorrow, Saturday, I shall
finish it then. What I have lived through and don't know
about! I remind myself of my girlhood. Do you remember
how I used to go about in our Lombard Street garden
armed with a big volume of *Weltgeschichte?*

[TO ALICE L. SELIGSBERG]   *Jerusalem, July 14, 1931*

With temerity unprecedented, I am charging myself with
the task of organizing the Central Bureau for the social
work being done in the whole of Palestine. This Bureau is
the undertaking of the Vaad Leumi of the Keneset Israel.
At the present moment I have not got beyond the point of

discussing the methods and the purposes of the Central
Bureau with various agencies, such agencies as through their
work have acquired a somewhat wider view of the situation
than the rank and file of volunteer workers in specific institutions can be expected to have.

What do you think of my temerity in undertaking such a
task? When I came to Palestine, I acted as though I were
an expert on medical affairs. Fate made me pretend to be
an expert on educational affairs in 1927. And now, in 1931,
having passed the Psalmist's term of years, I dare go into
another field in which to expertize is imperative. But what
am I to do if experts on the spot like Mr. Viteles and Dr.
Hexter, who might be helpful, refuse to tackle the job, and
tackled it must be? The situation is becoming daily more
chaotic. If only there were at least money for administrative
purposes and we could invite a real social expert to take
hold of the thing! But even if money were available, we
must not think of exorbitant salaries. We shall never get
anywhere in Palestine if we invite experts with the promise
of large emoluments. I think the attitude is all wrong, but
one cannot run counter to a determined public opinion,
especially not in these days of economic crisis in America
and Germany and Hoover moratoriums.

Jerusalem, July 22, 1931

Talking of letters, mine must be true, for both my sisters
remark upon my greater tranquillity of spirit. Quite right!
To what do I attribute it? The demands upon me are as
exacting as ever, and this year I am getting no funds with
which to assuage and help. I think I am more callous or
more experienced. No single individual can make a dent in
the welter of conditions. So I don't go to the office at seven
as I used to, but at nine. I leave the office when all other

well-regulated humans leave it; and I listen to woes and shake my head sadly, and I refuse. The two hours gained in the morning I devote to reading, systematic reading. And I sleep more, I even take a nap during the day.

Not all this sense is to be attributed to "sense" but, I fancy, to age. I am not so vigorous as I was, I imagine. Not that I am sick or weak. Not at all—wonderful sleep in spite of autos and their aggressive horns, too wonderful appetite and too much to eat. A part of my calm I attribute to my bookcase.[5] How could I live without one at my side (or back) all these years? Of course, it makes me even more homesick than I have been for my very own books in storage. What a silly business I have made of it all!

Jerusalem, July 31, 1931

In my work the plot thickens. We of the Vaad Leumi are caught in a vicious circle—no money, hence no organization of the local communities, hence no tax levy, hence no money. I feel like a squirrel in one of those barbarous cages they used to have. In one respect I am less stirred up than I was at first. I am no longer so concerned as I was about my ignorance of the technique of social work. The situation we have to deal with is so intensely, cruelly, multi-fariously human that I have come to the conclusion that ordinary common sense, with even a few grains of general experience with men and their affairs, will go a long way, and will have to be permitted to go a long way toward clearness and organized relations before the fine points of social service science or art can usefully be applied.

My room and my bookcase continue a delight, and for

---

[5] After her years of living in and out of Palestine, she procured a bookcase "all her own."

the last two weeks I have been enjoying my garden, consisting of a pink hydrangea and a pot of varied cacti. It is
queer about the hydrangea, a plant I've never had any fond-
ness for. I classified it in my mind (or heart) with the old-
time dahlia. Someone gave me the plant, with not a vestige
of a bud on it, and I was speculating how decently to dis-
embarrass myself of it when, lo and behold! I found myself
getting very fond of it. Why? Because it's a toper. It claimed
my attention morning and evening. If I didn't water it
abundantly—more generously than the Jerusalem water
supply permits—it drooped so pathetically that I had to
devote myself to it. The result: six great blooms such as
they print in the seed catalogues, and more coming. And the
cactus also has bloomed gloriously. You see, I am getting
to be as domesticated as Adele's cats.

Tel Aviv, August 18, 1931

I am writing from Tel Aviv, not from Jerusalem. I came
here for a full meeting of the Vaad Leumi and stayed over
to talk on social service organization plans with various
individuals and organizations. My intention was to go on to
Haifa today, but the meetings there were canceled. My trip
was to wind up after Haifa at Ben Shemen—one of the three
and the most successful of the Children's Villages; I mean,
successful pedagogically—where there was to be a peace-
day celebration for the youth of the country.

The celebration was to have taken place last week-end
but was postponed on account of the disturbed state of the
country's mind. This morning's paper contains the notifica-
tion of the Arab Executive that on August 23, this week-end,
a strike is to be put into effect as a protest against the sealed
armories and against the legalization proclamation which

will remove disabilities from those who all these years have "stolen" into the country without visas. The proclamation is designed to benefit Arabs as well as Jews.

But the Arab Executive chooses to look upon it as a measure favoring only Jews. The Arab papers give the number of such "illegal" Jewish residents as 25,000. That is a gross exaggeration. As a matter of fact Arabs have been "stealing" in too. But no one remarks upon them, while Jewish immigration and population increases are watched with Argus eyes by government and Arab leaders.

I should be going back to Jerusalem early this morning, if late last night there had not broken out a hot labor-capital dispute in one of the orange-growing regions adjacent to Tel Aviv. So I am to stay and help settle it! Life in Palestine is not monotonous! If I were to give you a description of my interviews yesterday and carry you, as I was carried, from the sixteenth to the twenty-first century as illustrated by the views of various circles on the way social service work should be conducted, you'd realize the synthesis we stand in need of.

[TO ROSE A. HERZOG]   *Jerusalem, October 2, 1931*

I believe I gorged myself with letter-writing while I was in America to such an extent that I shall never again be able to get down to it with avidity. In fact, does one ever do personal correspondence avidly? I have just finished reading a book of letters, those of Gertrude Bell written to her own family while she was roaming through the deserts of Syria and Arabia again and again. In her letters, as printed at least, one finds no intimation that she ever was an unwilling correspondent. I envied her.

By the way, her letters, two big volumes, demonstrate what a live, active, intelligent, and energetic woman can do in the field of politics. I am convinced that she did more than Lawrence for the Arabs. And she served her government well, especially in that she influenced them to deal uprightly with the native population.

I am sure you will read between the lines that the weight of the Arab question hangs upon me. I admit that to my mind it grows more menacing every day. I see the menace in proportion as I begin to understand the ways that are being taken by the nationalist movements in the Near and Middle East. India, Sir John Simon's Report on India, and Gandhi opened my eyes, Gertrude Bell added her mite, and I am now reading Dr. Hans Kohn's book on nationalism in the Orient. We Jews and our Zionist movement are but a speck of dust on these huge scales. There is the possibility that the League of Nations will understand the highest demands of world justice and will have the power to enforce those demands. So be it.

From this you will see in what direction my thoughts are running. As for the situation right here, it is difficult, difficult beyond words, and promises to become more difficult as the year wears on. My own work, of course, suffers from the lack of funds, while I have every opportunity of seeing the seamy side of life. And yet I believe that the Yishub will emerge victorious, not perhaps in my day but eventually.

Jerusalem, May 7, 1932

Tomorrow—no, by now it is today, for I am writing after midnight—I shall have the opportunity of seeing the fruits of another sort of investment I have made. In various ways —two cash birthday presents, a gift of cash from Mr. Straus, and my fee as executrix of Mrs. Kantrowicz's will—I accumulated about $2200. I don't know why—I didn't want to use these gifts for myself. So I established a Rural Clinic

Building Loan Fund. The first such building erected with
it is to be dedicated at Nahalal, and the colonists have invited me and my friends to be present.

I ought to complete the story of my Palestinian invest-
ments. Mrs. Rosenwald gave me $5000 before her death,
and with that I established a Rural School Building Loan
Fund. The first school building was erected at Deganiah. I
haven't seen it, but I am told it's a very fine building. It was
dedicated last year while I was in America.

[TO ANNA KAPLAN]   *Jerusalem, June 7, 1932*

What a fascinating and what a bewildering subject Russia is. At this moment, I am reading Maurice Hindus's *Red
Bread* (not so good as his *Humanity Uprooted*), and on my
table lie two issues of the *Nation* devoted largely to the plea
for the recognition of the Soviet Republic by America. And
a few minutes ago I finished reading in *Ha-Aretz* an ex-
cerpt from a private letter written by a rabbi to friends of
his in Palestine. That is the trouble; the testimony that
comes out of Russia is so baffling. I am also reading Schmid's
Die Republik der Strolche, and not long ago I finished reading *Die Volga füllt das Kaspische Meer.* At the same time
I am a regular contributor to Magen, the Palestinian society which collects money to send to the "persecuted" Zionists in Russia. How can one reconcile Julian Huxley's statements and Louis Fischer's enthusiasm with the rabbi's
wail?

I was completely thrown off my base the other day when
I heard from Dr. Hans Kohn, who is lecturing on his impressions of Russia, that what I thought a passing feature
is an inherent element in the new system. He maintains that
the iron consistency which ruthlessly mows down all opposition is not, as I thought, a temporary means to an end,

but is an inseparable characteristic of the communistic form of life.

With us here things go on as usual. Those who come here from abroad maintain that our state is far better than that of any country in Europe or America. Certainly I can say that there is much less wailing and gnashing of teeth than there appears to be in the United States, if I may judge from letters and newspapers. However, I find in the course of my undertaking, the organization and co-ordination of the social service work, that in all conscience we have suffering enough and to spare. And we are facing a year of the acid test, when the Keneset Israel, still untried, will be expected to carry education, to an increased degree health, and the social service, in a country of immigration.

At this moment I do not see where the financial and the moral strength is to come from. I do not see the technically trained forces that are to supply the intellectual, the planning currents. As a matter of fact, the resistance to technically trained forces is as outspoken as ever, the prevalence of the partisan spirit as dominating as ever. Shall we have to suffer and suffer still more before we realize that we can't kick the world's experience aside? Look at Russia in that respect. The best technicians the world can produce are just good enough for her, and the fact that American treatment of the Soviet Union has been despicable in no wise creates an attitude averse from Americans.

Jerusalem, June 9–29, 1932

My chief occupation at the moment is dealing with the juvenile offender. He is so much less an offender than the people who want to reform him. They talk from start to finish in terms of reformatory institutions, when all that the little wretches need is larger opportunity for recreation and for education of the hand. Certainly the Russians know how to take hold of children's problems, beginning with the babies. If I had money . . . !

It was very interesting to have Bertha write about her all-day conference in Juvenile Courts. One of my new obligations is probation work with juvenile offenders, who are very juvenile and not offenders at all, but sick, defective, undernourished, mentally and physically starved children.

The Palestine government took a great step forward on April 1 in the appointment of a probation officer. He is a Britisher and was in despair as to how he was to deal with the Jewish boys, whose language or languages he cannot understand. The result is that I became his deputy for Jewish cases. It is a big job when it is taken in with other jobs and when there is no money to meet primitive necessities. One of the basic problems here is the remanding of children to a reformatory in which there are big boys charged with and convicted of murder. And the first punishment decreed by the court according to the statute book is—flogging.

I am writing on the thirtieth anniversary of our father's death. It seems so short a time ago and it seems so endlessly long ago.

Jerusalem, August 19, 1932

I ended my last letter to you with a travel plan which you may have thought the fancy of the moment. It wasn't. It's been years since I first thought of your coming out here and retrospectively becoming acquainted with what has been my background for twelve years.

Within less than a year I want to "devolute" here and return to America for the remainder of my days. If you come, I shall see five times as much showing you the country as

I ever saw before. On the way back we'd have a few weeks in Italy—we'd enjoy it together, I think, as we enjoyed the Shenandoah Valley and Charleston. (By the way, what is the name of the Gorge or Pass between Staunton and Lexington that one ought to see in rhododendron time and that we saw snow-covered? The Maury Monument stands half-way between the two ends. I have been torturing myself for days trying to remember the name.)

If I hold out for another half-year it'll be my last chance for a jaunt in vigor. These are my arguments in favor of the plan. I know none against it, except that I may not have saved enough money to do it. I haven't yet reckoned the cost.

Jerusalem, September 2, 1932

Among the tourists this week—the heat does not deter them, they come in shoals—was the daughter of Lombroso; she is the wife of another criminologist, Carrenga. My intercourse with her would, I am sure, have been delightful but for the barrier of language. Apparently she speaks only Italian well. Nevertheless, I enjoyed my talks with her.

It was so different from being accosted by an American, a Hadassah member, from Kalamazoo, with a half-indignant, half-amazed "Don't you remember me?" I've given up prevaricating on that point, for I have found out that these same people don't really recognize me. They are informed of my presence at the hotel [6] by the tout who, I heard recently by chance, uses my name as a bait when he goes fishing for guests on the arrival of a train from Egypt. I am considered, it appears, as a good card of recommendation. So the Americans know I shall be on show, and they spot me with a little prompting, I fancy, from the waiter,

---

[6] For years the Hotel Eden had been her residence.

who is a good-natured, officious individual. He takes excellent care of me, sometimes too excellent, but, alas! bathes only once a season.

I am keeping busy, very busy, now with the promotion of a good idea which unfortunately occurred to me—unfortunately because it was promptly accepted and thrown back at me for execution, on the principle that the maker of a motion becomes the chairman of the committee to whom the resultant decision is referred. You probably know that education was transferred from the jurisdiction of the Jewish Agency to that of the Vaad Leumi. The gift is accompanied by a deficit of £8000 in the proposed budget.

My idea is a stipend fund, $25 being the cost of a pupil in the schools for one year—cheap enough, isn't it? But the appeal is to be directed not to individuals but to organized groups. One stipend of $25, for one child, for one year, from one group, like a Hadassah chapter, a section of the Council of Jewish Women, a lodge, etc. On paper it sounds good, doesn't it? But it means the writing of endless personal letters—3000 at least—and then there may be total failure. The plan recommends itself because it does not compete with the regular Zionist fund collections. We'll see!

[TO ALEXANDER DUSHKIN] *Jerusalem, November 20, 1932*

Today came your telegram: "If plan put operation would undertake fifteen to twenty-five scholarships Chicago schools kindred groups love Alex."

I confess that I had hoped that you might be willing to influence "schools and kindred groups" elsewhere outside of Chicago, and I reveal to you that I shall live in the hope that Chicago schools and kindred groups will yield twenty-five rather than fifteen scholarships. For the rest, I am deeply grateful to you.

As a matter of fact, a change in the situation has occurred. The balancing of the budget was effected by the sacrifice of many items, among which is the grievous elimination of all the kindergartens in the whole country. We have therefore decided that all the receipts from the Stipend Fund will be devoted to the reopening of the small number of kindergartens that were in operation last year. The scheme now depends upon our being able to secure within the country a guarantee sum on the basis of the expectations from the Stipend Fund. Ye gods and little fishes, did I ever think that I would involve myself in these financial transactions—*combinatziot!* My head is whirling.

[TO ROSE A. HERZOG]   *Jerusalem, October 21, 1932*

There has been an almost uninterrupted succession of Hadassah leaders visiting here during the last year and a half. The connection between Palestine and America becomes more and more intimate year after year. All the Americans insist that Palestine is much more comfortable than the United States. I heard it only last night from Dr. Hexter, who has just returned. He said: "You and I"— meaning me—"ought to be happy that we are here and not there."

In not one of your notes to me do you fail to warn me against overwork. Your warnings are in vain. It seems to me that I do nothing but ward off new commitments. And still they come. For me apparently there will be no salvation but to remain on the ocean between America and Palestine. However, so far as my work is concerned—the organization of the social service of Palestine—I have not been wholly unsuccessful and that gives me a certain degree of satisfaction. The only self-criticism is that I should not have begun a piece of work that requires a long expectation of life.

CHAPTER FOURTEEN

The Advent of Hitler

I

THE apparent tranquillity of the two years following the return to Palestine was shattered by the Nazi triumph in Germany. Outside that frantic and unhappy land itself, the first people to understand the universal scope of the destructive forces which Hitler embodied, forces that have since engulfed the globe, were naturally the first victims—the Jews.

How deeply the corrosion of civilized values had already gone can be discerned in Miss Szold's unwonted and poignant outbursts of pessimism and despair as witnessed by her letter (September 29, 1933) on the "ledgerizing of the soul." The *Sturm und Drang* which seemed to come so late in her life—for old age no less than youth sometimes has its growing pains—were reflections of a world irremediably out of joint.

Fortunately, Miss Szold repaired at once to her favorite medium—hard work. At first it may have been distraction. But eventually it led to what became the crowning achievement of her career, the direction and upbuilding of the Youth Aliyah, an organized effort to rescue scores, then hundreds, and finally thousands of boys and girls from the Nazis.

As usual, the procedure was from the outset a matter of laying stone on stone. She began—shall it be said, innocently?—by heading a campaign for funds to meet the needs of German refugees pouring into Palestine. In October she

was sent by the Vaad Leumi to participate in a general conference called in London to consider the German Jewish
plight. What kept her worried, as she said, was the children. She kept her mind, too, on her efforts in the department of social service, for the one need paralleled the other.

Because it summarizes both her mental state and her activities during the first few months after Hitler seized power,
the initial letter of this chapter is placed out of chrono-
logical order.

[TO DR. SOLOMON SOLIS COHEN]
En route to Marseille, October 24, 1933
Last spring I determined to cut loose from Palestine and
return to America for my remaining years, to be coddled by
my sisters. Hitler disposed otherwise. I should have felt like
a renegade if I had not remained to do my bit, seeing that
my many years in Palestine naturally mean experience of
the sort useful in the emergencies created by a large immigration.

I am not, indeed, as you write, "in charge of the settlement in Palestine of exiles from Germany." I have been
heading the "drive" for funds, and in connection with this
enterprise I am a member of the executive committee of
three which allocates the moneys collected. The result of the
campaign, £12,000, seems pretty good for the old *halukah*
land,[1] doesn't it? It must be remembered that this was the
first campaign of its kind in Palestine.

Presently our *ad hoc* committee will merge its allocation
activities into the new Department for German Jewish Affairs recently formed and attached to the Executive of the
Jewish Agency, under the chairmanship of Dr. Weizmann

---

[1] The *halukah* is the traditional collection of funds in every land
for the support of indigent and pious Jews in Palestine.

in London and of Dr. Ruppin in Jerusalem. The new department insures centralized, co-ordinated action. I am now on my way to the London conference called by the Joint Foreign Committee, to consider the various aspects of the German situation. I go as a representative of the Vaad Leumi of the Keneset Israel.

I want to thank you particularly for having taken the trouble to write me of your reactions to the Hitler assault and to the methods proposed for combating it. I agree that we Jews have often derived values from persecutions, and doubtless the German crusade will add a chapter to the history of our spiritual consolidation. In Palestine it is obvious that our young community there, almost in the first stages of development, will receive an accession of trained, experienced forces whose coming will be of decisive influence upon us. Some of them are saturated with the Zionist ideology; their assimilation to Jewish life will proceed naturally, without effort. Many of them, however, are as visitors from another planet. They know nothing of the Messianic hope, even in its modern form of Zionism; they are strange to the whole gamut of Jewish ideas and principles. If we win them, your prediction will be verified.

Seeing the beginnings of the process before me, I cannot accept your fear that your view may be condemned as mystical. Our history seems to be full of examples of the preservation of our fundamentals by persecution. Whatever betides, our *idea* gains; and there is always the saving remnant to carry the idea. However, the processes are painful. I again agree with you in not choosing Nazism as even a providential instrument to effect spiritual good.

While naturally I am concerned chiefly with the Jewish aspects of the German outrage, I am also unhappy over the general calamity. It hurts me to think that violence is being done to a culture created by Lessing, Goethe, and Schiller. So much of my own education was impregnated with the German language and its literature, and I loved it so dearly, that this phase of the catastrophe needs must harrow my feelings. But I believe I should not react otherwise if a culture remote from me, the Italian, the French, had been violated by such brutality. At bottom it is a question of faith in the perfectibility of man. As a Jew, can one afford not to cling to such faith? And yet is one encouraged by what happens before one's eyes?

During the last few months my mind like yours has been traveling back fifty years. It was in 1883 that, as a young woman, I was drawn into the activities that sprang up around the East European immigration into America as a result of the Russian pogroms. I remember well how helpful was American Jewry's action, how despicable was American Jewry's refusal to recognize the Russian fugitives as equal brethren. American Jewry of those days was chiefly "German." The wheel has turned. In Palestine today there is helpfulness in full measure, yet no lack of unkind criticism of the refugees as Jews of inferior rank. Palestinian *Mayflower* Jewry is East European!

There are the two half-century mileposts: Russian pogroms and Hitler's Nazidom. Then there is the failure of the Disarmament Conference and the dark war-forebodings in Europe; and there is the disunion in our own ranks carrying one back beyond the half-century to the Kamza and Bar Kamza incident in Temple times and one wonders whether the Messiah *can* come.[2]

In Palestine at least there is the heart-warming reflection

[2] Kamza and Bar Kamza are two personages in a Talmudic legend which attributes the destruction of Jerusalem by the Romans to an accidental misunderstanding between their names and the subsequent perfidy of Bar Kamza.

that the Zionist idea has been justified. It is stirring to think
that the ardor of a handful of idealists, having faith in the
efficacy of the age-long nostalgia of the Jew for the Land
of Israel as a regenerative force, prepared the remedy before
the ravages of the disease appeared. But in Palestine, nevertheless, a tangle of problems is developing around the German immigration which will require more than a London
conference to solve. And on the horizon hang the lowering
clouds of Arab discontent! And in Jewish circles land speculation running riot! I leave you to fill in the others—and
don't forget Great Britain's place therein.

Jerusalem, June 2-9, 1933

Getting into the drive is proving difficult. The public
doesn't like the German Jews apparently any better than
Hitler. My campaign is coming on slowly, too slowly. The
arguments against giving and in favor of not giving multiply from day to day. It is amazing to me that some of the
most thoughtful people here fail to take in the implications
of what has happened and is happening in Germany.

The other day there fell into my hands the official paper
of the Kehillah in Berlin. I was surprised and pleased to
observe the dignified acceptance of their fate by the German Jewish community. Their one aim is to find the thousand ways that may lead to what they call *Berufsumschich-
tung*.[3] Not that they think that success in that direction will
return them to anything like their former place in the economy of German life. They seem to know that they are
doomed to inferiority, to citizenship of second grade. But
can 600,000 persons flee? Palestine will probably receive
10,000 within the next twelvemonth. I hope we shan't bun-
gle the business of absorption and adjustments too badly.

[3] Change of occupation.

What keeps me worried is the children. They are already beginning to come, and without their parents—who cannot come away without risking the loss of every penny they own. How we are going to provide places for 3000 to 4000 children passes my comprehension. And I am not thinking of the funds. I am thinking of the forces of organization at our disposal.

Jerusalem, September 1, 1933

I can't say it's been a dull week. Plenty of work, as usual, several trips to Tel Aviv, and an accumulation of reports from Germany on the throttling process. Some of the sanguine Germans who have come here cherish the hope that the Hitler regime must come to an end soon. They don't seem to realize that the mischief has been done for a generation—perhaps forever. The very children in the primary classes have been taught contempt and hatred and methods of applying both, developed as never before with such refined cruelty in the history of persecution.

It is said that on the average two hundred German immigrants steal in nightly, under cover of darkness, over the northern boundary of Palestine, having made their way from Germany overland. Many of them are caught without visas in the countries through which they pass and are forced to return to their hell. And those who escape into Palestine—there is no telling what their fate will be if by frequent chance their illegal status is discovered. And the way these "illegals" are skinned and fleeced at the border by those who are making it a business to help them across —it's fiendish!

We have settled about three hundred at work near the villages, but of course we are not able to execute any large scheme of either agricultural or urban settlement with the

sums available. Besides, the need for actual emergency help
—"social service"—grows with every day. Today, exactly
today, I succeeded, after three months' constant pegging
away at the demonstration, in proving to the rest of the
committee that certain sums must be allocated to social
service—philanthropy, they call it contemptuously—for the
care of children, for the sick (especially the mentally disor-
dered!), the aged, and to release [craft] instruments and
tools from the customs.

Well, a New Year is approaching, and we shall follow
our habit and wish each other happiness. I suppose habit
is the best safeguard against cynicism and despair. But
whether it conduces to improvement, that's another question.

Jerusalem, September 20, 1933

I didn't know that it was possible to sink to lower depths
of dejection than Hitler had dropped me to. Last Friday,
instead of writing to you, I went up to Haifa to meet Mrs.
Wronsky, the Jewish woman who, with Dr. Alice Salamon
(baptized but nevertheless ejected), stood at the very head
of all social-pedagogic work in Berlin. She was the archivist
of the city of Berlin, the founder of a library of 55,000
volumes, all of which she herself collected, the editor of a
number of sociological journals, and a lecturer much sought
after. She is a woman of fifty.

I heard her personal experiences. She told them in the
most objective, unemotional way conceivable. The greatest
stress, if stress there was anywhere, she put on the demonstrations of sympathy and disgust by her associates and sub-
ordinates. She said nothing of atrocities. It was a tale of
spiritual suffering, of relinquishment of all cherished values, the passion of the German Jew, in the same sense in

which the nuns of the Dames de Sion speak of the passion of their Saviour—also a Jew, as was the founder of their church, Father Ratisbonne.

The tide of German immigrants is constantly swelling. In Tel Aviv, the goal of eighty percent of them, the housing problem has assumed gigantic proportions. Whole families are sleeping on the beach for want of vacant rooms. On the last day of September our German collection ceases —on the first of October Tel Aviv begins a local collection for the erection of barracks to meet immediate needs, and cheap dwellings in view of the large volume of immigrants announced for October.

Meantime the question of the transfer of the children still hangs in the balance. I have had interviews with the Director of Immigration and with the High Commissioner. At their request I have written letters packed with details; but no reply is forthcoming, and groups of boys and girls are waiting in Germany.

I shall not repine when the end of the drive comes. It's been hard drudgery. But when I heard Mrs. Wronsky's description of the Hitler system, placidly philosophic and analytic though it was, I could not but feel that I had acted rightly in staying here. I do wish it had been "right" to do the other thing. Here I am writing on Erev Rosh Ha-Shanah,[4] all alone. It is true I am writing in my room heavily fragrant with roses, lilies, and carnations sent to me by all sorts of people. But . . .

Jerusalem, September 29, 1933

My answer would be appropriate to this day, the eve of Yom Kippur,[5] because it should be a sort of confession, not

---

[4] The eve of the Jewish New Year.
[5] The Day of Atonement.

of sins unless errors of judgment as to how life should be ordered should be accounted sins. The confession would be what they call in Hebrew *heshbon ha-nefesh*—the ledgerizing of the soul. Bertha might have told you something of what I should write, if you had had a chance for a real conversation with her when she got back from here.[6] Not that I ever had or took an opportunity to pour myself out to her. But a summing up of a long succession of short comments upon life and work here and upon Zionism and Zionists, and upon Jews in general, must have given her a survey of my soul. She must have seen just as much cynicism and so much pessimism as drive one to do the duties that have come to one, in large part uninvited, the very, very best anyone knows how to fulfill them, without thinking of ultimate goals. Do you see what I mean? Can you read between the lines that I am approaching your Omar Khayyám attitude—almost a Calvinistic attitude—that nothing matters because everything is as bad as it can be, and it means to stay bad, no matter what you and I do or anyone else does?

But I am not fair to myself when I write in such general terms. I should really go into the details of the Jewish situation as I see it and as it affects me, to let you understand why all grace and faith are threatening to desert me. Somehow or other I have lost the harmoniousness of living of which I used to boast to myself—fortunately not to others. My *Sturm und Drang* period came so late. It culminated in the Arlosoroff murder.[7] Devastating as that tragedy was on

---

[6] Bertha Levin, Miss Szold's sister, had visited her. The present letter is addressed primarily to Adele Szold (Mrs. Thomas Seltzer).

[7] Chaim Arlosoroff, a prominent labor leader, was mysteriously murdered in the summer of 1933. The trial of a number of suspects, which continued through the succeeding year, stirred the labor and rightist elements of Palestinian Jewry into bitter conflict.

the personal side—a fine mind was annihilated—it was even more destructive to the philosophy by which I had lived. Not that the one incident broke me. It summed up what I had been gathering for several years bit by bit, confirmed the moral judgments I had passed on disparate acts and tendencies, and consolidated them into one comprehensive judgment. Let me hasten to say, it's not all the fault of the Jews. It's the fault of this world of ours; I only see its iniquitous stupid ways in and through my Jews.

Jerusalem, September 29, 1933

Whether the German immigrants are going to adjust themselves to the Palestinian life remains to be seen. The three hundred or four hundred men whom we have pushed into the *kibbutzim,* the workers' groups who are employed in the agricultural villages—while gradually in their "leisure" time developing their own plots of ground—are fitting themselves into the conditions as they exist, but not too easily. It is their will that is making them successful, not their natural inclination.

There is a great gap, emotional and social-economic, between the German and the East European Jew. The latter is the disciple of Russia, the former its opponent, conscious and unconscious. So much for the young. Those who have passed the forty-year milestone are bound to suffer. They long for the fleshpots of their German Egypt. They would return—they say so themselves—in a jiffy if the Hitler regime were ended. And many of them believe it will end soon. The wish is father to the thought. And if it were to end, they forget that a whole generation, now sitting on the school benches in Germany, has had its mind poisoned forever and aye. I ought not to fail to say that it's only the non-Zionists who believe Hitler's reign will be brief and who speak of the return to Germany. The Zionists among them have an entirely different attitude. The privations (I don't know what they are) of Palestinian life don't affect them. In other words, their philosophy is practical.

[TO ALICE L. SELIGSBERG]   *Jerusalem, September 30, 1933*

When people combat my pessimistic outlook, I am secretly elated. I hope I am wrong, and their optimistic cheerful interpretation of Jewish life is right. Is it not possible that when the main principle [in Russia] is vindicated, demonstrated, and firmly established, the implacable leveling process which seems now to be grinding the Jews out of existence will be relaxed? Then the "saving remnant" in Jewry which has never failed us in our long history will assert itself, and a purer Judaism will emerge. You see, I refuse to be a consistent pessimist.

The Arlosoroff trial and the Nahalal bomb-outrage trial are revealing depth after depth of depraved revolutionary tendencies among the Jewish as well as the Moslem youth. In both camps terroristic movements have been laid bare. You can imagine how startling some of the revelations are, if at a meeting of the Vaad Leumi held two or three days ago Dr. [Ben-Zion] Mossinsohn brought in a resolution that immediately after the holidays a special meeting of the Vaad Leumi be called to consider the state of the Jewish youth of Palestine. Paper resolutions—the issue of lengthy speeches—are not going to put a dent into the situation. First there must be some very incisive self-criticism, then some hard intensive work, detailed work, that will require so much thinking and acting that our teachers of youth will have no leisure for politics and professional grumbling. First and foremost, the elders will have to forgo their favorite sport of discussion.

[TO THOMAS SELTZER]   *Jerusalem, October 1, 1933*

The times are too serious for one to be writing pleasant nothings. Every letter ought to be a self-revelation—an attempt to analyze the world situation in relation to one's own inner self. If that were done, we might in the course of time—from out of the mass of self-revelations and subjective reactions—arrive at that objective judgment which not even our wisest and most experienced and best-trained thinkers have succeeded in offering a distracted world. I am too lazy intellectually for such self-analysis. It would mean painting in backgrounds, and molding foreground figures, that is, presenting one's microcosm as the foil to one's reflections. I just can't get down to that. So I am silent for the most part, at least in writing.

However, I *am* busy, heart-breakingly busy. This German Jewish business is devastating. Zionism apparently justified itself by having Palestine in readiness, with doors at least ajar, to receive the German refugees. But Palestine is so small, and the means are so limited, and the need so cruelly great. So far as I personally am concerned, I ask: doesn't it seem unfair that a person should be subjected to the same barbarous experience twice in a lifetime? Exactly fifty years ago I was engaged in America on behalf of the East European Jews in absolutely the same makeshifting as I am now engaged in in Palestine on behalf of the German Jews.

Tonight a stranger was seated at my little table at suppertime. I entered into a conversation with her. She spoke very simply of her experiences in Berlin. Indeed, very few of the Germans who come here resort to heroics. But their very directness stirs the listener to his depths. And it's no use trying to find out, ecclesiastically or scientifically, why the

Jews are the eternal scapegoats of the nations. Conceded, we have repelling characteristics. So have others, who are not made to suffer supremely. The worst aspect is that a cause for persecution that defies explanation cannot be removed. It will go on forever without loss of potency. And as for the educability and perfectibility of the human race, can we go on believing in them? Millions upon millions are alive who underwent the horrors of the Great War. Yet international conferences fail and another war is preparing, while simpletons—or are they knaves?—talk of disarmament.

So I just work.

[TO MRS. ROSE JACOBS]   *Jerusalem, October 9, 1933*

The Arab community is agitated over the volume of immigration. Today's paper reported the resolution of the Moslem Supreme Council to arrange a big protest demonstration on Friday of this week. The Police Department published posters today, warning against incitement to excesses. I anticipate no violence for the present. As long as we continue "prosperous" and Trans-Jordania suffers want, nothing serious will happen. But the promise is being stored against the days of adversity.

An incident happened a few days ago that stirred me more deeply than the announced demonstration. The counsel for the defense in the Nahalal bomb case pleaded for mercy for his convicted [Arab] clients on the ground that they were led on to their misdeed by the false policy of the government. The judge meted out no rebuke, and I understand that the plea for clemency has been granted.

The holiday season has been exquisitely beautiful. Nature takes no note of man's degeneration.

II

In October Miss Szold attended the London conference on the German Jewish situation. Threads of an organization for settling German youngsters among the Jewish co-operative colonies were already being spun before she left. Other threads, she learned, were being spun in Germany among the Jewish youth groups. "Yet I am looked upon as the head of the movement," she complained two years later. "I cannot understand it, it is unfair." The plans, however, were haphazard and disjointed; the threads were at loose ends. So she proceeded to Berlin, still quivering under the first lash of the Nazis, to tie the threads together at one end. Then she returned to Palestine and with patient toil knotted them at the other. Social fabrics—the Hadassah or now the Youth Aliyah—are not born or led; they are valorously woven out of the strands of life. "She layeth her hands to the spindle and her hands hold the distaff, and her candle goeth not out by night." If Miss Szold cannot consent to be considered a leader, she must permit anyone who knows the work of her hands to call her, too, "a woman of valor."

S.S. Naldera, *November 19, 1933*

How I can put time, ink, and paper on the high cost of living and lucky strokes of fortune, after my experiences in Germany, I fail to understand. I heard nothing new factually, but I felt—I felt the atmosphere.

I was in Berlin on the Friday of Hitler's pre-election address [8] and heard part of it over the radio, standing among the hotel personnel, every last bootblack of whom had been

---

[8] The "election" was the plebiscite of November 12, 1933, which endorsed the Nazi regime.

shepherded to the loud-speaker. I did not listen in long, because the apparatus was unclear. The passage that caused much excitement was the one in which he referred to the emigrants who had left and were leaving the Third Reich as gypsies—*Zigeuner*. The interpretation is that he referred to all fugitives—Jews, liberals, pacifists, and socialists. The audience in his hall, by means of *Zwischenrufe*, referred it expressly to the Jews alone. They cried: "The Jews, the Jews!"

The city is placarded with every sort of propaganda poster that imagination can devise. In the hotels, in the restaurants, in the synagogues, in the office buildings, on the streets, poster after poster. A favorite one consisted of Lloyd George's recent sympathetic utterance. What cannot be described is the atmosphere, the *Stimmung*, and apparently it is a depressed *Stimmung* that holds not Jewish Berlin alone in its clutches. The streets of Berlin are dead, empty. The shops are empty (but so are they in London and Paris!).

The worst manifestation is the startled look people cast around when they have been betrayed into uttering a free and critical word, to assure themselves that none but the interlocutor heard it.

My visit to Germany was entirely in the interest of the children. I believe I achieved something worth while. I found much confused organization, no understanding of Palestinian conditions, and much talk at cross-purposes. I don't flatter myself that I straightened out the whole tangle but I think the path is somewhat leveled. If only there were funds. In Paris I went to see Dr. Bernard Kahn. He insists that the Joint Distribution Committee has practically nothing to give until its next drive comes off, which cannot be soon.

Jerusalem, December 15, 1933

I wanted to say a word to you about the jobs, such as at the Federation, which, as you write, call for only a superior sort of clerical ability. I sympathize with that description. It fits my work too. When I view even this new undertaking of mine, the children's immigration, which ought to throb and pulsate with life—when I sum it up in its day by day aspects, what is it but just that, superior clerical work? I admit that, by some fluke, I have an advantage over you: my clerical jobs are continuous, overlapping. I have come to the conclusion that only the few, the creative scientists and artists, rise above the clerical. Nine-tenths of what is called "writing" is no better. It's hackwork and that's clerical.

Jerusalem, December 22, 1933

My new job, the organization of the transfer of the children from Germany to Palestine, is growing under my hands from day to day. It deals with children—it is not child's play. The responsibility is great. If and when I carry it through, I think I should let my active life come to an end with it. Not that I feel too tired to contemplate more. But I should make room for the younger, better-trained forces that are coming into the country.

Jerusalem, January 4, 1934

The transfer of young people from Germany involves me in endless correspondence. So much of it is superfluous. There was no proper adjustment at the first between Berlin and Jerusalem. The result is that there must be daily readjustments. Another source of confusion and consequent trouble is that so much of the arrangement depends upon governmental administrative action. That means delays and misunderstandings. We haven't yet succeeded in bringing over the first group. It is destined for Ain Harod; and there are to be sixty-three girls and boys, between the ages of fifteen and seventeen. It's a serious experiment. My sense of responsibility toward it grows every minute.

I was ungrateful when I called the week barren. One really amazing thing happened—a conference of social workers. I have been holding such conferences every six months or thereabouts, chiefly for the purpose of thrashing out intercity technical difficulties. This time I widened the scope. In the course of the two years and a half since I began the organization of social service bureaus, the number of volunteer workers has been astonishingly enlarged; and latterly the influx of German trained workers has given a strong impetus to popular participation. It seemed the psychological moment to bring social questions before the public, or what one might call an intermediate public. It was a great success. About sixty persons came from all parts of the country and sat through three perfectly unsentimental, ungushing sessions, discussing problems the solution of which means primarily the conscious organized cooperation of the loosely connected elements in our population. It was most encouraging.

If, now, we could only get down to organized collection of the funds that are flowing unregulated through a thousand channels, something genuinely useful might be achieved. But we still have a long way to travel. Perhaps if the depression in the United States continues a little while longer to baffle our President, Palestine will learn how to stand on its own feet. Hitler, too, has done his share in inculcating a sense of independence among Palestinians. One of the interesting facts was the insistence upon an early development of social legislation. That is the fruit of Russian

Jewish social-political philosophy united with German Jewish social-political experience.

Jerusalem, January 26, 1934

It's cold, cold. The very marrow is freezing in my bones, and my brain is an icicle. Oh, for Adele's coal stove or for an over-steam-heated New York apartment! The little oil stove standing in the center of my room makes no impression upon the cold. We even had two attempts at a snowfall this week—sub-tropical attempts.

The week had an outstanding event for me—the Huberman concert, to which Max Schlossinger invited me. It was superb—exquisite as to program and indescribably beautiful as to execution. He played Bach, Mozart, and Beethoven. The concert had its quite extraordinary human interest too. We have had an orchestra here for some time. Whenever it played we would say complacently: "Good for Jerusalem." This time it was good, absolutely good. Huberman himself had practiced with it all week and had whipped it into shape. Besides, latterly, there have been good accessions from among the German immigrants, and there was a German conductor.

Huberman has taken Palestine by storm. He arrived enveloped in a cloud of glory—the glory of his snub to Germany, to which he refused to go for a brilliant engagement. That adventitious virtue (from an artistic point of view) was enhanced by the generous aid he gave to the musicians here and to their attempts at a musical center. He organized, at the end, a philharmonic orchestra and assured its existence, first, by securing the patronage of the High Commissioner, and then by creating the possibility of obtaining funds. The proceeds of his all-Beethoven concert he gave to the struggling Jerusalem Conservatory of Music.

He, too (like me), went to the Emek,[9] and played for the settlers who streamed to Ain Harod from all parts undaunted by the muddy roads.

Jerusalem, February 8, 1934

The reason I can do what you can't—shut my eyes to the hellishness of the world we live in and push it aside from my consciousness by allowing the details of my various tasks to absorb me to the exclusion of analytical thought— the reason I can do that is that I know I can't think to any purpose. I can't understand what is going on around me. I don't understand the stabilization of exchange, the good of purchasing gold, the value of raising the price level— nothing, nothing do I understand. I am befuddled by all I read. Strachey—I understand him sentence by sentence, but the whole of the argumentation means nothing. So I have resigned myself to be a hewer of wood and a drawer of water.

On the other hand—perhaps I am contradicting myself or perhaps I overrate myself in what I am going to say now —I do not say, as you say about your going to Russia, that it is too late. I find that, old as I am, in a certain sense I have not stopped growing. While I don't understand, while my intellect is an organ of narrow limitations, my inner world —perhaps it is my world of feeling, of instinct—expands.

[TO MRS. ROSE JACOBS] *Jerusalem, February 10, 1934*

The transfer of the youth from Germany is not only chock-full of time-consuming details, but the undertaking is so overwhelmingly responsible that I sometimes am all

---

[9] The Valley of Esdraelon, converted from swamp and wasteland into the most fertile region of Palestine by Jewish pioneers who live mostly in co-operative or socialist settlements.

but mastered by the impulse to flee from it. Recently I took a trip to the Emek settlements—to as many of them as the heavy roads permitted me to reach—in order to choose the places to which the next group to be organized is to be directed. The discussions on the spot, the visualization of what is involved physically and spiritually in the transplantation, took away the breath, as it were, of my mind and soul. And when I have to deal with the delays and obstacles which the government delights in interposing, I rage and despair. The beginnings are naturally difficult, and naturally weighted with responsibility. On their success hangs the fate of what should be a movement of several years' duration.

This children's undertaking is, of course, added to my social organization work. In it I am fortunate in having won the devoted assistance of Mrs. Wronsky, along with her friendship and personal sympathy. All of which sounds as though my labors had been lightened. Not at all! The interpretation is that now I am able to execute numberless undertakings of the necessity of which I had always been cognizant, but for which my strength did not suffice. If anything, I am busier than ever with the social service. But, at least—if it were not for Tel Aviv, which is more obstreperous than ever—I work with more satisfaction to myself. Besides, the addition of the special service to the German immigrants, which has been put into the Vaad Leumi frame, gives me a budget to handle. That forms a sort of springboard for all the work.

CHAPTER FIFTEEN

Youth Aliyah—The Children's Migration

I

THE preliminary plans were executed for the reception of the young newcomers, and the first open-eyed group arrived in February 1934. As reported by Miss Szold, the plans provided for a two-year apprenticeship in Palestinian life: "The youth will have received two years' instruction in practical work on the farm, in stables, in workshops; they will have received two years' instruction in the Hebrew language and adjustment to the conditions of their new home through the study of Jewish history, Jewish literature, and the geography of Palestine. They will have been made to understand what their work is because they will have had the auxiliary studies that make their work understandable —botany, physics, and chemistry. They will have had the opportunity from time to time of wandering in excursions through the land with their leaders and teachers, who are ready to explain the nature of the land; ready to tell them the meaning of the social experiments that are being carried on in the laboratory of Jewish life."

The boys and girls were received at the ages of fifteen to seventeen when the migration began; later the age limit under pressure of grim circumstance was lowered. After their two years of preparation in the Youth Aliyah, the young people were to choose their permanent occupation and residence. But even then, Miss Szold continued to report, "We are going to watch them; we are not going to abandon them, though they may not any longer receive financial aid from us." And she added: "Can you imagine a colonization scheme more beautiful?"

In her letters we follow her putting the beautiful scheme to work—staggering through the mud of a Palestinian winter, supervising every detail for the children's needs and comfort, providing teachers and helpers, corresponding with the parents left behind, worrying over the finances; and, as they landed at the dock or entered their new village home, personally greeting each boy and girl. Long ago she had written: "I should have had children, many children." Her wish came true.

Floods, delinquents, nursing along the social service work, Arab-Jewish relations, the death of a poet, the beauty of a concert, the dedication of a hero's monument, laying the cornerstone to a long-cherished dream, all these are part of a life which, as we try to keep pace with it, we can hardly believe to be nearing its seventy-fifth year.

[TO MRS. ROSE JACOBS]   *Jerusalem, February 17, 1934*

Day after tomorrow, the first detachment, a group of forty-four of "my" children, arrive from Germany. I go to Haifa to meet them, have them examined medically, and get their possessions out of the customs. Then I accompany them to Ain Harod, to see them installed there. I want to see them tucked away in their beds. I feel weighed down by the responsibility of this children's immigration. It's a terrible experiment. What next?

I had thought in the remote days of my youth that one attained to serenity and wisdom with old age. What do I find in *my* old age? Vagueness, eternal wonder at the meaning of things, inadequacy to the daily tasks, anything but tranquillity.

Jerusalem, March 2, 1934

At this hour a week ago I returned to Jerusalem after four days spent in Haifa, Ain Harod, and Kfar Giladi. It took me two hours and a half to remove mud from my shoes, my overshoes, my coat, my dress, my unders—for from the moment on Monday morning when the train reached the environs of Haifa until the moment on Friday when I escaped from the environs of Kfar Giladi, it rained and hailed and blew and stormed and then began all over again. Such depths of mud as I trudged through! Every time I took a step I dug up great clods and by the time I approached any destination I was bound for—dining-room or my bedroom in the *kvuzot*—I was dragging with me a mountain of earth.

What was it all about? The first group of boys and girls arrived from Germany at Haifa, the detachment of forty-three destined for Ain Harod. I went up to meet them, and then traveled to Ain Harod with them and stayed with them there for two days. It was a great experience for me. I am going to send you an account I have written of their arrival and their reception at Ain Harod as soon as it is stenciled. The account is intended for the committees that are raising funds for the Youth Immigration. I did not succeed in conveying in the account the beautiful attitude of the Ain Harod community toward the young people, and how solemnly and yet joyously they assumed the responsibility for them. The way they introduce them into the *kvuza* life is a religious poem. I don't mean a ceremonial. They work out a plan of gradual adjustment that is of the essence of delicacy and tact. The boys and girls felt the forethought instinctively. I wish I might have stayed with them a month.

The evening of the second day I returned to Haifa in order to set out from there the next morning to Kfar Giladi via Tiberias. I had been commissioned to inspect the place —not Kfar Giladi, but the neighboring Tel Hai—as a possibility for a youth settlement. The monument to Trumpeldor [1] was to be unveiled, and the members of the Executive of the Vaad Leumi were to be present. As I had ostensibly come for the unveiling, I considered it my duty to labor up that hill in the teeth of wind, rain, and hail; but I never got to the top. Thirty or forty steps from the monument, I suddenly felt that if I lifted my feet once more in that direction, I'd have no breath left. So I turned about face and descended.

The farmers of Kfar Giladi then sent a wagon for me— the mud was preferable!—and insisted I stay for a talk with them about the advantages of the place for the German girls and boys. They had heard that I considered the isolated position in the midst of Arab tribes a danger. The storm went on unabated, darkness fell, and I had to stay at Kfar Giladi for the night. The accommodations at Ain Harod had been uncomfortable enough. They were royal as compared with what Kfar Giladi offered, and it offered me its very best. The wind and the rain and the hail continued all night, and the next morning was lowering and cold. At six I was off, and after eight hours in autobusses got to Jerusalem, too muddy and too exhausted to write you my weekly letter.

Jerusalem, May 17, 1934

I have just returned from Tiberias, and I feel as one feels after a five hours' autobus ride on a hot, a very hot day. I

---

[1] See footnote 4, page 128.

went to Tiberias to look after the arrangements made for four hundred Jewish families whose homes were flooded. Some of them collapsed at once, some must be demolished in short order. I am too tired to attempt a description of the scene of destruction and devastation. There were two cloudbursts, on two successive days, over the same spot, at exactly the same hour of the day, high noon. The water has torn deep clefts into the side of the hill behind the city; it ruined one-third of the city park, it brought down into the city streets big boulders from the mountainside, it filled the streets to the choking point with the muddiest mud ever seen. There were thirty deaths, a large number of them little children.

By the time I got there, the social service worker from Haifa with the Hadassah nurses had organized the camp admirably with the help of the government. The government is equal to the task. It put its best foot foremost. It was prompt and has been efficient. The Vaad Leumi permitted me to send a social service worker up there—the first recognition I have got of the value of my organization of the department.

On account of the Tiberias calamity—my having to deal with the social service aspects—I did not participate in the Asefat Ha-Nivharim, the delegates' assembly which takes place only once a year, the assembly that elects the Vaad Leumi. It was not a bad by-product of the cloudburst, because I am finding it increasingly hard to listen to speeches.

Jerusalem, June 2, 1934

I am heart-broken because the Jews don't seem to realize that the Arab question and the way they are going to solve it are the supreme test. I hate the nagging ways the Jews have adopted toward the English government, whether the question be the big one of restriction of immigration or petty daily inadequacies. I am unhappy because we Jews here have no feeling for order, system, self-discipline, character-building in our educational work, indulge in unending partisan bickering, while arrogantly believing ourselves superior to all others with whom we come in contact.

The more remarkable our achievements are, and they are remarkable, the more I long for an Isaiah to show up our littleness and our demoralization, which obtrude themselves glaringly the more successful we are in shaping the externals of civilization. Our actions here, during the last few prosperous years, have not shown either will or ability to live up to the Zionist ideal of communal responsibility. You see that instead of objecting to "perfidious Albion," my mind dwells on our own inadequacies.

Adele asks whether the future menace to my "Jewish homeland" is not so grim as it seems to her. Yes, it is grim; England is not keeping her word, we are just as much despised here as by Hitler in Germany. Arab nationalism, bettering the nationalism of its Jewish teacher—this is an alarming combination. But to me the worst of the situation is our own small stature. You should listen to the "political" quarrels of the children in the kindergartens; you should read our daily papers and note the character of the constant labor disputes—and you would understand my depression and my instinctive avoidance of the whole subject.

Jerusalem, June 7, 1934

It has been again a full week. It started with the arrival of another group of German children, this time not a very large group. I went down to Haifa to meet them and accompany them to their destination, a *kibbutz* [2] near Petach Tikvah. I had visited this *kibbutz* several times before. They are in Palestine a unique group, for the most part pre-Hitlerite German Jews, all young, and all deeply religious, not only outwardly, not only observant of the ceremonial law, but religious from the same sort of conviction that dominates the thoroughgoing communist or socialist—by which I mean that their human relations are regulated by their religious principles. It is still a struggling group. While they have land and are cultivating it and have begun to develop every branch of agricultural economy possible on that strip of land—a good strip—they are at the same time day-laborers in the adjacent villages.

Jerusalem, July 6, 1934

I don't think I'll be able to write about anything—as I can talk and think about nothing else—except the death of Bialik. His loss is irreparable. That sounds commonplace. At this time of internal rupture among the Jews in Palestine and Poland more particularly, he was the only hope. His being taken is a misfortune nothing short of diabolic.

That he was a poet, a genuine poet, for children and adult thinkers alike, is one thing. He was a re-creator of the Hebrew language. He was a rare scholar. Those who knew him intimately consider him the pattern of what a noble man should be in every respect and relation.

I did not have intimate personal contacts with him. What I lament is the passing of a prophet. At the moment I can't think of anything to say that will convey to you the essence of my mourning except that his death leaves me with the

---

[2] A *kibbutz* is a large *kvuza*, i.e., co-operative settlement, which is part of a country-wide organization of similar settlements.

same hopeless empty despair as the failure of the Disarmament Conference. I wonder at myself, for I don't think I have great capacity as a hero-worshiper. And as I write I almost come to the conclusion that my confidence in his powers and the expectations I fastened upon his personality were due not so much to a primary personal judgment of his character and his ability as to the influence he wielded over the public, the response he evoked whenever he made a public utterance, the exaltation of spirit his addresses produced.

He did not resort to sentimental evocations—he was sober, full of knowledge and information, which he utilized to carry home his points with almost cold logicality; and yet his audiences—and they were always great in number —responded enthusiastically, the sort of enthusiasm that led inevitably to action, if that was the end to which he wanted it to direct itself. And how scathing his words were when he scourged the Jews, as he did on rare occasions. It was to be expected that this prophetic aspect of his make-up was going to manifest itself with frequency in the period ahead, because his creative ability in poetical form had to a certain extent come to a halt.

If you had witnessed the dumb grief of the masses of the people when the news of his death came, and the spontaneous expressions of mourning on every side, you would realize that I am not exaggerating.

Jerusalem, July 13, 1934

It was a full week and a hot one. Sunday, a meeting in Tel Aviv; Monday afternoon, off to Haifa to investigate possibilities for apprenticeships; Tuesday afternoon and evening meetings on social service problems; Wednesday and Thursday dashing in an auto from *kvuza* to *kvuza* to arrange for groups of boys and girls and visiting the groups already settled. If one went into particulars, there would be much to write about. Our mother's saying—I wonder whether you remember how often it was on her lips—*"Man wird so alt wie eine Kuh, Und lernt noch immer dazu,"* occurs to me so frequently.

The outstanding impression is the incessant striving of the people to create, create values particularly in the form of living. Their interest in life is painful in its intensity. It glorifies—for them—every daily act, no matter how lowly, from dishwashing and cleaning to the vintage and the discussion of an educational program. In the rural districts, at least within the four walls, as it were, of the *kvuza,* one does not feel the irritation of party strife, though the *kvuza* builders are the most determined and consistent of the partisans. They live their principles while talking them. In the city communities they only declaim.

Jerusalem, August 24, 1934

This week the only incident that broke the usual round was a visit to the women's prison near Bethlehem, in which over fifty Jewish women are confined awaiting deportation. Why they are sentenced to imprisonment for two and three months before deportation, I cannot fathom.

The business of illegal immigration, with all the excitement it arouses among the Arabs, gets on one's nerves. The Jews maintain that the illegal Arab immigration from Trans-Jordania and Syria is many times greater than the Jewish from Germany, Poland, and the Asiatic countries, but that the government sees only the Jews. And it is true that while one reads in the papers from time to time of the deportation of some Syrians and Hauranites, the long lists of deported contain ninety-nine percent Jewish names.

The Arabs from the surrounding countries are crowding in, lured by the tales of prosperity in Palestine; the Jews come away from intolerable conditions called persecution, which probably are no less due to economic causes.

Last night I was carried away, far away, from all such sordid conditions. It was full moon, and a concert was given in the amphitheater of the Hebrew University on Mount Scopus. The night was magically beautiful, and the moonlight on the Moab hills bathed them in an atmosphere and in colors that have no name. The program was exquisite. It consisted entirely of dance music—beginning with Bach, Handel, and Gluck, through Beethoven and Mozart, down to Strauss. The orchestra consisted entirely of strings. The effect was fairy-like. There was a huge audience that sat spellbound while the music lasted and broke loose into applause of genuine appreciation when it ceased. I hated to come back to automobiles, deportations, juvenile offenders, and crass poverty in the teeth of prosperity.

Jerusalem, October 19, 1934

I have survived my own Hebrew speech and all the rest of it connected with the cornerstone-laying of the Hadassah-University Hospital on Mount Scopus.[3] It was really a very dignified and impressive ceremonial. Events can't help being so when they come off on Mount Scopus, on the spot from which Titus hurled his firebrands into the Temple area.

And, of course, one cannot help being impressed by one's own funeral. That's what it was to the "mother" of Hadassah, and the "founder" of Hadassah, and the "or-

---

[3] She was chairman of the ceremonies of laying the cornerstone of the Rothschild-Hadassah-University Hospital and Medical School, the largest medical institution in the Near East. The Hebrew University is likewise built on imperial Mount Scopus.

ganizer" of Hadassah, and the "inspiration" of Hadassah. What were my thoughts? Should I confess to them—to the cynical ones? I couldn't ward off, first, the thought that in spite of all the respect and even homage shown me—and I don't doubt its sincerity—I have so little power. I can't get a thing done because I can't get co-operation. Then came the thought of the price I should have to pay. I knew the price—that the next day and thereafter the seekers after place and the unemployed would come or would write and tell me, as I had so much influence, wouldn't I secure for them what they wanted or needed, since I could do it by simply uttering a word. And they did come the very next day! But something else crept into my mind. I went whizzing through the Shenandoah Valley, the apple country, and across to the Atlantic Coast, to and through Charleston, and I gloried in that other time, nearly four years ago now, when I was threatened with a similar funeral. I had made my escape with you in Adele's little Ford. Even the skidding after John Brown's monument danced through my mind. That one time at least I cheated an audience.

I suppose you read that we, the speakers, broadcast to the Hadassah Convention at Washington. I confess I got a thrill out of that. But even that was enveloped in a funereal atmosphere—the solemn silence enjoined upon the participants, the hangings and floor-coverings that shrouded the room, the cryptic technical words that passed between, "Hello, New York," and "Hello, London," and doubtless "Hello, Jerusalem," and the expectancy until the red light flashed up to announce that the connection between the two distant continents had been established—it was awesome.

I am writing this letter after a strenuous day and a half at Tel Aviv, all given to social service adjustments. I came to the conclusion that I ought to accept the funeral rites at the cornerstone-laying as the end of my active life—I ought to vacate in favor of younger forces. I am losing patience with my own futile efforts at "organization." I think this letter should be read only by my sisters. It's too pessimistic for the young people—too revolting.

Jerusalem, October 26, 1934

Did you succumb to the wonder of the England–Australia air race? It moved me as much as talking from Jerusalem to New York. Both are black magic. As I read the details of Scott's flight, the words "Langley's Folly" constantly flashed into my mind. To think that I am in a position to remember the scorn and sarcasm that were poured out on Professor Langley, when again and again his flying-machine thumped down into the Potomac and finally was allowed to lie there water-logged—and to see the triumph of his principles, aeronautic and mechanical. If one could forget a whole lot, such as, for instance, the ugly demonstration against Jews by Jews at Haifa last week, what a wonderful world and life it would be.

Bertha's description of the autumn woods increased my homesickness a hundred percent. These last few weeks I have been telling everybody who would listen to me how much I was longing for a glimpse of our woods at home. The Palestinians who hail from Eastern Europe cannot understand my calling America "home." Neither nature nor man binds them to their former abodes. I wonder whether I shall ever think of America as a stepmother.

Jerusalem, November 8, 1934

We have had our first loss by death among the youth groups, and I am not easy in my mind as to the care the boy got in the early stages, when he ailed and the typhoid fever diagnosis had not yet been made. I was informed of his illness exactly twenty-four hours before the end, and even then the information reached me accidentally. I believe that is what worries me most, that I haven't yet got it across to those responsible for the groups that I must be informed of every exceptional state or happening. To be sure, illness in its early stages is not always alarming, and I suppose I'd be furious if I'd get information about every cold and discomfort felt by one of the young people all over the country. Nevertheless, the boy's death discouraged me. I constantly see his parents in Hamburg before me.

This week, too, the General Secretary of the German Department left for Europe, and I am left to struggle with problems which I announced from the start I would refuse to be responsible for—the problems involved in the financing of the Youth Immigration. They are complicated and perplexing, and I don't like financial botherments in any form.

The enclosed letter from Dr. Hess gave me a peculiar sensation. It put me into a sort of trauma. It took an effort to attach myself to that other self of two generations ago. That other self of two generations ago, I remember, scouted the idea of old age! I wasn't ever going to have the peculiarities of old age that I deprecated in the aged of those days—but I have them!

Jerusalem, December 14, 1934

I have been northward, to pay a flying visit to a *kvuza* of the Ha-Shomer Ha-Zair.[4] The country abutting on the Sea of Galilee was itself a sea when it wasn't a swamp. The auto couldn't approach the *kvuza*. We had to leave it on the

---

[4] The leftist wing of the labor movement.

main road, and trudge on foot through the mud to the houses. Mud! Great clods stuck to my rubbers and very soon I could hardly lift my feet, they were so heavy with mud. However, it was a blessed rainfall.

The reason of my trip was a rumor that the Ha-Shomer Ha-Zair *kvuza* had not fulfilled its obligation to prepare houses and all that goes with dwellings for a group of twenty-eight German youths to come in two weeks from that time. I was due at a meeting at Haifa at three o'clock in the afternoon. So it was a race against time. We managed it, and confirmed the rumor. You can imagine my state of mind and conscience. I got the promise that all hands would be put to work and things got half-way ready. They are coming eighty-six strong on Monday, and I shall be posting up to Haifa again to meet them and distribute them among seven different places. The undertaking is getting tremendously big. Naturally not all the boys and girls stay with the groups they come with. There are all sorts of reasons for making changes. Such individual cases cause me no end of correspondence—and wondering thought.

Another event—and it happens that it was an eventful event for me—was the Delegates' Assembly which was called together for a short session, primarily to adopt the budget of the Vaad Leumi for 1934–1935, and secondarily to render a report on the activities of the Vaad Leumi. I succeeded at last in putting the social service on the map. How? I don't know. I confined myself to the problem of the child— the delinquent, the psychopath, the defective, the behavior problem, as well as the normal, for whom no provision is made here. The child never fails to make a stirring appeal, naturally; and with us neglect and poverty, in spite of our vaunted prosperity, have worked havoc these last two years. Juvenile offenses have multiplied cruelly. It's poverty that does it, with the absence of all opportunity for children to occupy themselves in their leisure time—no libraries, no organized sports, no clubs, and particularly no manual training. Palestinian children are an outstanding example of the mischief Satan finds for idle hands.

So the child appeal registered. But I am inclined to believe that I succeeded because, strangely enough, I spoke freely and forcefully in Hebrew. I was surprised, for I had had no time to prepare myself and spoke from English notes. I was tired from my long jaunt in the rain, and yet the words flowed. It only proved to me how right I am when I insist, as I do, that my usefulness in Palestine has been cruelly curtailed by my having to use a language that is not intimately interwoven with all my experiences from childhood on.

Jerusalem, December 28, 1934

Two weeks ago eighty-six children arrived from Germany. I met seventy-five of them at Haifa and escorted them to the Emek Ha-Jordan settlements. I remained with them until the next day, saw them well bestowed, assured myself of the presence of screens, mosquito-nets, and sanitary installation; I celebrated a charming reception with them, at which there was feasting, singing, dancing, and speech-making, and for which the settlers of five neighboring *kvuzot* had come together at Deganiah Aleph. The *kvuzot* were naturally not established as educational institutions, but they might have been if one was to judge by the way they make these fugitive youths at home and prepare for their training.

My pessimism regularly vanishes when I spend a few hours in a *kvuza*—I forget that I am a cynic. It's a life of hardship, but not of strain. And the hardship has its com-

pensation in the form of achievement and the consciousness that both the hardship and the success are a common
responsibility and a common advantage.

[TO MRS. ROSE JACOBS]   *Jerusalem, February 22, 1935*

In all the fourteen winters I have spent in Palestine, I
haven't ever experienced such constant rain. There is, of
course, great rejoicing in the country districts—and great
mud! I met a new group of young immigrants last Monday,
sixteen of them, and accompanied them to Mishmar Ha-
Emek, Irma Lindheim's *kvuza*. So I tested the mud, but
also became more intimately acquainted with Mishmar Ha-
Emek. Mrs. Lindheim's enthusiasm over it is justified.

Its members are not above thinking about and caring for
externals. For instance, families do not live in congregate
houses, but in separate one-room huts. That means securing
that precious commodity—privacy. Mishmar was selected
by all the Ha-Shomer Ha-Zair groups in the country as the
fittest place for the central school of the movement. A remarkable building has been erected, in many respects the
last word in construction, especially in the sanitary arrangements, which are equal to those at the King David Hotel at
Jerusalem. The teachers are superb men. It is an intellectual and a spiritual experience to acquaint oneself with the
institution and its aims. I am not prepared to speak of its
achievements. It is very young. I shall never be able to speak
of them, for I cannot expect to live long enough to see the
ultimate results. A generation at least must pass over the
heads of its pupils for such judgment.

Your letter also gives me your suggestion about securing
the names of the relatives of the German newcomers resi-
dent in America. From the propaganda point of view the
idea is good; less so from the point of view of the develop-

ment of a Jewish Palestine. While I take every occasion to stress that we Zionists want Palestine for all Jews, at this stage it would be well if there were not too many Hitler-made Zionists developing it. I am told there will be an influx of 20,000 immigrants in the course of the next three months, most of them from Poland. Our inner organization is woefully inadequate. Hitler came too early. Jewish Palestine had not found itself; and Zionist Palestine, the Palestine of the honeymoon days of the pioneers, had lost itself. Meanwhile, the speculator, the fanatical politician, the advocate of fictitious marriages as a counterpoise to an illiberal immigration policy, took possession. Those elements should not be fortified.

On the technical side, your suggestion would demand minute organization, and we haven't too many organizers here. Doubtless the chaos will resolve itself some day soon, but just now we are living here in the most chaotic chaos conceivable.

Jerusalem, April 19, 1935

Last week the hurry and scurry of Palestinian life got the better of me. . . . To all this there has been the bass-drum accompaniment of so-called peace talk around Germany's "unilateral" action in disposing of the Versailles treaty.

I *must* find time to get my passport into shape! There's bound to be war. And if there is, what will be the fate of, for instance, this hardly built-up "homeland" of the Jew? It will be scattered bloodily to the winds—that's my opinion. That will be only one of the many still remaining values to be shattered and dissipated.

Jerusalem, May 3, 1935

Next week I again go off on a German children investigating and visiting tour in the Emek. I shall spend a few days at a gathering of the teachers and leaders of all the German youth groups in the country, at which pedagogic and organization questions are to be discussed. At this moment the chief point under discussion is the possibility, from the political and financial point of view, of extending the movement to embrace youth groups in other countries, Poland foremost among them.

It is interesting that a movement started by children— the initiator was the Jüdische Jugendhilfe, a federation of Jewish, chiefly Zionist, youth organizations in Germany— gives promise of developing into a Jewish world movement for youth. It *is* something to be attached to such a movement when one is seventy-four, isn't it? But one pays for the honor. It demands every scintilla of time and strength and involves one in endless minute details of organization.

Jerusalem, May 31, 1935

It is really next to incredible that a person of my age can keep going at such a pace. But it must be admitted that I am absolutely juiceless. Life rides by me at full speed. Nothing makes any impression, certainly my memory retains no impressions. Such an old age! And when I was a little girl I expected a serene old age, such as it seemed to my unsophisticated years the Quakers among whom I then lived were enjoying. But now I am sure that their demure gray Shaker bonnets hid turmoil.

The week was crowded even beyond the usual on account of a Social Service Conference that lasted two days, and the preparations for which took many more. But it was extraordinarily successful. Two years ago I arranged my first conference. There were twelve or fifteen persons present. At this conference the number in attendance ran up to over two hundred and the discussions were lively and to the point (for the most part). Today I got the left-overs, the people who always must add something in a particular way.

The other event of the week was the death of Schmarya Levin. I went to Tel Aviv for the funeral. I had gone to see him only ten days before his death—for which I am grateful. He was as animated as ever I have seen him, and spoke with the same bubbling fullness as always.

II

In August 1935 Miss Szold set out for a conference in Amsterdam summoned by the various European groups raising money for the Youth Aliyah. En route she attended the World Zionist Congress in Lucerne. To her surprise— for such things always surprised her—she was greeted by an overwhelming ovation; and the German Zionist organizations announced the founding of a Palestinian settlement to bear her name. Dearer to her heart, the Congress created a committee on social service work in Palestine and moreover voted it funds. Then the Amsterdam conference converted the Youth Aliyah from an emergency undertaking "into a movement to include not only the thousands of young people who must be removed from Germany, but also from Lithuania, Poland, France, and Carpathian Russia." She might well exclaim: "We are facing gigantic tasks!"

From Amsterdam she went to Berlin. There her heart-rending experience gave her—and she tells us why—the heart to meet the tasks.

Off Cyprus, August 15, 1935

The week previous to this one of preparation for the journey, I spent in visiting all the groups in their new habi-

tations—nearly 600 children. Everywhere I was met with
individual problems, the problems of the adolescent, until
I felt that the undertaking was a failure. But when I summarized the complaints, I found that all together—health,
sex, activity, education, parents (the last cause is the most
persnickety)—amounted to less than five percent of the
whole number enrolled. And when I summarized the advantages and the achievements, I was—I write the word
even now so threadbare—thrilled. I keep on saying that this
is the most worthwhile undertaking I have ever been connected with; and after my grand tour, I am convinced that I
am right in my appraisal.

The achievements lie on both sides—for the main beneficiaries, the youth, and incidentally for the *kvuzot*. The
latter must bring themselves up to a better mark in sanitation and in developing educational systems for the youth
of the country. I wish I were younger—my broken back
after getting through with packing up the contents of my
room warns me of my age.

[TO BENJAMIN AND SARAH LEVIN]

Lucerne, August 29, 1935

It is amazing how successful a Zionist Congress is in preventing you from doing anything, even from doing the
business of the Congress. At the same time one's sense of
duty keeps one chained down; and with the Lake of Lucerne and Pilatus and the William Tell country and the
Rhône Glacier calling out to you to come and see, you stay
put and enjoy none of the beauties that beckon and tempt.

I wonder whether the news of the honor done to me has
penetrated to you. My German associates have announced
the foundation of a settlement to be named after me. It is
thrilling, but the surprise nearly paralyzed me. Now I've

got accustomed to the idea, and all I can think of is how they are going to adapt my awkward name to a Jewish Palestinian village.[5]

Lucerne, September 5, 1935

I was induced to come to the Zionist Congress only in the interest of the Youth Immigration. My duty done to it, I had expected to go to Berlin, but then, suddenly, the possibility loomed up of doing something for social service. The Congress Committee had for the first time in the history of Zionist Congresses provided for a Committee on Social Service. There was nothing to do but stay on and see that business through.

And it turned out worth while. We put social service on the map. All I asked of the Budget Committee was a modest allotment for service to the immigrant. The allotment was not granted in the sum asked for. It was reduced by two-thirds, but my claim was declared just and proper. That recognition is bound to be worth a great deal in the future.

Vienna, October 1, 1935

I have lived a century since I last wrote. Where was my last news from? From Amsterdam? Amsterdam was interesting and stimulating—I refer to the Conference. But when such a thing as Berlin lies between Amsterdam and Vienna, nothing counts. I don't think I shall ever be able to describe what Berlin was and means. To be there is living history in a stirring time, at once depressing and elevating. The Jews, whom Jeremiah and myself criticize unmercifully, are a wonderful people—even the German Jews.

---

[5] Nothing was easier. The settlement, located in southern Judea and manned by young Germans, is called Kfar Szold—Szold Village.

En route to Alexandria, October 10, 1935

I entered Berlin at the very moment, almost, at which
Hitler was delivering his speech at Nuremberg, in which
the new legislation was announced.[6] More or less, the Nazi
intentions were known before. But with the saving grace
of humanity, one hopes up to the last moment that the
worst will not supervene.

I knew that in Berlin all sorts of preparations had been
made to press the most out of my visit for the good of the
propaganda for the Youth Immigration; and I could not
bear the thought of the public demonstrations which had
been intended for the previous week and were now going
to be kept to the letter, though the dreaded blow had fallen.
The Jewish organizations went through with the program
with grim determination. They used each of my public ap-
pearances as an occasion to assert their undaunted courage
in the face of the degradation inflicted upon them, and to
announce plans chiefly of an educational character to remove the sting from the persecution and maintain the cultural standard of former days, at least in dealing with their
young people.

I am writing in general terms. The meaning is not clear
unless one enters into the details of the planning, which
is designed to give opportunity for a junior high school
education to the young people, thus bridging over the
dangerous period from fourteen to sixteen. At sixteen the
Youth Immigration carries them to Palestine—if there are
means! At present, before their plans materialize, the boys
and girls are left totally without occupation and without
hope during those two or three years.

I cannot begin to describe to you what indignities they

---

[6] The Nuremberg laws which turned the Jews from citizens into
pariahs.

are exposed to, not so much in the large cities as in the small towns. In the populous centers, like Berlin and Hamburg, the Jews are living, as it were, anonymously. They are affected of course by the legislation, but less by the malice of the Nazi madmen. In the small towns every Jew is known, and Nazi persecution strikes deeper. While I was in Germany, the Jews in Berlin had to send milk and bread to the small places all over the Reich, but principally in the northeast, the Nazis having forbidden the victual-sellers to dispose of their wares to Jews. Little children were starving.

With my own eyes, as I passed through villages, one after the other, on my way from Berlin to two youth camps, one in the Mark [of] Brandenburg, the other in Silesia, at which our young people are trained for immigration into Palestine, I saw huge signs stretched across the main road with the legend: *"Juden nicht erwünscht"* or *"Mädchen und Frauen, Juden sind euer Verderber."* [7] And with my own ears, while I was making an address, I heard the marching Storm Troops yell: *"Jude, verrecke!"* [8]

To be sure, there are many Germans—I myself met some of them—Aryans who hate the regime. Here is an illustration: In Berlin I was living in the house of a Mr. and Mrs. X——, a family of the highest caliber, intellectually and in social position. An Aryan friend of Mrs. X—— asked her to allow her to come (from some small town) to live with her as a guest for a week or ten days, and bring her daughter of ten with her. Her reason for the request was, that in case her child became infected with the Nazi virus, she wanted to be able to remind her that she had been the guest of Jews, and that she had found them lovable.

A very well-known artist sent me the copy of a picture

---

[7] "Jews not wanted"—"Girls and women, Jews are your depravers."
[8] "Death to the Jew!"

in recognition of the Youth Immigration movement. The artist insists that Hitler will not rest until every last Jew has been hunted out of Germany.

The Jews themselves—I mean those who see clearly—think so too. You would know it to be their opinion if you saw the crowds that beleaguer the rooms of the Palestine Office in Berlin to apply for certificates of immigration. The success of Zionism and Palestine is ghastly!

Oh! before I go on with a description of my personal experiences, I must warn you that, though we, you and I, may think ourselves obscure individuals whose utterances are of no public concern, you must not use any incidents mentioned by me, at least not in connection with names like A—— or X——: the consequences may be dire. Sticking harmless people into concentration camps is still a daily occurrence.

On the evening of my arrival in Berlin, the first public meeting arranged on account of my presence took place. It was a small meeting limited to the chosen representatives of the various organizations that had originated the idea of a village to bear my name. There were about 125 persons present. After the formal introductory address came a surprise that took me off my feet. The speaker, a Mr. Seeligsohn, began by saying that fifty-three (I think it was fifty-three) years ago the Philadelphia community which had arranged a commemoration service in honor of Moses Mendelssohn's hundredth birthday could find none better to deliver the address than the rabbi of the Oheb Shalom Congregation of Baltimore. The speaker then proceeded to analyze the address our father delivered; and he used it to demonstrate the love of the Jew for German literature, the German language, the German people, and his identification with them. He continued to quote from our father's sermon striking passages, many of which I remembered. The inference was that in this way I was prepared to take up work for the German immigrants, especially German youth.

Can you imagine my consternation and embarrassment and pride? Or doesn't the incident affect you as it did me? Perhaps my fortunes make a difference. You have remained more or less in your milieu. You have no need to legitimize yourself. Your background is known and recognized. Ever since I have been living in Palestine, I have had the feeling that I hadn't the protection of the rock from which I was hewn. And here suddenly the rock was the important feature. I confess I felt solemn and touched.

It is impossible for me to describe, even to you, my sisters, what was done to me in Berlin. My reception was nothing short of homage. Even the little children knew me. If I get time I'll send you a copy of what two boys wrote about the luncheon given in my honor at their Children's Home, part of which has already been transferred to Palestine.

The other meeting that I should like to describe, if I could, is the one with the parents of the boys and girls— 750 of them—under my charge in Palestine. Again can you imagine my consternation when I entered a hall packed with 800 persons, with whom I was to have an intimate conversation about the children from whom they had separated voluntarily?

Wherever I came they told me—and I have no reason to doubt their sincerity—that my presence, the presence of an outsider interested in their affairs, had fortified them to bear the new trials imposed upon them. And I myself, when the time came to leave, felt that I was abandoning a dear sick child, mortally ill, who needed my ministrations. I still feel regretful. Will you think me sentimental? You would not, if you had been in the Berlin atmosphere a half-hour, in which no three Jews can gather together and not speak of *the* nasty, black thing. That is one of the accursed aspects of the situation—one cannot escape from it. The whole of life is permeated with it, negatively and positively. Jews keep away from the theater and the concert and the lecture hall and the opera and the cafés and the restaurants—they refrain from a thousand normal activities. They might as well be in a ghetto—indeed, they would be better off behind ghetto gates.

And outside the Jewish precincts, the Italian bombs were beginning to explode at the threshold of the innocent Abyssinians!

Up till now—and I am writing this chapter thirty-six hours before the scheduled landing time—the passage on the Adriatic and the Mediterranean, in among the Greek islands, has been smooth and placid. The alarmists predict trouble for us on landing. At Brindisi, the air- and seaplanes darkened the skies above, and we have sighted English war vessels; but I do not believe there is any foundation for alarm. I shall mail this letter from Palestine. If you get it, you will know that all went well.

I wonder whether this endless letter will impress you as self-centered, when the world is waiting with bated breath to learn whether it is again to be convulsed by international complications? And yet I could not but write and tell you about myself in Europe. I cannot hide from you that what happened to me there kept me in a state of bewildered wonderment. I have been trying to analyze why the routine administrative work I did should have impressed the German Jewish community so deeply. I have reached a conclusion: it is all a matter of language. My mastery of the German language brought me near to them and them to me. In so far as that is correct, Mr. Seeligsohn was right in stressing our father's distinction, his love of German litera- ture, and all the rest. The remainder of the exaggerated praise is ascribable to the excited state of Jewish feeling in Germany. But you had a right to know what happened to me. I had to write about myself.

[She must have written likewise to Hadassah in America. When the Youth Aliyah goal seemed far out of reach Hadas- sah sent her a surprise cable.]

Jerusalem, October 26, 1935

I am breathless from the effort to catch up with all that has accumulated during the two months I was away. The goal is still at the other end of a long stretch of road. And here comes a cable from Hadassah to come to its Conven- tion at Thanksgiving time for a single day to present the new project. It is thinking of going into the Youth Im- migration movement. Of course, I am wickedly tempted to accept the invitation. Perhaps we could repeat, for my seventy-fifth birthday, the wonderful experience of my seventieth. Is it credible that five years have passed since that snowy dash through the South? The temptation must be resisted. My commitments here are too heavy, and we are in for a terrible winter—a mass immigration and no funds!

And so I wonder whether I'll ever get back to America again. I've never been away so long before.

Jerusalem, November 22, 1935

My work flows on as usual on a heavy tide of work, and not a little anxiety. My big family keeps me in a stew. There is much illness and serious illness at that. I believe I wrote you that there are also engagements, and I am expected by the parents at the other end to investigate the prospective bridegroom. I find I am much better at nursing, at least by proxy, than I am at such delicate investigation. And what happens after the investigation, even supposing that the prospective bridegroom has a record that qualified him for the process of being kicked downstairs? The girl marries him and it remains to be seen whether they lived happily ever after. I don't find it funny—not a bit. Nevertheless, the movement I am engaged in is beautiful!

. . . Here in Palestine it is a daily occurrence, my meeting people whose families were known to me and by me more or less intimately in the old Oheb Shalom days. The two ends of my life are joining themselves into a circle.

CHAPTER SIXTEEN

The Arab Sword

I

"It was a fairy tale and you were one of the fairy god-mothers," Miss Szold wrote of her seventy-fifth birthday celebration to Tamar de Sola Pool, president of Hadassah. Besides the chapters of Hadassah, thousands of friends and admirers not only in America but throughout the world gathered in meetings to do her honor—"rare and notable," she called it. The rarest part was the days she could spend in the countryside with her sisters.

She relished profoundly the renewal of the fast-dwindling ties with her early youth. "Girls" from the Western Female High School and "young ladies" from the Baltimore Woman's Literary Club forgot their white hair and their wrinkles, as she forgot hers, when they looked into one another's eyes. In Baltimore it was Dr. Harry Friedenwald who addressed the celebration in her honor. When she read later what he had said, she wrote him: "I am not the one to judge whether your characterization of my personality and ability is true to fact. Of another aspect I can judge—your evocation of our past, its beauty, its simplicity, its genuineness, its warmth. That touches every chord of my being and plays upon them. That gives me a sense of harmony, joining the latter end to the beginning, as though there had been no transformations." Only age—and then by good fortune—can experience this integration, rounding-out, and completion of the inner life.

The best of the fairy tale was, as it should be, the end. Miss Szold sailed back for Palestine with the pledge that

Hadassah with its 50,000 members, which meant 50,000 workers and contributors, would support the Youth Aliyah.[1] In Palestine more honors and fetes and a jubilee fund of $20,000 awaited her. And the second day after she landed she went back to work.

Haifa, March 4, 1936

My advice to humankind is either not to attain to seventy-five or flee to the North Pole or to the innermost Sahara when it comes along. Benjamin[2] maintains—he has been following me in the papers—that, despite all that has happened to me, I have not attained the pinnacle of fame because no sardine has been named for me. It appears that there is a Bialik sardine and an Arlosoroff sardine.

And to think I can write in this silly way when tomorrow, according to all signs and tokens reported in the press, the cymbals of war may be sounding. This morning's papers report that the German Consul-General in Jerusalem published a notice addressed to the German Jewish citizens living in Palestine of a certain age to register for military service! Does Germany really want the Jews who have had to seek refuge from her barbarity in Palestine to take up arms for her greater glory?

I must return to celebrations to tell you at least one thing —that a jubilee fund for a social purpose amounting to £3500 was collected while I was away in my name, I to decide its purpose. The last few words indicate the fly in the ointment. A thousand different decisions have been suggested to me.[3]

---

[1] The present membership of Hadassah is 100,000.

[2] Her nephew, Benjamin Levin, then living in Palestine.

[3] A month later, when the sum had reached £4000, she decided to devote it "as an endowment fund for child and youth care, in the hope that similar endowment funds will be co-ordinated with it."

Jerusalem, March 6, 1936

Just now a letter from Bertha was handed to me dated February 16, in which she mentions a reception at Haifa and the freedom of the city of Tel Aviv. But what you read about me is not a tithe of what there is to tell. One function after another, one obituary after another, until I actually wished myself a corpse with unhearing ears. And the flowers and the letters and the other "attentions." [4] I have never been so heartily tired of anything as I have been made of myself.

All the time my work lay untouched, except that from the second day on I hopped off, whenever an escape from "affairs" was possible, to visit the groups of youths who had come in during my absence, or the social service stations. During my absence the individual problems among my nearly thousand young people have multiplied and been intensified; and I must stay put in order to solve them, not to speak of social service, in which the care of the immigrant has obtruded itself until one sees nothing else.

Jerusalem, March 13, 1936

I have never been busier and kept longer hours of work than since my return. I have an idea, nevertheless, that the excitements of this recent period, since the middle of August when I left for Europe, have left their marks upon my physical vigor. At that, if you get your information from the press, you can have no notion of the "adulation" that has been paid me here. I believe I have now passed the crisis. Each mail still brings in belated congratulations, some of them from Poland, coupled, in many cases, with requests for a certificate of immigration, for the placement of chil-

---

[4] Elsewhere she speaks of more than a thousand letters of congratulation lying unanswered in her desk.

dren, for money with which to do all sorts of outlandish things. A favorite epithet of my eulogists has been "the mother of children in Palestine." Utter strangers, reading this in the press, appeal to me to be a "mother" also to Polish and all sorts of other children.

By now I have accustomed myself to regard myself as an object for dissection. As it were, I stand by and watch the process, and am curiously impersonal. I have really cultivated a scientific detachment.

Afuleh, March 19, 1936

At Tel Yosef the German youth group is discussing its plans after the end of its two years of Youth Aliyah instruction. I wanted to hear reports of the group as such and of the members of the group, and their wishes, and discuss all possibilities with them. They are to leave Tel Yosef on August 1.

Seventeen of them have already determined to remain together as a group, and form together with a similar group of Palestinians a new settlement—with nothing to start on. Five others will go to another *kvuza* and undergo additional agricultural training. That leaves eighteen who haven't yet made up their minds what to do. There are a few among them who have special desires, one to become a nurse, another a teacher, another a carpenter. A large part of the remainder, I fancy, want to go to the cities and earn money to bring their parents over from Germany. They are facing a terrible disappointment. It is one of the saddest of my many sad individual experiences, the letters which I receive from a large number of the young people who write that they cannot enjoy their happiness and their good luck because they know how their parents are suffering.

The beginning of the week was no less exciting for me.

Our annual Social Service Conference, the fourth, took place. The first, three years ago, was attended by fifteen persons; the second, two years ago, by sixty; the third, a year ago, by two hundred and twenty; and this one by over three hundred persons, many men among them, and also many from among the circle of the Labor Party, a recognition of the fact that the work is being done to their satisfaction, not philanthropically, but constructively. The subject was the immigrant. The discussions were satisfactory. Now we only need a little cash! . . .

Jerusalem, March 27, 1936

Where did I leave off? . . . The day carried me from climax to climax. The next stop was at Gevah, with another group of boys and girls whom I had welcomed but had not seen to their settlement. A very special reception had been planned, and I couldn't be there to take the part assigned to me. When the boys and girls filed into the *kvuza* and had been relieved of their impediments, they were at once, each one of the twenty, equipped with a young sapling, and marched off to the edge of the settlement, where a stretch of twelve acres had been prepared for tree-planting, a future piece of woodland to bear my name. Each young immigrant planted a tree, which will always bear his name. Only my place was left vacant. When I got to Gevah the youth group again formed into a procession; and my solitary tree-planting was made an occasion for speechifying, and afterward some more festivity around a well-furnished table. It was all charmingly done; and the boys and girls felt the poetry of being bound, rooted, to the land as their first act.

II

In a few days such idyls and the very trees that evoked them were to be swept away. On April 19 the smoldering Arab revolt broke into the open. For one hundred and seventy-five days bombing, murder, destruction, and terror were rife in the land.[5] Miss Szold continued to write to her sisters; there was no lack of news to relate.

Jerusalem, April 24, 1936

I get bewildered beyond the possibility of extricating myself from contradictory thoughts and views when I read the accounts [of the week's events] in the Jewish papers and extracts from the Arab papers. Who sees straight and clear?

The government of course sticks to cold neutrality bordering on lies. Certainly it holds back evidence and facts that might help to point the way to a genuine evaluation of the state of affairs: as, for instance, that among the first to be attacked, of course by Arabs, were eight Britishers, who were more or less lightly wounded. If that were published in England, let us say, the public would be interested in fixing the blame. And in these uprisings fixing the blame is important; for if, as we believe, the aggressors are Arabs, then the next thing that will be revealed is the fundamental item that the disturbance was the patiently carried-on work of agitators throughout the length and breadth of the land.

A day or two ago, for example, a sheik of prominence issued a proclamation urging the Moslems to resort to their mosques in numbers, for who knows how long they will still enjoy the opportunity of praying in their houses of

---

[5] A readily available account of the Arab uprising is to be found in William B. Ziff's *The Rape of Palestine* (New York, 1938).

worship; the Jews intend to appropriate them as quickly as possible, and they will have the ability to do it, for their numbers are growing prodigiously.

On account of such incitement the whole country looked forward with apprehension to today, Friday, in Jerusalem, when the armed villagers stream into the city and crowd into the narrow streets leading to the Aksa Mosque. The fact that the strike of Arab shopkeepers and laborers was made to spread by well-organized picketing did not tend to lessen the danger. However, it appears that the government was stampeded by the Jews into taking effective measures of prevention. I am writing between three and four in the afternoon and the report is that all's quiet.

Even I, a Jeremiah-like critic of ourselves, must admit that since last Sunday the Jewish communities, nervous and jumpy though they were, have behaved with exemplary self-restraint.

Acts of terrorism have been occurring on all the roads these many months past. As the acts multiplied, it became evident that not pillage but political murder was the object. Ten or twelve days ago the political intent became particularly obvious. Autobusses were stopped on one of the roads, and the passengers divided into two groups, a non-Jewish and a Jewish. The Jews were threatened and one of them shot down.

After the funeral of this victim in Tel Aviv last Friday, a demonstration took place, staged, it appears, by a group of young hot-heads. The Histadrut [6] came out with an attack on the Revisionists as the originators. It cannot forget the murder of Arlosoroff. Feeling continued to run high in consequence. On the following day, the little Arab shoeblacks who ply their trade in Tel Aviv were cuffed and

[6] The Federation of Jewish Labor.

kicked, and the Arab fruit-vendors beaten up, by Jews of course, and sent bruised and bleeding to Jaffa. At the same time news came in of two Arab dead found in the southern section, in the vicinity of Tel Aviv; and the cry arose among the Arabs that it was a Jewish act of reprisal. Today the government is offering a reward of £200 for information about the murderer. All this was fuel for the fire that burst out in Jaffa on Sunday and shot its tongues of flame to all parts of the country.

The Hebron Jews were evacuated from their city and brought to Jerusalem by the government—I should add against the will of the Jewish authorities, who are, rightly I think, of the opinion that the government owes protection to the Jews in every place. To me, by the way, the evacuation of the Hebronites and the provision for them in Jerusalem was a source of pride. The social service system in Jerusalem worked to perfection. In Tel Aviv the problem is much more serious. The Hebronites brought to Jerusalem count 95, the fugitives from Jaffa to Tel Aviv number 5945! It is just possible that this emergency will convince the Tel Avivans that they, too, must accept a modern system of organized social care.

We are forcing the government to take upon itself at least fifty percent of the outlay involved. I think it should have been one hundred percent, for whether the Jews or the Arabs "began," the casualties are to be laid at the door of the government, which has had endless warnings that it is not providing adequately for the public security.

We shall emerge from this with the number of widows and orphans to be cared for augmented, but otherwise we shall go on as before. Perhaps our faces will be set forward even more determinedly than hitherto. Only a select few will remember that the chief task and lesson is how to solve the race problem.

There has been a terrific amount of tinder accumulating —the Legislative Council, the Parliamentary debate on it, the increased immigration of Jews, the government's discriminatory land legislation, the recent plan of sending a delegation of Arabs to London to offset the favorable Parliamentary debate. The High Commissioner is very distressed. I have the impression that he thought that under his just rule, his even-holding of the Arab and Jewish scales of the balance, nothing of the sort could happen. I think, on the contrary, cold neutrality, especially with an undeveloped population like the Arabs, can work great mischief. Children must be told when they are wrong; punishment is not important, or perhaps it is important not to punish but to explain and train.

Jerusalem, May 1, 1936

It has been a tense week. The Arab agitators sitting in high places have openly and frankly been plotting (if plotting can ever be said to be frank and open) incitement. The instrument is a general strike in which even schoolboys have been made to participate. Their part is to strew nails and bits of iron and glass on all the roads in the country and thoroughfares in the cities, to puncture the automobiles. They succeeded well. So did the sneaks who set fire to houses, shops, forests, and machinery, and uprooted hundreds of fruit trees already bearing fruit. At Ain Harod five hundred and fifty orange and grapefruit trees were destroyed. Can you see the farmers [who had been] working over these trees for years, day by day, standing in the devastated groves? And we were so proud of our afforestation.

Fortunately the forests were rescued after suffering slight damage.

The whole country, north and south, is unquiet; and, if for a moment one forgets, a patrol bobs up in an unexpected place to remind you that a state of siege prevails. Among the Jews there is a constant whispering game going on. Either it's rumor-mongering or it's speculation about the Jewish Self-Defense. It is said that the Self-Defense has been admirable, admirably watchful and admirably restrained. The eastern communities—the Kurds, Persians, Yemenites, Bokharans—are in a particularly high-tension state of apprehension. They are in constant readiness to take to flight. Jaffa has emptied half of its 18,000 Jewish population into Tel Aviv, where eighty-five places— schools, synagogues, halls, private houses empty by chance —have been arranged as camps. Over a thousand volunteers, men and women, came forward there to render service. All the Hebronites are encamped in Jerusalem, all the Jews of Beisan in Tiberias. In the "old city" of Jerusalem, the people have settled in the synagogues. They are unable—they are not permitted by Arab pickets—to go to work. So they move into the list of social service clients.

Rumor says that the commotion has been created by Italian money. It is Italy's way of fighting Great Britain in revenge for sanctions and for stationing a fleet in the eastern Mediterranean. Others say it's German money. Some say it's the example of the Syrians, whose long strike reduced France to a state of submission *vis-à-vis* the Arabs. However that may be, the cry of the Palestinian Arab is: forbid immigration of Jews, forbid land sales to Jews, renounce the mandate with the Balfour Declaration.

The High Commissioner is, I think, a sad man. Many of us have the impression that he felt certain of the rightness of his policy. We think he considered it impossible that under his regime such an outbreak could occur. Yesterday in opening the Levant Fair, nearly ruined by the riots and the strike, he deplored the loss of life and the lawlessness. But he showed no indignation. I still think a dose of right-eous indignation coming from a righteous man—and I believe Sir Arthur Wauchope is a righteous man—might do good.

It's humiliating. I went down to Tel Aviv on two differ-ent occasions during the week. I felt ashamed when the car made a detour in order not to pass through Ramleh, the usual route.

Over the fence of the little fruit garden of my Youth Aliyah office a honeysuckle vine drapes itself. I have been bringing bunches of the blooms home with me and making myself homesick as I draw in the fragrance that fills my room.

I spoke of interference with work. Don't imagine that I am idling. I have never been busier in my life. There is one easement—curfew. What a blessed institution! Why was it ever given up? I am sure of my hours from seven in the evening until five in the morning. And the quiet!

Jerusalem, May 8, 1936

There still is only one subject—the disturbances. My opinion is that the end is not in sight by a long shot. Today the Arab Supreme Committee announced "civil disobedi-ence" as the order of the day. Unless the government stops immigration of Jews, interdicts land sales to Jews, and es-tablishes a national Arab government by May 15, not only will the present strike be continued but the Arab popula-tion will refuse to pay taxes.

The Arabs still do not seem to understand that Palestine is situated differently from Syria. In Palestine, besides Arabs, there are the Jews. They carry on in the face of all sorts of dangers—knifing, stabbing, beating, wrecked automobiles by nails strewn by schoolchildren (under the tutelage of the Central Strike Committee) on all the roads, within and outside of cities, trees uprooted by the thousands, arson in fields, in woods, of factories, grain in storehouses and unripened—every sort of danger that can be created by cruelty and chicanery. The Jews go right on.

Underground there is an effective, restrained, marvelously disciplined Self-Defense. All the stanch youth of the country is enrolled in it, to one's pride and one's regret. It's not the way—that is certain—of adjusting the Arab problem. This time, when even the basest prejudice cannot blame the Jews for the outbreak immediately, there is less disguised talk among the Jews than ever to my knowledge, on the ways and means of establishing a *rapprochement*. Even the chauvinistic patriots do not deprecate peace and compromise talk. I wonder whether the mood will outlast the danger, the inconvenience, the economic losses.

Jerusalem, May 15, 1936

The sickening business goes right on, and is so omnipresent to all the senses that one can speak and think of nothing else.

It is superfluous to speak of what it means to me to hear day after day of the slaughter of innocent, guileless men— Jews and Arabs alike. But one tries to express one's feelings about the destruction of trees and crops. The beautiful woodland at Mishmar Ha-Emek, the pride of the settlement, as it might well be, has been set afire eight times. The other night the incendiaries applied the match to ten different places, and the blaze had to be fought simultaneously

by ten fire-fighter groups. Saplings are uprooted ruthlessly.
The other day one hundred and fifty olive trees of seven
years' growth were cut down—in this treeless country!

The High Commissioner remains inscrutable. He expresses formal regret over murder, arson, destruction, and
sympathy with the sufferers and the bereaved; but his words
sound formal and official. He has, to be sure, brought in
additional troops to avoid a great outbreak today, the date
for the commencement of the resistance in the form of non-
payment of taxes. To a delegation from the Jewish community he said yesterday: "You may be sure in a few days
there will be quiet." That has a sinister sound—it may
mean yielding to the Arab demands. If that happens, we
may as well crawl back into the German rat-holes and the
Polish rabbit-warrens.

An interesting incident happened to me a few days ago,
which in the retrospect I realize might have been *fearfully*
interesting. I went by auto from Haifa to Nahalal to visit
a group of German young people whom I had not been
able to welcome at the harbor. When our auto was in sight
of the Nesher factory (Portland cement), where Arabs as
well as Jews are employed in considerable numbers, and
where the agitators have been particularly active and successful in influencing the Arab workmen to strike, it suddenly stopped.

We saw before us two long lines of Arabs, men and children, drawn up in white holiday attire, looking very dignified and picturesque. They signed to us to come along, as
though to assure us that there was no evil intent; and we
rode through between the two rows as though a guard of
honor had been commandeered for us. We wondered what
it was all about, and came to the conclusion that it was
meant for the reception of some distinguished sheik.

When we returned to Haifa in the evening, we heard two things. The distinguished sheik was the Mufti himself, and the village we had seen on parade, which has a bad reputation for truculence and probably is the home of many of the striking workmen of the Portland cement factory, had sent a delegation to the Jewish community settled adjacent to the village, to deliver a declaration of peace and harmony. The Mufti, on the other hand, was on a propaganda tour in favor of the strike and civil disobedience. He had that morning delivered an inflammatory address at Jenin, describing the Jews as murderers and incendiaries. Probably he harangued the very people who had invited us to run the gantlet and had told them of their folly in treating with the Jews.

What simple, non-political-minded people—that's myself—want to know wonderingly is why the High Commissioner permits the Mufti to incite to violence—the Mufti, who is a government employee; why he allows dozens, perhaps hundreds, of government officials in all the departments to strike without filling their places; why he permits the departments to requisition the striking taxi-drivers and their machines and pay them £2 a day besides the salary of the drivers and the cost of the petrol; why Jewish passers-by are suddenly held up by the police and searched for arms, while Arabs go along unmolested. Other questions of the sort are being asked, and no reply is forthcoming. I have a reply: 200,000,000 Moslems in India, Arabia, Egypt, Syria, and Iraq. A powerful reason in these days of aggression by Italy in Ethiopia.

However, we Jews should have found a way by now to meet the race problem. Our complete failure is not to our credit.

Jerusalem, May 20, 1936

Life—and death—goes on as usual, and has become usual all of these six weeks. The slaughter of innocents and of doubly innocent trees shows no sign of abating, though five battalions have been brought in from Egypt.

Certain things have become clearer to me, though I should hesitate to say that they are proved. I am convinced that Italy is behind the agitation. The strike fund is too large for the theory that it has been gathered by Arab patriots. Why I should conclude that it's Italy and not Germany or communists, I cannot tell. I feel instinctively that Italy at this moment is more interested than the others in making trouble for the English.

It is also clear to me that this trouble bears a fundamentally different character from the previous riots and disturbances. The most prominent difference is that the [Arab] Youth Movement is far more in evidence than ever before. If instead of sending a royal commission over to "investigate," Great Britain would set up a body of wise men with the task of studying the race antagonisms between Jacob and Esau and determine the thousand ways that might lead from Arab heart to Jewish heart and back from Jew to Arab, and from Arab head to Jewish head and vice versa, the tripartite problem might be solved.

I am sending you yesterday's *Palestine Post*. It struck me, as I read it, as giving an epitome of what we are undergoing. What it does not and what it cannot convey is the tension under which we are living. One works, but always there is the feeling of "before the war" and "when the war will be at an end."

Jerusalem, June 26–July 10, 1936

This week there was a meeting of the members of the Zionist Executive Committee who live in Palestine, called to give the Executive the opportunity of rendering account of its action during the long season of turmoil. A story was revealed of uninterrupted efforts to influence the government and get closer to the Arabs.

Yet the strike goes on. Violence is still practiced in the same measure as before. Innocent men are shot down by stray bullets entering their homes. Bombs are thrown in public places among crowds, and the naïve Yemenite or Kurd Jews who report the matter to the police are stuck into prison for indeterminate periods. Traveling on the high roads is a most dangerous pastime. And the pitched battles between the marauders and the troops, occurring every day, produce no improvement. The most atrocious act this week was setting fire to the Baby Home with a hundred infants in it. The act—but not the perpetrator—was discovered and the fire put out in time.

The toll of trees has now risen to 96,000. I didn't know there were so many in this desert country. . . .

Some days the papers claim that the strike is weakening —that intimidations [on the part of the Arab strikers], such as throwing lysol or petroleum on the vegetables brought by the Arab women from the villages into the cities, are ceasing. The next day the assertion is revoked. As for the spoilt vegetables, it is interesting that the typhoid record for these months is the best yet. The vegetables eaten by Jews are either grown on Jewish farms or brought from Egypt. The elimination of vegetables raised by Arabs in Palestine with their use of sewage for fertilizer has in turn eliminated typhoid. It has always been known that in Palestine typhoid is not water-borne. Now it has been proved that the source is the primitive methods of the Arab farmer.

Jerusalem, July 31, 1936

A few hours ago I returned from a visit to Tel Aviv, the first I have made, I think, in two months. It was a humiliating experience. The arrangement now is to travel only in convoys under military escort. Our convoy consisted of three omnibusfuls of passengers, in each omnibus a British soldier occupying the front seat opposite to the chauffeur, and a cartful of soldiers besides, provided with a machine gun and accompanied by a second cart equipped with signaling-apparatus.

Our soldier was a dear young lad, with a delightful English, half-Irish accent, and a fresh complexion, who kept assuring us: "See, the danger is past," until he warned us that a danger spot in the hills was coming or pointed out the places at which he was engaged in some action. For you must know, if your papers haven't told you about it, that we are now having daily pitched battles in all the hill country.

It's sickening. How sickening I didn't know in fact until I was actually being "protected" by this young slip of a boy, sitting opposite me, his rifle in his hands, in position for instantaneous action when the moment of danger announced itself. I went down yesterday and came back today unharmed, except for the scar to my spirit, inflicted by the consciousness that a young life might have been the ransom for mine.

III

"The Jews," wrote Miss Szold, "go right on." For herself, in addition to her incessant work with the Aliyah, it meant supervising the liquidation of the camp for the Jaffa refugees.

Jerusalem, August 7, 1936

I have this minute returned from a sizzling hot trip to Tel Aviv. The purpose was to take charge of the "liquidation" of the camp of the refugees from Jaffa who have been "demonstrating" at the government and municipality offices because they are hungry. At the start there were 9000; now only 3000 are left. Obviously they are the weaker vessels. And the government refuses to help. I can't understand its attitude.

The flight from Jaffa to Tel Aviv took place because the Jews in the former place were being shot down—the fifty-second victim lost his life this morning in the no-man's land between Tel Aviv and Jaffa—like birds of prey, and there was no adequate police protection. What were they to do? They had to run for their lives. Meantime their property has been stolen and their houses burned and more. Doesn't it seem that the government must meet at least part of the damage? In this morning's paper I notice that the United States government has issued a notice to Spain —goodness knows to whom in Spain, loyalists or socialists or rebels—that they will be held responsible for injuries and damages to Americans. How much more should a government be held liable for the losses to its own law-abiding citizens whom it fails to protect adequately.

Talking of law-abidance—in Jewish circles the feeling is growing that our tactics of restraint and discipline have been inapplicable to the situation. The opinion is that the Arabs do not appreciate our higher morality; they look upon us as cowards. I can't agree. In the first place, they know from their own papers—even their own papers which do not distinguish themselves by truthfulness—that the Jews are constantly besieging the government with petitions to allow the guards of the rural settlements to use rifles instead of shotguns (I'll be jiggered if I know the difference; I hate both and fear both). In the second place, there have been enough witnesses of brave self-defense to convince them of Jewish self-reliance and even heroism. In the third place, I still believe that the majority of the Arab population is not in sympathy with the acts of their terrorists, and values Jewish standards.

Jerusalem, August 21, 1936

I have just returned from one of my regular trips to Tel Aviv in connection with the liquidation of the refugee camps. It was a beastly journey. It took more than two hours each way, four hours and more cut out of my short life before me, and among the most unpleasant in my long life. Machine guns accompanying me, machine guns pointing at one from all the hilltops. We are living, you see, in a veritable state of war. And the occurrences of the past week were among the worst of our four months' adventure. The three busses making up the convoyed caravan were full. Apparently the travelers were quiet, even unconcerned. But it was obvious from the instantaneous stir that ran through the car at the slightest jolt, cry, whistle, or commotion on the road ahead or behind, that nerves were jumpy. How could they not be?

Everyone is asking: "How long?" No one answers. I don't see how our young people can be held in much longer. They have been and are wonderful. At the time of the funeral of the two nurses who were felled ruthlessly in the yard of the Jaffa government hospital—perhaps your papers did chronicle that misdeed—there were something

like fifty thousand persons thronging the route to the cemetery in Tel Aviv, and there wasn't an untoward incident.
But *"Es tut nichts! Der Jude wird verbrannt!"* [7] No one has
a good word to say for the Jews. The hatred we are held in
is an amazing phenomenon.

To be sure, we are not altogether innocent in this de-
bacle. Some of us have been warning for years that the Arab
relations question should be given first place on the Zionist
program. Our "patriots" wouldn't hear of it. No one can
assert that consideration of the problem would have averted
what is happening. But we should at least have done our
duty. Certainly, it would still not have earned us the sympathy of the English officials here. They damn us if we do
or if we don't.

When I alighted from the convoyed omnibus in Jerusalem, I ran into a big crowd—a funeral! Whose? Of a
professor—Billig—of Arabic at the University of Mount
Scopus. He lived at Talpiot, the Jewish suburb. He was
sitting at his desk in his room, poring over an Arabic manuscript, when a dum-dum bullet was shot through his iron
shutters, tore off the back of his head, and he fell dead in-
stantly, his hand sweeping the Arabic manuscript from the
table with him as he dropped. His body was found only the
next morning. A great deal of shooting had been going on
all evening, and this particular shot had not aroused special
attention or investigation. He was the mildest man conceivable, absolutely incapable of harboring an evil thought
against anyone. On the contrary, he was one of those eager
to find the way to harmonious co-operation with the Arabs.
Two days earlier one of the most promising students at
the University was shot down. And as I write shots are

_____

[7] "It doesn't help—The Jew will be burned!"

heard all around. It's probably not so bad as Spain, but bad enough.

Rhexia virginica! My! How long since I have either heard the name or seen the flower. But I remember it well. Your mention of it made me homesick.

Jerusalem, August 28, 1936

Obviously we are nearing the end of the strike, and the report is that the reign of violence is then to be called off. This promise of calling off the terror is interesting, since all along the Arab Supreme Committee has been insisting, though not too vigorously, I confess, that it does not favor brigandage, assault, and murder.

One thing amazes me anew every day. If I had read a description of the details happening here every moment, these one hundred and twenty-five days, as of an historical event, I should have pictured the bulk of the citizens standing around terrified, unable to think of going about their business and cooking their dinners. As a matter of fact, we even give teas and receptions and have to go to them. In Jerusalem, on account of the curfew, there are no cinemas; but Tel Aviv and Haifa pursue their pleasures with zest. Also, serious matters receive the same earnest consideration as in normal circumstances, and the business of hatching projects for the betterment of our state and of human society in general proceeds as though there were no bullets whizzing through the air seeking out innocent victims.

Jerusalem, September 4, 1936

The same story still—murder, sniping, ambushing, bombing, indiscriminate shooting, lying, slandering, and so-called negotiating with all the forms of diplomacy. In such diplomacy as there is, the Jews are not drawn in. The struggle is frankly between the Arabs and the government, with the Jews as the "objects." Behind the observable tactics there looms a formidable war of international dimensions. It seems to me to be only a matter of weeks for it to break out. The Mediterranean basin, from Spain to Palestine, will not be one of the lesser scenes.

Here is an illustration of our terror! In the bus in which I traveled to Tel Aviv last Tuesday there was a single Arab. In the valley we stopped to wait for a part of the military convoy. A number of persons took the opportunity to descend and stretch their legs. So did the Arab. When we were ready to start, all the Jews returned—not so the Arab. Great excitement, and a search of the bus to make sure he had not left his visiting-card behind in the form of a bomb under his seat. One Jewish passenger happened to know the Arab and to know that he was an employee of the government in the Water Department, and that when he left the bus he had walked across the fields to one of the pumping-stations. A sigh of relief!

That is the way we live. And yet, we eat, we drink, we build homes, we work our heads off over Youth Aliyah and social service and all the rest of it.

Don't worry! Unless an international war breaks out!

Jerusalem, September 12, 1936

One hundred and five boys and girls arrived from Germany at Haifa, our last batch for who knows how long a time. Recently, the government granted, after much supplication, one hundred Youth Certificates instead of the four hundred and fifty we had asked for in March; and to this pittance was attached the condition that no more were to be petitioned for until after the Royal Commission had submitted its report and the report's recommendations had been acted upon. Who knows when that will be?

To be sure, the tension in Jewish circles has relaxed somewhat since the publication of the London government's Statement of Policy. The outrages, however, continue; and the Arab Committee of Notables refuses to acquiesce in any proposed steps toward calling off the strike and the acts of violence. The Mufti himself is said to be the nigger in the woodpile. Today the new military commandant probably arrived. Unless the Arab Committee has at the last moment changed its tactics, his coming is the precursor of martial law.

The other urgent business is the liquidation of the refugees' camps in Tel Aviv. The job is hard enough, but it is made still more onerous by the niggardly and pestering attitude of the government. No use going into details. It would take a disquisition to make the thing plain. The governmental methods may drive me into abandoning it. I don't do the actual work involved. I act only as moderator at the discussion of plans to be implemented, but it is precisely negotiations with the government, particularly the Treasurer—and he is a super-Treasurer—that fall to my lot. I'd rather work for a day than talk to the Treasurer, that one or any other, for ten minutes.

[TO DR. HARRY FRIEDENWALD]
Jerusalem, September 13, 1936

I believe you know that I have always held that Arab-Jewish relationships should have been the central point of our Zionist thinking in Palestine. It has not been so. We are reaping the harvest of our neglect. At least during the catastrophe our people have behaved with marvelous dignity and self-restraint. This is compensating to a certain degree; but I wish we had all along measured up to the highest standards.

Jerusalem, September 25, 1936

A week of traveling between Jerusalem and Tel Aviv and the writing of reports at the demand of all sorts of bodies and authorities. I still have to travel convoyed and escorted—because my friends insist upon it. It's almost as slow as stage-coach traveling was a hundred years ago and, I believe, no safer. This week's experiences made me resolve to have done with it. With the ordinary automobile one covers the distance in an hour; with the convoy it takes nearly three, if one includes the half-hour one must anticipate the start in order to assure oneself of a seat. Now, imagine, this week when I made two day trips to Tel Aviv and back, twelve hours gone. For a woman of seventy-six that's more time than she can afford to waste.

My second trip to Tel Aviv this week was to attend the funeral of Mr. Dizengoff, the mayor, indeed *the* mayor *par excellence,* the builder of Tel Aviv. It was a notable occasion. It was an ocular and, so to say, aural demonstration of the spiritual self-restraint the Jews of Palestine have been exercising these many months. Tens upon tens of thousands marching through the streets after the bier; other tens of thousands fringing the windows, the balconies, and the roofs of the houses along the route; and only the sound of marching feet audible, and that in a city which is as a rule loud, noisy, aggressive, obtrusive, clamant.

It was hot, for the funeral took place in the middle of the day; but there were no accidents to mar the commemoration. I am content that I was in the procession—I hope I won't have a funeral in the remotest resembling it. Such thoughts attached to my years are natural, because Mr.

Dizengoff was only three months younger than I am. Three days before his death I had a letter from him regarding a plan connected with Arab-Jewish relations which Dr. Magnes had worked out and in which Mr. Dizengoff was interested. I happened to be the go-between for one phase of the plan. In a postscript to the letter he wrote me his wishes for the New Year and congratulations on my having been made Nurse *honoris causa,* and he added that he expected by the time I reached eighty I'd be Mother *honoris causa* to all the children of Palestine. Perhaps! If somebody gives me a few hundred thousand pounds.

IV

With the calling off of the "strike" against the government, the insurrection came to a technical end the middle of October. It had accounted for 700 lives and thousands of wounded. All told there were 1996 attacks on Jewish settlements and communities, besides forays directed at busses, police stations, and public buildings. The property loss was estimated at £3,000,000. The government had spent almost as much for extra police and military forces.

The succeeding peace, however, proved to be only an intermittent truce. Violence and sporadic warfare continued until the outbreak of the second World War in 1939.

Jerusalem, October 23, 1936

This was one of my fullest weeks on record. One of the incidents—a pleasant one—was breaking ground on Scopus for the Nurses' Training School as the first of the three buildings constituting the Medical Center. The newspapers here are carrying photographs of me handling the pick and spade vigorously. The ceremony—simple but very attractive—was appealing after the strain of the last few months. It was held at eight-thirty in the morning, and I had to rush off at once straight for Tel Aviv for the weekly meeting of the Refugee Camps Liquidating Committee.

It *is* amazing how we Jews go ahead—we are such thoroughgoing humans, like the Galvestonians after the tidal wave, the Chicagoans after the Great Fire, the Pompeians after Vesuvius. We go right ahead as though nothing untoward had happened. Take this, for instance: on the previous Tuesday's meeting at Tel Aviv, my associates urged that I go with them next morning to Rishon-le-Zion, or, rather, the neighboring village Nahalat Yehudah, to which 175 families of refugees were to be transferred. Houses are to be erected there by the refugees themselves for their own use, they meantime occupying either rented rooms at Rishon-le-Zion or tents near Nahalat Yehudah. The quarter is to be developed on the sand dunes.

I resisted because I was to take the ten o'clock train for Haifa from Tel Aviv. They paid no attention to my refusal and came the next morning to fetch me away, promising to get me back to Tel Aviv in good time. Well, I climbed those sand dunes, and all I could think of was the work it would be to level them for buildings if climbing them made one's heart palpitate and one's brain throb. The ceremony was brief—also breaking not ground, but sand. Then I hurried back to the taxi, only to find it had sunk about three feet deep into the sand, and it took fifteen minutes to dig and lift it out. Was I going to catch that train—so it was two hours late!

From the papers you know that the strike has ended and that curfew has been lifted. That, too, was an amazing experience. It was as though a magic wand had been waved over the country. The roads were at once alive with traffic, the city streets swarmed, the people wore an entirely different aspect. Nevertheless, while I sat at supper in Ramat Gan, between the afternoon and evening meetings, forty shots rang out in our immediate vicinity. The attacks continue, but daily more sporadically. Nothing else could have been expected. The violence that has been nurtured and extolled as heroism will have to be allowed to die down gradually.

If it were not for the presence of the military swarming everywhere, every trace of the disturbances would have disappeared from the range of physical vision. Our inside worlds, of course, are not so serene. We are either remembering atrocities or wondering what will happen when the Royal Commission starts and conducts its superfluous investigations. It could have found out all it thinks it wants to know while sitting comfortably at its English fireside and reading all sorts of reports that have been written in the course of the years.

Jerusalem, November 14, 1936
This week I finished my big job in Tel Aviv; the refugees' camps are liquidated.

I can't recall whether I ever wrote you the figures that tell the story of the flight from Jaffa. Over 10,500 Jews fled to Tel Aviv during the few days that followed the fateful nineteenth of April. A couple of thousand were received by relatives. The public had to make arrangements for about 9000. There were 85 camps. During the summer the most independent gradually departed and established themselves in Tel Aviv or elsewhere. None could go back to Jaffa to their former abodes. At the beginning of August there were still 24 camps, 4650 persons, comprising about 962 families, in synagogues, halls, empty houses, and in tents. A plan was worked out to cost £10,800, half of which sum the government contributed on certain conditions. The other half came from a popular collection. One of the government's conditions was that the liquidation must be completed in three months. It was!

The committee that had it in charge worked marvelously —devotion, understanding, and experience did the deed. But . . . there were three categories of families. The first, the largest contingent, could not be helped beyond getting them settled in Tel Aviv, paying their rent and their maintenance for a stated period, and letting them find their way back to their normal occupations. The second class were (89 families) pitiable derelicts—widows, paralytics, blind, old. They had been charity pensioners before and, to our shame, they will remain charity pensioners. Perhaps they can't be rehabilitated even with the application of large funds. The third section, 270 families, were the picked class who were found adaptable to a new life. For them a special plan was worked out. Parcels of land were to be acquired near Petach Tikvah for 75 families, near Rishon-le-Zion for 120, near Ness Ziona for 25, and near Kfar Saba for 50 families. In all these places, the refugees themselves, under instructors who were to teach them the handling of tools, were to build their own houses, and pay rent at the rate of half a pound a month, which would make them their property in the course of fifteen years. The building plans were to dovetail into the liquidation plan. They didn't.

The houses were to be finished on November 1. They began to build them this week. So there is a new problem. The liquidation period and fund are at an end. The people are in part living in tents. The rainy season is on. There are no schools for the children. There is sickness. There are sanitation problems, water problems, and only part-time work to be had. So the end of my job, as always in this awfully imperfect world, is the beginning of a job; and one this time for which the means are not in sight. Instead of going to Tel Aviv once or twice a week, I must fly around to Petach Tikvah, Rishon-le-Zion, etc.

Jerusalem, December 18, 1936

Last Friday I returned from an exhausting trip exactly five minutes before the Sabbath came in. Today I have exactly five minutes for a bite—no more. The week has been swallowed up, every moment of it, day *and* night, by the Royal Commission. The Vaad Leumi laid upon me the task of putting all the material in shape for its memoranda of grievances. I hate grievances. And the grievances I have are mostly against my own people! Also, I am to appear before the Royal Commission. That requires preparation, too. So there was not a moment for human intercourse—what I did was unhuman.

Jerusalem, January 22–29, 1937

This week we bade farewell without regret to the members of the Royal Commission. What a nightmare it was! But probably there is worse to come. Worse to come for all of us, at least all of us in this Eastern Hemisphere. I wonder whether you feel the war-clouds hanging low above your heads as we do?

The country is not quiet. The unrest beneath the surface is disturbing. Terrorist bands are forming in all parts. At present ninety-nine percent of the victims are Arabs, Arabs of position who refuse to pay blackmail. Every Arab suspected of wealth is being assessed. Obviously another strike fund is being scraped together. Even if the Report of the Royal Commission turns out to be moderate, an attempt at appeasing both sides, I feel that the Arabs will continue their opposition and show it in violent, murderous measures. And the government, which is well informed I am told, sticks to its *laissez-faire* policy. It has not disarmed the gangs, it has connived at the escape of the ringleaders in violence.

Jerusalem, June 4–26, 1937

This is the season of report-writing for the Zionist Congress and the Asefat Ha-Nivharim; it is also the season of all sorts of annual meetings, two occupations highly time-robbing and sterilizing. Besides, I can never get those pesky reports completed on time. Then there are the attacks from administrative headquarters to parry. Here in Palestine and at this period of three official languages—German, not Arabic, is the third for the Jewish community—report-writing is a linguistic exercise. Indeed the whole of our life is linguistically tedious and *anspruchsvoll*. Sometimes dealing with a matter means for me calling in at once the three secretaries—the Hebrew, the English, and the German— and all of them itch to correct my style and then it turns out that they have corrected the thought out of the document. . . .

A new job fell to my lot this week. It is keeping an eye on the testimony of the claimants for compensation from the government for injuries to life and limb during the disturbances. Fortunately the investigation is in the hands of a commissioner who is just and sympathetic. All went well. But it's another job, and all the others seem to grow in complexity from day to day.

Jerusalem, July 9, 1937

The strain is over, and now the pain! I heard the conclusions of the Royal Commission Report at Ben Shemen day before yesterday evening over the radio. There was a conference at Ben Shemen of the leaders and teachers of the Youth Aliyah groups all over the country. All together, between three hundred fifty and four hundred persons gathered in the dining-room to hear the verdict. The silence that descended upon the group was thick, ominous. Even the young children sat awed.

The sentence that stood out glaringly to my eyes and my eardrums because it was such a monumental lie was the one used by the High Commissioner when he said that with a clear conscience he could maintain that the British government for the last seventeen years had done everything in its power to bring the Jews and Arabs together. I have been in Palestine all these seventeen years, and I can say with a clear conscience that the British government never attempted to do a solitary thing to bring about co-operation between the two races. Apparently *nothing* was in its power with respect to the reconciliation of Jews and Arabs.

August 27, 1937

We who have been close to the situation in Palestine can say that the British administration has deliberately thwarted every effort made by the Jews to find a method of conciliation between Jew and Arab. Here lies my attitude: we must have another five years of sympathetic trial to solve the Arab-Jewish problem. I believe there is a solution; and if we cannot find it, then I consider that Zionism has failed utterly.

Jerusalem, October 1, 1937

These have been trying days here. The assassination of Andrews [8] has thrown us all into mourning. He was an

[8] Lewis Yelland Andrews, District Commissioner for Galilee.

unusual character and an able official. He was not pro-
Jewish, but the fairest of men. In all his actions he was objective to an unusual degree. Today our excitement reached
its culmination. The government is resorting to energetic
measures. The inciters to rebellion have been arrested and
the ringleaders deported. The Mufti himself has not been
deprived of his liberty, but he has been deposed from his
post as president of the Moslem Supreme Council which
gave him great means to carry on his subversive campaigns.
I can't convey to you the atmosphere of tension, expectancy,
not unmixed with joy, also not unmixed with fear. Everybody wonders what the morrow will bring—more assassination? Or are the bandits intimidated? And is the policy
of suppression a thought-out plan or only a spurt?

And such a Palestine is competing with Japan and China,
with Spain and Morocco, while Mussolini and Hitler be-
fuddle a public as hypocritical as themselves, and the judicial murders go on merrily in Russia.

V

The horrors of this one-sided and treacherous war moved
Henrietta Szold to a public protest, which disclosed the
spiritual root and source of her Zionism. At the height of
the outrages, in August 1936, the Arabs murdered two
Jewish nurses as they were on their way to the Jaffa government hospital in order to tend their *Arab* patients. In
the name of the Jewish women of Palestine, Miss Szold requested an interview with the High Commissioner, Sir
Arthur Wauchope.

"We cannot refrain any longer," she wrote him; "we
cannot suppress the impulse to cry out before you on whom
fortune has laid the great trust of securing peace and pros-

perity in the Holy Land. We are impelled irresistibly to cry out, but not in protest alone. Protest implies indignation. What moves us is something that lies deeper than righteous indignation, a something whose roots are imbedded in the same soil as the self-restraint and discipline we have encouraged our sons and husbands and brothers to practice at the very risk of having them condemned as cowards. Our indignation, our reproaches, our self-discipline, our patience, our subjection of natural passion, they all together are the outflow of our inherited Jewish way of life which demands respect for the soul and the life of others and enjoins holiness of living upon ourselves. . . ."

A few years later she found herself impelled to protest again, when respect for the soul and life of others was violated among her own people. Rival elements in Palestinian Jewry had resorted to unwonted violence, settling political scores with bombs and conducting an internecine terror. In such a crisis Miss Szold seldom or never considered herself a public figure endowed with the privilege of issuing public statements. This particular appeal she called "a most unusual act, perhaps unprecedented in my life." In it she revealed once more her high philosophy of Zionism and her conception of what a Jewish homeland must be if it is to deserve the habitation or the name of the Jew.

Under the date of September 10, 1941, she published an open letter to the Jewish community, the Yishub. Speaking in behalf of the thousands of boys and girls transplanted to Palestine by the Youth Aliyah, she pointed out that "these wards of our people, whose ties to parents and home we severed, were brought here by us to be trained as citizens and builders of the new-old land sanctified by the words and the lives of legislators and prophets as well as by our own fervent faith in an honorable future." For their sake and the sake of all the youth she appealed for an end to intolerance, partisan strife, and violence. "License," she wrote, "is tending to replace law among the people of the Law. Our hallowed ethical standards are in danger of declining. These are evil things of which our camp must be cleansed."

She concluded with a patriotic allusion to the thousands of Palestinian Jews who had enlisted in the British army. "We lay the task upon them to save from annihilation the precious bits of culture amassed since the remote days when our fathers were bidden to 'proclaim liberty throughout the land unto all the inhabitants thereof.' These young warrior-builders . . . demand of us to be mindful of the teaching of our people's history: the Jew and his cause have persisted through the ages not by the might of the fist, not by the power of brute force, but by the spirit of divine law and love."

For Miss Szold and like-minded Zionists, a Palestine inhabited by a Jewish majority, governed by Jews, rendered fertile and prosperous by Jews, is not enough. To be worth the cost of the struggle, such a Palestine must be pervaded with "the Jewish way of life"—that way which her father, the rabbi, taught her and which prepared her for Zionism. She wrote in one of her letters during the Arab uprising that if the Jews cannot find means of living at peace with the Arabs, "Zionism has failed utterly." It will have failed no less, she implies, if Palestinian Jews cannot find means of living at peace with one another.

It may appear easy to raise objections to this point of view. Why must Jews, one might ask, exercise more self-discipline, more respect for the life and soul of others, more holiness of living, more faithfulness to divine law and love than other peoples? Are not Jews entitled to indulge in the same amount of partisan strife and violence as the inhabitants of other lands? No doubt she would answer: Jews who wish to behave as other peoples should remain where they are, in whatever land it may be; why wander thousands of miles to build a new land with incredible toil and sacrifice, against bitter and almost insuperable obstacles, if the new land is to perpetuate all the old vices? And why, except as a masterstroke of irony, call it a Jewish work and a Jewish land if it is to be devoid of the Jewish spirit?

The answer may sound Messianic. She is fond of the word, and I believe she would embrace the epithet. When the Pittsburgh Program, with its plans for a co-operative commonwealth, was adopted back in 1918, she said she felt as though Amos and Isaiah were present. A new Palestine without Amos and Isaiah would be a Palestine without the two halutzim who alone can pioneer the way to a truly Jewish homeland.

CHAPTER SEVENTEEN

Where All Roads Meet

I

DURING the summer of 1937 Miss Szold attended the Zionist Congress in Zürich and paid a last brief visit to Germany, where she found that two years under the Nuremberg laws had reduced the Jews to "living corpses." Then she returned to Palestine for more trying days, as described in the concluding letter of the previous chapter.

October found her in America for another Hadassah Convention. In January 1938 the indefatigable traveler sailed once more for Palestine, where she has remained until the present writing.

In these last four years her gait has begun to slacken—she is calling twelve hours a day's work—but she still marches sturdily along a highway into which all the familiar roads have converged. Hadassah, Youth Aliyah, Social Service, the bomb-torn *aliyah*, the rocky "ascent" to Zion—she treads all these roads as one, marching onward, an undaunted little figure and not the least of her people. Admirers have dotted the road with trophies—gifts and funds for her disposal—and, more triumphal still, new tasks for her to perform. Moving onward, she in turn places wreaths for those who have dropped from sight. Almost forgotten paths run at her side, where she catches a glimpse of a little red Hungarian pitcher and the black-embroidered front of a dress. The grandson of her father's best friend is tending the flowers by the way—among them a slip planted by Adele. Golden Bantam corn is waving in the fields and there are ferns in the woods. As she nears the crest, befitting the ascent to the city and the land of *shalom* she breathes the prayer of every Jew—the prayer for peace.

Trieste, August 27, 1937

Emotionally the Zionist Congress was devastating. I felt shattered by it. But it was to be followed by worse—the meeting of the Council of the Jewish Agency. That I know only from hearsay, for during its sessions I was away in Germany, taking part in the farewell "party" arranged for the one hundred and twelve young people for whom, after a considerable interval, we succeeded in securing certificates. In all I was away from Zürich only seventy-two hours, thirty-four of them being spent on the railroad.

Either I was so played out by the Congress happenings or, indeed, the emotional strain produced by what I saw and heard in Germany was so inordinately great that my powers of resistance proved inadequate. At all events, those three days will be unforgettable for their misery. What I saw in Germany two years ago was a grueling experience; what I saw this time cannot be described in language at my command.

The Jews are living corpses. They are capable of only one emotion—fear. They are furtive, listless, scared. Those over forty-five or fifty have resigned themselves to their fate —they will rot in Germany. Their one cry is: Save the young! I wish I could describe the scenes I witnessed and of which chance made me the center. Besides the parents of the young people now on their way to Palestine, there came to the farewell "party" many parents whose children have long been in Palestine in the Youth Immigration groups. They crowded round me, many of them with photographs of their children, which they thrust at me wanting to know whether I recognized them. While most of them expressed their happiness at their children's experiences in Palestine, some of them had petitions. I was nearly torn to pieces.

On my return [to Zürich], the Second Biennial Conference of the Youth Immigration began—constructive, hopeful, unpolitical. It was balm to all who had been through the struggle of the Congress and to me who could not get rid of the thought of the specters in Germany, not by a long shot all of them Jewish specters.

I am tired, very tired. I hope to get some rest on the boat, the *Marco Polo*. I shall need it, for I have five strenuous weeks ahead of me in Palestine before I set out for America to attend the Hadassah Convention. I cannot recollect whether I wrote you of the pact between me and Hadassah. I consented to come only if no Hadassah publicity is set in motion. I suppose publicity cannot be avoided, but at least it is agreed that I am not to be made the center of it.

Atlantic City, October 29, 1937

The Hadassah Convention is a spectacular demonstration. I have been enfolded in affection on all sides. For me the climax came today, when Hadassah voted $25,000 as a memorial to Felix Warburg, to be incorporated into my Children's Central Fund. Besides, I am to get my birthday gift of $5000 for the placement of children. Handsome, isn't it? Worth while coming five or six thousand miles. And Hadassah is a marvelous, flexible, well-oiled machine.

I am sorry I could not get here sooner, to see the country in its early October glory, the sight I always long for.

[TO THOMAS SELTZER]   S.S. Galilea, *January 28, 1938*

I had meant to respond to your note—it is dated January

1!—before my leaving America, the return to which you urge upon me. If you could look into my soul, you would discover that I am not at all averse from returning to America, which today appears to be the only abode of semi-security, even if not of security.

I am literally afraid of what will meet me in Palestine. The economic conditions prevailing there are the worst we have known since the beginning of our adventure. The organization is being disrupted by the various opinions held more or less honestly. And in my thoughts this central interest and responsibility of mine is veiled and darkened and in a measure buried by China-Japan, by Spain, by Germany, by Italy, by the fascistic tendencies manifested by the smaller European states, by misery and lack of vision everywhere. England talks armament, Paris is stupefied, dead, Italy bristles with arms, hope non-existent, fear and anxiety prevalent. Personally, a mountain of accumulated problems awaits me. Isn't it clear that it would be easier to remain in America, to return to America? But one has a conscience.

When my mood is apprehensive to the point of pain, there arises before my eyes your little white house set in green shaded by elms, and its warm cozy interior, and my conscience almost vanishes. They were idyllic weeks in Connecticut.

Jerusalem, April 1, 1938

I am writing at the end of what has been perhaps the most murderous week since the beginning of the disturbances all but two years ago. I have lost count of the victims, young men, old men, women, and children, with practically not a word of condemnation of the outrages in the Arab press. Last Sunday I felt closer to the ruffianism than ever before. I traveled up to Haifa in a taxi. At less than twenty minutes' distance from the end of our journey, we had a puncture. It delayed us by over a half-hour. Less than an hour later —at five-thirty—two taxis were attacked by armed bands on that very spot. It happened that one of the cars was driven by an Arab chauffeur. All the passengers were wounded, the chauffeur was killed. It's gruesome. And there seems to be no end to it—or to the funds with which the gunmen are kept supplied.

And all this is happening in a country poignantly beautiful and peaceful-looking. Such a riot of bloom, such verdure, such blue skies (but not zephyr winds; winter refuses to depart from the temperature), such rich promise of crops, with oranges gleaming from the trees, in heaps under the trees and on the roadside waiting to be carried to the packing-houses, from the lorries filled to the brim.

Today cables came from Hadassah: Eddie Cantor collected $32,000 for the Austrian Youth Aliyah. Meantime it seems certain that we shall have to tackle Rumania, too. There should be many Eddie Cantors unless the Hitlers and the Francos can be made innocuous.

Jerusalem, August 27, 1938

On Friday a bomb exploded in the Jaffa marketplace killing as many persons as are killed, according to the newspaper reports, in a regular pitched battle in the Chinese or the Spanish war. Nevertheless, we are having "disturbances" —not a war—in Palestine!

In the afternoon my associate in the Aliyah, Mr. Hans Beyth, met a friend of his in the streets of Jerusalem. The friend had just arrived in town, his taxi having managed to escape from Ramleh. Ramleh is on the road between Jaffa and Jerusalem. As soon as the news of the bomb explosion in Jaffa reached Ramleh, the hoodlums there

jumped to the conclusion that the dastardly deed was per-
petrated by the Jews; and they stoned and shot at every taxi
carrying Jews. Mr. Beyth's friend was covered with blood
from top to toe, but not his own. He escaped unhurt, but
the woman who sat next to him in the taxi was wounded in
the cheek and her blood ran profusely.

And who was the woman? One of the Burgenlanders, the
Austrians, seventy in number, who for months had been
living on a raft in the Danube, not permitted to land in
Austria (their home for centuries) or to take refuge in
Czechoslovakia or Hungary on which their Danubian perch
abutted, scourged daily by the Nazis who boarded the raft
for the purpose, stung by swarms of mosquitoes by day and
plagued by rats at night, their clothing dropping from them,
undernourished by the food other Jews managed to get to
them. For months all sorts of efforts were made to secure
for them United States affidavits or Palestinian certificates.
Two weeks ago some certificates were obtained; and she,
this bleeding woman in the taxi, had been among the first
to be released from her Danubian open-air prison, and
promptly she dropped from the frying-pan of the Nazis into
the fire of the Arabs.

It's no use warning me not to overwork; it's no use telling anybody in Palestine to take care. One has to grit one's
teeth and take a chance.

[TO MRS. DAVID B. GREENBERG]
Jerusalem, October 11, 1938

As for my health, it is completely restored. But the warning administered to me was impressive, and I find I must
heed it. I cannot work as I used to. I must give myself more
sleep; and I do, with the result that I fall behind more and
more each day in my work. I cannot keep up with the pro-

cession. The march is too rapid. As it is, I am actually at work twelve hours daily. To do what is required calls for at least eighteen, and at that I should not be responding to the demand for personal contacts, not to mention articles, etc., that should be written and visits that should be paid to institutions—*kvuzot,* social service bureaus, and all the rest. As you see, it is not a question of more secretarial help. I have no doubt that others could work faster than I do.

What was the warning? The doctors said "a tired heart." I said "a heart that has been beating for seventy-eight years." He agreed and then said more technically: "A cardiac-vascular disturbance." So that's that.

Jerusalem, October 21, 1938

This week taught me what I could never make myself understand when I read history or a description of a war in the daily papers. I have not been able to imagine how ordinary people went on living in Spain throughout the frightful upheavals in city after city. This week I have been living in a beleaguered city with airplanes whizzing and buzzing through the air, and the reverberations of shots assailing my ears. And what did I and thousands of others in the city do? We picked up the circulars dropped by the planes, we read almost with equanimity that the military commander whose troops had taken possession of the Old City advised us not to leave our houses, we gobbled up all the details of the beleaguerment of the Old City by the soldiery—and we went about our business.

My business the morning of the beginning of the siege was to get out of the city and travel by auto to Haifa via Tel Aviv and from Haifa to Kfar Yeheskiah near Nahalal to attend a meeting of the teachers of the Youth Aliyah.

And again I was struck by the sang-froid with which we

accept war, for latterly it has been war. There was a reference in the opening address to the difficulties under which
we are carrying on and to our sorrow over the loss of some
of our forces—almost a formal reference to the situation—
and then on to the thing we had come for. And who were
the teachers who had assembled there? For the most part
young men who work in the fields in the morning, teach
our youth in the afternoon, and stand guard all night.

If a war breaks out, I am afraid I shall not get back to
America. Your analysis of my attitude about leaving my responsibilities is correct. In any case, however, I am working
unceasingly toward the end of relieving myself of public
responsibilities. I keep saying that I always knew it was
hard to get a job, but I never knew it was so hard to get
out of a job as I am finding it.

Jerusalem, January 6, 1939

Though I extricated myself from the Vaad Leumi, that
is, the Social Service job, a day plus a week ago, the week
was as full as usual. In the first place, I must clean up in
the Vaad Leumi. I had fallen behind in my work rather
considerably, and in the second place a number of really
involved problems had arisen in connection with the refugees' plight.

We are having a large illegal immigration. Shiploads arrive on Greek vessels from Austria and Czechoslovakia—
2400 during December. They come naked, hungry, sick.
Their voyage, instead of taking four days from Europe,
takes four to six weeks. They have to land in the darkness
of night, with signal lights from government airplanes playing on them; and they land, not at a port, but at any place
along the shore that offers security. Many of them must
swim ashore, holding a child and their clothes over their

heads (they have no clothes but those on their person).

And on shore begin new troubles—no employment! It's ghastly. The Jewish Agency, for political reasons, cannot deal with them as it deals with legal immigrants. As the director of the Social Service, I took it upon myself to treat them as if they had come in by the front door, with a passport, a visa, and a certificate. But the money! There is none. This morning we had a four hours' meeting with the Agency on the subject. Result: much talk, little planning, no money! I was not a little plagued by my conscience when I considered that it was my last official act in the Social Service. Has one the right to protect oneself?

That is the dragnet which caught me up on my return from my birthday vacation in Nataniah. I stopped over in Tel Aviv on my return in order to meet people interested in the problem. They all had heaps of advice and no one had money. If I had money, I'd need no advice. There is one heartening feature. Last week, 600 arrived on one of these illegal transports and spilled themselves into Tel Aviv. By evening hundreds of families had volunteered to take them in and in large part feed them.

Jerusalem, June 14–17, 1940

In spite of all my resolutions to "jump off the band-wagon," I am traveling on it faster than ever. Emergency organization is the order of the day; and protest as I will, I am drawn into the hurly-burly. Italy's entry into the war was depressing, but not half as depressing as the peril of Paris.

I had a gardener—Perles, the grandson of our father's best friend!—re-pot my window plants. Most of them are now ranged on the table on my porch. The fuchsias bloomed, but wanly. There is too much sun, too little moisture for them; they are now standing *under* the table for protection. Mr. Perles insists upon my keeping the begonias and the amaryllis indoors. Do you remember the begonia that bloomed so incessantly? It is still blooming. The other one, from Ayanot, is gorgeous as to leaf and bloom. The aralia did not survive the winter well. The cacti are flourishing. The maidenhair fern could not be resuscitated. The most luxuriant pot next to the Ayanot begonia is the one planted with a little slip by Adele from the Ehrlich garden. Your enumeration of the spring blossoms in Eva Leah's woods made me homesick beyond words. But it was right for me to stay here!

. . . We who get together and discuss the news of the day—and how we discuss it!—are heartsick over France. I feel, foolishly I admit, that I am being treated badly in particular. It is the second time in my life that I am experiencing a German victory over France. I remember well the war of 1870 and the Commune in Paris.

Apart from the world situation, and my constant brooding over Adele's going from us,[1] and over your having to settle so much of what by right is my business, a huge unanswered personal correspondence stares me in the face and all my papers still lying on the shelves as you deposited them. Nor do I ever "catch up to myself" in my work—the old, old story.

[TO MRS. ROSE JACOBS]   *Jerusalem, November 20, 1940*

My working days are far shorter than they used to be. I can't any more extend them far into the night and until the

[1] Miss Szold's sisters, Mrs. Louis H. Levin (Bertha) and Mrs. Thomas Seltzer (Adele), visited Palestine for several months in 1939. In the spring of 1940, after her return to America, Adele died. And what were hitherto "family letters" are now addressed to Bertha alone.

morning after. And my Youth Aliyah and Kehillah obligations fill my working day, such as it is, to repleteness. Yet
honesty compels me to confess that not lack of leisure alone
is the explanation of my silence. There are so many reasons for not pouring out one's soul on paper these days,
again for both external and internal considerations, that
words of all kinds dry up on one's lips and in one's pen.

On one happening I did long to speak to you—the passing of Alice.[2] I know you were prepared for her going, I
also know what her going at any time meant to you and will
always mean to you. To me it means parting with the
purest, the truest, the most stimulating of friends—with a
friend in the highest sense of the word. In my early girlhood, while I was a pupil at the High School, I had such
a friend—a Methodist. For a number of years, until her
early death, she was a conscience to me, an intellectual and
a spiritual conscience. The experience was not repeated until, nearly thirty years after the death of my friend at school,
Alice came into my orbit. Superficial onlookers might have
thought that she came under my influence. The reverse was
the case. How often, when I was faced by a (for me) momen-
tous decision, I found myself asking how Alice would approach the solution of my problem, how she would dissect
and analyze it, how she would relate it to her past, to her
surroundings, to the vital things of existence. I confess that
not always could I accept her principles. Even when I could
not, her attitude rectified my thinking.

It is hard to realize that the force she had made of herself is no longer in action. Such realization neither life nor
death has taught. This reflection puts meaning into so hackneyed a phrase as "may her memory be for a blessing."

---

[2] Alice L. Seligsberg.

Jerusalem, December 7, 1940

I wonder whether I shall survive those eightieth-anniversary celebrations of which rumors reach me day after day. One of them at least I scotched and I succeeded, I hope, in influencing its character. There was to be a public meeting at which speakers were to tell the Palestinian world —or perhaps they were to tell me—who and what I am. I have attended one funeral like that. It was in celebration of my seventy-fifth birthday. I cannot stand another. So, when an occasion presented itself, I suggested a program: The Developments in Jewish Life during the Last Eighty Years: (a) in Zionism, (b) in Palestine, (c) in America. The suggestion was accepted with alacrity. In what spirit and with what vim, honesty of purpose, and analytical ability the speakers will execute it remains to be seen. They probably will introduce me as the heroine, because they won't believe that eulogies are distasteful to a person who has never considered herself (and never will consider herself) as a public character, and who knows her own shortcomings as a simple member of a community—whose eighty years have served primarily to teach her that years alone are not important. Well, we shall see.

Jerusalem, January 31, 1941

I have plunged into a new organization problem. You probably know that Hadassah gave me a birthday gift of $25,000 to be applied as I see fit. How do I see fit? Not so easy to answer. One of my difficulties is to decide whether I have the right to organize something which the community or Hadassah has to support and develop. The alternative seems to be to divide the handsome sum into small parts and help an infinity of lame ducks of institutions for the next year—a plan that does not satisfy me.

Jerusalem, April 3, 1941

Today we began with the organization of three urban
groups on the model of the Youth Aliyah groups—a dream
of mine fulfilled by means of a special allocation of funds
by Hadassah. We are going to choose sixty from among the
[Palestinian] city children and give them two years in the
meshakim.[3] The difficulties are proving not small; but if
we succeed, we shall have achieved a worthwhile enterprise.
The fact that I led the discussion at this meeting today
should be proof to you that my illness is not serious.

Jerusalem, July 11, 1941

I am writing as formerly on Friday afternoon, because
last evening I had no choice but to tumble into bed after
a full day spent in visiting two youth groups on the road
between Tel Aviv and Haifa. When I call yesterday a full
day, it is not only that I was on the go (by means of an auto
and Hans Beyth), but because the contacts with the young
refugees from a variety of war-stricken countries crowded
my soul with emotions indescribable. My only escape from
their bitterness was the feeling I *ought* to rejoice that by
chance I am an instrument in a movement which saves a
tiny remnant of humans who have suffered torments and
would have suffered far more if the Youth Aliyah had not
stepped in.

As a matter of fact, they are still of the tormented. They
have only one thought—the fate of the parents and brothers
and sisters left behind. The strange effect upon me was
that, in spite of the agony the young people innocently
enough caused me, I returned exhilarated as I haven't been
these many days—indeed, I may say, since my birthday,

---

[3] Farm settlements.

which proved a celebration beyond my physical and emotional strength.

One of the incidents of the trip was that we picked up one of our runaways who asked a lift of us, not having recognized us. He was a lad of twelve and a half, with a rucksack as big as himself on his back containing all his worldly possessions. The outcome was that he had a delightful auto trip through gleaming country, and by evening was snugly bestowed in his own bed at Mrs. Nathan's Talpiot school. We'll have to go into his case!

Jerusalem, August 1, 1941

I regret more and more that I did not keep a diary. My association with my young people of the Youth Aliyah brings home to me impressively, almost painfully, that I have outlived or, to use a Germanism, overlived myself. I keep on day after day contrasting ourselves with the young generation in my charge. The system that formed our minds and—I say it with special emphasis—our hearts is dead, dead as a doornail. But like many other dead things dug up by the archaeologists, there is much to derive from us, from our records. With all my heart I now wish that on my various visits home I had had the strength of mind not to let Hadassah's need for publicity absorb me and prevent me from carrying out my successive resolves to get at our family documents. For instance, there must be somewhere the last will and testament of Papa's father, in which he directs that a certain field be sold to enable his son, Benjamin, to secure his rabbinical education. . . . We, our generation, should not throw away such memorabilia. Leave that to your children who belong to the present.

Jerusalem, August 25, 1941

I wish, oh, how I wish I could be going over the old household gods with you! Perhaps it is well that I am six thousand miles away from your cellar storehouse. If I were sitting next to you, you would probably not be so thorough a discarder of mementos and photographs and whatnot as your young people have made of you. But, on the other hand, I might recognize the canvas with "a handsome cross-stitch pattern embroidered on it." And I'd be looking out for some particular thing, as, for instance, a little red Hungarian pitcher, and the will (written in Hebrew or Yiddish, I don't recall which) of Papa's father, and the black-embroidered front of a dress which Rachel and myself did together for Mamma.

Jerusalem, September 26, 1941

For the rest, it is war, and Youth Aliyah, and Social Service without let-up. The start made in our new undertaking—three groups of boys and girls from the cities of Palestine, to the number of seventy-five, placed in three *kibbutzim* according to the Youth Aliyah system, approximately—has been auspicious. We had the candidates in two camps for observation for a little more than a month. The camps were a great success. I hope the results will be what we—enthusiasts as we are—expect. In that case Hadassah will continue to finance the undertaking.

And have you heard of *my* success with Hadassah? I cannot recall whether I wrote you of the plan for a Girls' Trade School in Jerusalem which I submitted as a fitting Alice Seligsberg memorial? The idea is a Girls' Trade School with a four years' course in trades now open in Palestine to girls—sewing in all its branches, housekeeping (cooking, household economy, etc.), clerical course (secretarial,

WHERE ALL ROADS MEET 341

bookkeeping, etc.). The school is to serve the girls who have completed the eight elementary classes of the general school system, and there are to be evening courses for working girls.

Jerusalem, October 3, 1941

To think of Golden Bantam corn and fish with flavor, and a walk through ferny woods! It's like hearing about the glories of the ancient Temple service and not having the privilege of witnessing them.

Today was another day of meditation for Jerusalem—Mr. [Menachem] Ussishkin's funeral. It gave occasion to one of the most impressive demonstrations I have ever participated in. I do not venture to estimate the number of persons who followed the bier—thousands. The order was perfect in spite of the vast, packed crowds—not a loud word, no jostling; only sincere mourning. The community feeling is that its Rock of Gibraltar has disappeared. There were no eulogies, no flowers, only the traditional prayers at several halting-places. I followed on foot as long as I felt I could with impunity.

Jerusalem, October 17, 1941

I returned from a two days' visit to Haifa and surroundings a little more than an hour ago, and it is now nearly half-past five. The interval has been spent putting away my travel equipment and getting dressed for the Sabbath eve. In spite of the brief time left before candle-lighting I want to have a little chat with you, because on my desk lay a letter from you to greet me. It was your Cumberland letter, with its reminders of the beauty of the country up in the mountains of Maryland, and the memories connected with it, historical and of the family.

The whole of the past week has been absorbed in writing or speaking tributes to Brandeis.[4] On Tuesday I disgraced myself on a really notable occasion, the meeting held in his memory by the Zionist Executive. I had to speak in Hebrew. On account of the holidays and of the various other tributes I had to devote myself to, my address, written in English, could not be put into Hebrew. So I had to speak it as best I could. My best was wretched. I was tired and nervous from late night work, and my Hebrew is not equal to solemn occasions.

But that isn't the whole of the failure. Yesterday there was a memorial meeting in honor of Brandeis at Ain Ha-Shofet, the settlement named for him,[5] whose original members are Americans. Exhausted as I was, I decided to use what I had written for the Zionist Executive meeting and, for the same reason, I decided to read what I had written and not even pretend that I was speaking extemporaneously. So it fell flat. But the tribute at Ain Ha-Shofet was as perfect as meetings can be made. The whole of the Emek sent representatives, and Ain Ha-Shofet is a marvelous achievement.

From Ain Ha-Shofet I went to Haifa for an intensive discussion on sexual education, which kept me so long I had to spend the night there. The morning and early afternoon were filled with attending to left-overs from previous trips. So I didn't get back to Jerusalem until after the middle of the afternoon. Too much for an eighty-year-old, isn't it?

Jerusalem, September 1941

In spite of all my sympathy with your desire to clear things away and gain space I cannot repress the hope that

---

[4] Justice Louis D. Brandeis, who died October 4, 1941.
[5] Ain Ha-Shofet means "The Well of the Judge."

you are not destroying the letters you write about—those to Sadie.[6] Your description of them clutched me. Perhaps I shall survive this terrible war and join you in America. Sometimes that hope is strong enough to buoy me up. But I lay no injunctions upon you—I do not wish—I only hope.

This is the third day of futile attempts to write you a letter in the spirit of the passage of the year from old to new. And now, when at last my room is cleared of visitors and the flowers sent to me by friends are bestowed in water-filled vases, I must light the candles and go off to synagogue. Perhaps just as well!

What can one say that is not in every mind not utterly diseased? There can be only one wish—for peace, for cessation of the butchering of a generation—another generation—of young men. I confess that I have so far left behind my old attitude that I cannot content myself with the wish for peace—I have learnt in the interval between the two wars that it must be a just peace, that is, a complete peace, a peace that solves *the* problem, if men are to live humanly, as becomes human beings.

I must stop. Love, love, love.

I I

It is the children's village of Ben Shemen in December 1940. Young men and women who were graduated from the Youth Aliyah, and boys and girls still in training, have gathered from all over the land to do honor to Miss Szold on her eightieth birthday. They represent the nearly eight thousand youngsters whom the Youth Aliyah had salvaged from the wreck of Europe.

A slip of a girl with blond bobbed hair—relates Dorothy

---

[6] Sadie Szold, the sister who died in 1893.

Kahn Bar-Adon, whose account we are quoting—rose to her feet. She was Margalit of Deganiah, who had come originally from Austria. Her family were dispersed "somewhere in Europe." In a few words she told of the change which Palestine had wrought in the lives of the youth. She told of the time that the youth had stood in the fields, sweat running from their brows. "And then the country seemed to say: Look at your land, love it, it is yours." Turning to Henrietta Szold she promised: "We will follow the road we have taken, forward and upward. And you will be with us on the road."

Index

345

126; educational credo, 13–5; eightieth-birthday celebration, 343–4; illness, 74–5, 115; pacifism, 100, 103–6; seventieth-birthday celebration, 223–4; seventy-fifth-birthday celebration, 291; sixtieth-birthday celebration, 161–2; social service work, 208–9, 228–41, 249, 259, 262, 267, 273, 276–7, 280–1, 283, 292, 295, 298, 333–4; teacher, 13–5, 33, 39, 47, 55; travels, 22–5, 60–8, 120 ff., 220, 225, 256–7, 284, 326–7; writer and editor, 56–60; Zionist credo, 54, 67, 101, 323–5

Szold, Rachel (Mrs. Joseph Jastrow, Henrietta's sister), 27, 34, 42, 120, 218, 340; death, 220

Szold, Sadie (Henrietta's sister), 26, 42; death, 343 n.

Szold, Sophia (Sophia Schaar, Henrietta's mother), 3, 6, 10, 67–8, 126; death, 89, 91–3; trip to Europe and Palestine, 60–8

Talpiot, 339
Teachers Association of Maryland, 27
Tel Aviv, 130, 178, 234, 250, 262, 273, 297–8, 308–10, 313, 316–8
Tel Hai, 128 n.
Tel Yosef, 294
Thomas, Miss M. Carey, 15
Tiberias, 140, 266–7, 300
Tourists, 203–6, 239
Trotsky, 146
"Troubles in Turkey, The" (Henrietta Szold), 10
Trumpeldor, Captain, 128 n., 266
Turoff, Dr., 67
Twain, Mark, 17
Typhoid-control in Palestine, 153, 306

Uriel Acosta (Gutzkow), 5
Ussishkin, Menachem, 341

Vaad Leumi, 227–30, 232, 240, 244–245, 253, 262, 266–7, 276, 319, 333
Viteles, 231
Volga füllt das Kaspische Meer, Die, 236
Voltaire, 18

Wald, Lillian, 56
Warburg, Felix, 328
Wauchope, Sir Arthur, 301, 322
Weinheim, Mrs. Emil, 166
Weizmann, Dr. Chaim, 168, 244
Western Female High School, 9, 12–13, 291

William, Prince, 29
William I, 31 n.
William II, 32 n., 35
Wise, Dr. Isaac M., 6, 20, 205
Woman's Literary Club (Baltimore), 15, 42, 47, 291
Workingmen's Party, 227
World's Parliament of Religions, 60
World War, 82–8, 90, 94–6, 98, 100–108, 110–1
World Zionist Congress (Lucerne, 1935), 281–3. See also Zionist Congresses
World Zionist Executive Conference (Jahres Conferenz), 137, 310–3
World Zionist Organization, 94, 147, 191–3, 212, 223; Palestine Executive Committee, 221, 223, 227 n.
Wronsky, Mrs., 249–50, 262

Yishub, 169, 222, 235, 323
Young Men's Hebrew Association, 16–7
Youth Aliyah, 243, 256–9, 261, 264–266, 268–9, 274–7, 284–9, 292, 294, 301, 312, 323–4, 327, 330, 332, 336–340, 343; Amsterdam conference, 281; Ben Shemen conference, 321; Zürich conference, 328

Zeitlin, Rose, 155
Zichron Jacob, 142
Ziff, William B., 296 n.
Zionism, 11, 21–2, 37–8, 49–54, 56, 65, 67, 69–74, 77, 80, 83–8, 94, 106–108, 116–7, 137, 152, 164, 185–6, 191–2, 203, 210–3, 217, 221, 223, 226, 281–3, 286, 320, 323–7; effects of World War on, 83–4, 96, 100–2; School of, 97, 108
Zionist Association. See Hebras Zion
Zionist Commission, 115–7, 128, 135, 138–9, 179
Zionist Congresses, 185–6, 191–2, 226, 281–3, 320, 326–7; Basel (1897), 52; Carlsbad (1921), 185–6, 191–2; Lucerne (1935), 281–3; Zürich (1937), 326–7
Zionist Executive, 226, 306, 342. See also World Zionist Executive Conference
Zionist International, 147
Zionist Organization, 147, 192–3, 212. See also World Zionist Organization
Zionist Organization of America, 108, 116–7, 217
Zionist Review, 110
Zunz, Leopold, 53